America's Dream at a Crossroads

America's Dream at a Crossroads

The 2024 Presidential Election and Beyond

Donald T. Iannone, Ph.D.

Wisdom Work Press

CONTENTS

CONTENTS

To the Honorable George V. Voinovich

This book is dedicated to George Voinovich, former Mayor of Cleveland, Governor of Ohio, and United States Senator, whose life and leadership epitomized the American Dream.

George taught me that public-private partnerships can effectively address challenges and seize opportunities in government and economic development through collaboration and integrity. Throughout his career, he demonstrated that one can lead with conviction while respecting individuals from all walks of life. His bipartisan cooperation and respect for taxpayers were highlighted in a Cleveland Plain Dealer editorial after his passing in 2016: *"After decades in an arena that has sullied so many, Voinovich's integrity remains unquestioned. He has never been afraid to work across the aisle and has never forgotten that tax money comes from the wallets of hard-working people."*

I was privileged to serve as Voinovich's economic development advisor during his first gubernatorial campaign in Ohio. Working closely with his administrations in Cleveland and the State of Ohio, I witnessed his dedication to public service firsthand. George's lessons have profoundly shaped my views on governance and public service, guiding my commitment to the American Dream. This book is a testament to his memory and lasting contributions to our nation.

I am grateful to all those who taught, supported, and walked alongside me during my four decades in economic development and public policy. Their guidance, encouragement, and insights have been instrumental in shaping the ideas and themes explored in this book.

I want to begin by thanking Dr. Nathan Grundstein, who cultivated my interest in political philosophy many years ago at Case Western Reserve University. I am grateful to Bill Bryant, former President and CEO of the Greater Cleveland Growth Association, who taught me the importance of doing my homework before tackling sensitive assignments, especially when navigating political circles. His advice has been invaluable in my career and the creation of this book.

My gratitude extends to Dr. David Sweet, former Dean of Cleveland State University's College of Urban Affairs, who showed me how to serve as a bridge between the world of ideas and the world of action. His mentorship allowed me to connect research and knowledge with local, state, and federal government policy, a skill that has proven crucial throughout my career.

I am truly grateful to Dr. Lloyd Williams, Chief Academic Officer at Transcontinental University, for writing the book's foreword and for his insights into how the American Dream remains out of reach for many African Americans and other people of color. Several experts reviewed this book and provided endorsements, including Jeffrey Finkle, Executive in Residence at the Voinovich School at Ohio University and former CEO of the International Economic Development Council; Dr. Don Holbrook, Ph.D., economist and best-selling author; Paul Raetsch, former Regional Director of the U.S. Economic Development

Administration office in Philadelphia; Dr. Larry Keller, Associate Professor Emeritus at Cleveland State University; Dr. Nick Bayat, University of Pittsburgh Study Council Consultant and retired Superintendent of Schools; Don Jakeway, Emeritus Board Member, Pro Football Hall of Fame and former Director of the Ohio Department of Development; Kirstin Toth, a philanthropy consultant and the former Senior Vice President of the GAR Foundation in Akron; and Craig James, Executive Coach and Co-managing Partner, CatalystStrategies LLC.

I also appreciate Paul Hertneky, author of the best-selling "Rust Belt Boy: Stories of an American Childhood," for his assistance in refining this book's concepts. My gratitude goes to Chris Brandt, my author branding and marketing coach, who guided me through publishing this book, and to Lisa Thomas-Tench, whose editorial advice was invaluable in helping me clarify my writing and align the book's content with my point of view. Ross Kleinberg, my publicist, has helped me greatly. My thanks to Ross. Finally, I thank Dr. Ned Hill, Professor of Economic Development at the John Glenn School of Public Affairs at The Ohio State University, for introducing me to the adjusted per capita personal income analysis technique, which I used in the Local and State Perspectives of the American Dream chapter. Ned and I were colleagues at Cleveland State University from 1986 until 2000.

I would also like to acknowledge my many economic development, academic, business, healthcare, legal, public policy, and planning colleagues, especially those who have become friends: Jim Alexander, George Ames, Mark Barbash, Terry Bailey, Dr. Ed Bee, Dr. Richard Bingham (dec.), Dr. Tom Bier, Tom Blanchard, Ladene Bowen, Paul Brehm, Hon. Paula Brooks, Ronnie Bryant, Steve Budd, Eric Canada, Tim Chase, Kurt Chilcote, John Claypool (dec.), Gary Conley, Karen Conrad, Leslie Cosgrove, Rod Crider, Michael Curley, David Dodd, Gene DePrez, Jim Devine, Ken Dobson, Dennis Donovan, Rick Duke, Dr. Tom Flynn, Dr. Maury Forman, Jay Garner, Vernon George, Dr. Lay Gibson, Victor Grgas (dec.), Jim Griffin (dec.), Howard Gudell, Blaine Henry, Cindy Hundorfean, Melanie Hwang, Don Jakeway, Mark

James, Dr. Jason Jolley, Joan Jorgenson (dec.), Todd Jorgenson, Michelle Keller, Steve Kelley, Bill Koehler, Dr. David Kolzow, Paul Krutko, Tom Kucharski, Ron Kysiak, Dr. Zara Larsen, Dr. Larry Ledebur, Benson Lee, Ray Lorello, Diane Lupke, Howard Maier, Hrishue Malhalha, Jerry Mallot, Chris Manegold, Joe Marinucci, Barry Matherly, Mike McCarthy, Trayce McDaniel, Bill McDermott, Kenny McDonald, Dr. Mark Miller, Leo Miller, Mike Montgomery, Jay and Mary Ann Moon, Dr. Ioanna Morfessis, Dr. Ed Morrison, Hunter Morrison, Carl Muller, Dr. Richard Mulligan, Ed Nelson, Nathan Ohle, Kevin O'Brien, Ken Oilschlager, Michael Olivier, Diane Palmintera, Dr. Kay Peterson, Dr. Phil Phillips, Joy Pooler, Jan Purdy, Paul Raetsch, Dr. Jim Robey, Judy Scalise, Paul Saldana, Dr. Mark Salling, Brenda Santiago, Wayne Schell, Karl Seidman, Dr. Robey Simons, Mark Smith, Dave Spaur, Dr. Michael Schwartz (dec.), Dr. Joanne Schwartz, Charlie Webb (dec.), Dr. Ted Sun, Dr. Ron Swager, Marilyn Swartz-Lloyd, Jim Trutko, Andi Udris, Patrick Vercauteren, Will Warren, Mark Waterhouse, Rick Weddle, Glen Weisbrod, Dean Whittaker, Roy Williams, April Young. Each has been instrumental in shaping my journey.

I cannot conclude these acknowledgments without expressing my deepest gratitude to my wife, Mary Iannone, who served as the copyeditor of the book and has supported me throughout my writing career. Her patience, encouragement, and belief in my work have been a constant source of strength and inspiration. I could not have completed this book without her unwavering support and understanding.

Without these remarkable individuals, this book would not have been possible. I am deeply grateful for their contributions and lasting impact on my life and work. Thank you for walking this journey with me and believing in this book's vision.

Introduction

I sought honest early reviews of my book from experts across various fields. The nine reviews I received are insightful, inspiring, and encouraging. For different reasons, three people declined to offer reviews of the book. The provided reviews come from highly knowledgeable and experienced professionals in economic development, academia, economics, writing and publishing, public administration, education, philanthropy, and communications. Their insights and feedback have bolstered my confidence as an author and budding political writer.

Endorsements

"Don Iannone's *America's Dream at a Crossroads* masterfully captures the stark contrasts between the attainable American Dream of the 1950s and 1960s when I grew up in Licking County, Ohio, and the harsh realities today's working families face. With insightful analysis and a compelling call to action, Don outlines the urgent steps America's next President and the Federal Government must take to restore hope and opportunity for all. This book is essential reading for the Biden and Trump policy teams because it points them in the right direction in fixing our government and strengthening the American Dream."

~Jeffrey A. Finkle, CEcD, Executive in Residence, Voinovich School of Leadership and Public Service, Ohio University, and former President and CEO, International Economic Development Council, Washington, DC

"A long-awaited primer for every voter on the American Dream and why it is the defining issue for the 2024 Presidential Election and America beyond the election. Don Iannone holds Joe Biden's and Donald Trump's feet to the fire on why their top priority must be reviving and reimagining the American Dream for all Americans."

~Dr. Lloyd Williams, Ph.D., Chief Academic Officer, Transcontinental University, Tuskegee, Alabama

"The American Dream is a beacon of hope and promise and the spark that ignites hunger for what is possible. However, it is in danger today! Don Iannone delivers the formula for keeping it alive and igniting a rebirth of what has made this country great. Read this to nourish your patriotic spirit of why it matters."

~Don Allen Holbrook, Ph.D., Economist, best-selling author, Las Vegas, Nevada

"What timing! Don's insightful take on today's America is spot on. His book *America's Dream at a Crossroads* should be mandatory reading for every high school and university student. Every politician at every level of government should also read it with an open mind to understand what all Americans want more than anything: An America that will protect democracy and freedom forever!"

~Donald Jakeway, Emeritus Board of Directors, Pro Football Hall of Fame, and former Director, Ohio Department of Development, Columbus, Ohio

"Don Iannone's reimagined American Dream is not a repudiation of prosperity but an expansion of its meaning. In this new vision, the pursuit of wealth is balanced with cultivating well-being, a holistic picture of success that includes health, education, environmental stewardship, and community connection. I encourage voters to read Don's book, and hopefully, the campaign teams for President Joe Biden and former President Donald Trump read and take Don's advice to heart."

~Paul Raetsch, Former Regional Director, Philadelphia Office, U.S. Department of Commerce/Economic Development Administration, Philadelphia, Pennsylvania

"Don Iannone's book is a realistic, poignant, and powerful examination of why the American Dream needs to be revitalized in our political ideology and national economic perspective. Equally important is ensuring that this dream continues to offer individuals and families security and remains within reach for future generations. The book is exceptionally well-researched, data-driven, and analyzed with clarity and significance, addressing our present-day social and political polarization. "America's Dream at a Crossroad" is an excellent resource for voters, students, and elected officials. This is a must-read now more than ever!

~Nick Bayat, Ed.D., University of Pittsburgh Study Council Consultant and retired Superintendent of Schools, Pittsburgh, Pennsylvania

"For any anxious voter concerned about the future of democracy, Don Iannone's book serves as a crucial guidepost to revisit and reignite our understanding of the American Dream. Don eloquently reminds us why this dream is more important than ever, especially in today's turbulent times. More importantly, he offers a robust plan with sensible strategies to avert our nation's systemic political collapse and advance the American Dream for future generations."

~Kirstin S. Toth, Consultant to philanthropy, education, executive management, and former Senior Vice President of the GAR Foundation, Hudson, Ohio

"At a time in history characterized by 'This side or that side' or 'Your view is not my view so it's wrong' ...'America's Dream at a Crossroads' helps us see things from all sides. It helps us look at the bigger picture and balances our thinking. The American Dream is the main character of the story. Don helps us understand why we should care about her deeply—and highlights our need to see her through a comprehensive, objective lens."

~ Craig James, Co-managing Partner, CatalystStrategies LL, Fairlawn, Ohio.

Scholarly Review

Don Iannone brings his varied, rich, and deep background to examining the American Dream in the current political context. He develops a comprehensive notion of the various conceptions of the elusive yet necessary American Dream. The Dream, which I capitalize in recognition of its importance to how Americans behave and see the world, is the centerpiece for a nation whose citizens are politically defined. As a nation, we are constituted by our political heritage. Immigrants are naturalized via a civics test (which many native-born citizens may need help to pass). This recognizes that we, as a nation and citizens, are political creations, reflecting the Constitution and other founding and revered political documents. We are not an ethnic, religious, ideological, or otherwise constituted people. These foundations create and express the American Dream, centered on core values of freedom, liberty, and a self-defined life, echoing Jefferson's notion of the "pursuit of happiness."

Iannone's book is a two-part examination of the Dream and the current context, with concluding recommendations to improve our politics and governance. While Iannone does not explicitly divide the book into two parts, it is helpful to recognize the different foci of the early chapters, the subsequent chapters, and the final chapter. The initial chapters explore the various conceptions of the American Dream, uncovering their historical and philosophical roots. The second part is a guide to the current election, explicating the views and personas of the two presidential candidates. Iannone is not polemical or biased in his evaluations of the American Dream or the candidates. He correctly notes the importance of the election, especially in its choice of American Dreams. For him, the two candidates are quite distinct in their conceptions of the Dream and how to enact it.

The book is a deep dive into these essential topics and rewards the careful reader with a fuller understanding of the Dream and the politics. From the founding of the American colonies to current state and local politics, as well as the global context, Iannone spells out the consequences of notions of the American Dream. These chapters look at the Dream in detail and how the particular setting impacts the various notions of the Dream.

Two chapters examine Biden and Trump in terms of how they approach politics, their perspectives, and the roots of their behavior. He notes how their views align with philosophies such as John Rawls' views on justice. He delves into illuminating detail with a balanced analysis, allowing the facts to speak without extraneous commentary.

The final chapter lays out twelve suggestions for improving politics and governance processes. He proposes agencies for auditing government performance, campaign finance regulation, and more transparency in government policies and the budget. He advocates for a third party and using Ranked Choice and Proportional Representation in elections. The suggestions are spelled out with articulate arguments.

One may not agree with all of Iannone's analysis or his recommendations. For example, one can question recommendations that require impartial professional agency administrators, which one party adamantly opposes and many Americans, regardless of party, categorize as undesirable bureaucrats. However, the book is both an education on the importance of, and the variety of views on, the American Dream and how current politics reflect and affect that Dream. The book is truly rewarding reading in our times.

~ Dr. Lawrence F. Keller, Associate Professor Emeritus, Public Administration, Cleveland State University, Cleveland, Ohio

Don Iannone's book provides much-needed guidance on redefining the American Dream in more inclusive and equitable terms. Aimed at the 2024 presidential election, it recognizes the high stakes for America's future during this pivotal moment. This book's lasting value extends beyond the election, serving as a primer for everyone on the American Dream. Don's book provides an integrated approach to federal policy that allows policymakers and citizens to see the "big picture" of the Federal Government. His "Twelve-Point Strategy" provides a bold but clear-minded approach to averting the systemic collapse of the Federal Government and the American political process, while at the same time offering a well-reasoned strategy for advancing the American Dream.

Don delves into the American Dream's definition, history, philosophical underpinnings, and positive and negative aspects. As Don aptly states, "When we think about the American Dream, all that glitters is not gold." The book offers multifaceted perspectives on the American Dream, examining its economic, social, political, educational, local, state, and global dimensions.

This comprehensive approach equips voters and the presidential candidates with a critical understanding of the American Dream. Don writes with clarity and conviction, presenting a new vision of prosperity and well-being that transcends the materialistic definition long associated with the Dream. This vision emphasizes greater opportunities for people of color and making the Dream more accessible to all.

Don highlights the need for an intergenerational perspective, from children to seniors. On college campuses today, the younger generation demands more from the American system regarding government, education, and humanity. Don provides insights and guidance on what needs to be done, regardless of whether Joe Biden or Donald Trump wins the presidential election, and what we must do as citizens and voters.

He clarifies that our vote is for a national leader and a new vision of the American Dream. The stakes could not be higher if we fail to reinvent the Dream inclusively and equitably. The very future of our nation is at risk, as the Dream has too often excluded and marginalized so many Americans. Don exposes the unintended yet devastating consequences of pursuing the American Dream in strictly individualistic and isolated terms. He shows how the Dream has become a vortex of consumerism, serving the wealthy at the expense of working people and marginalized communities.

Despite claims that the American Dream is dead, Don argues it is alive, shaping our marketplace and political system. However, he demonstrates how the Dream has often failed to serve the interests of working people and minorities, prioritizing the wealthy and powerful instead. Don shows that the American Dream is not an abstract ideal but a living force that shapes our economy, politics, and national identity. Failure to reinvent this Dream inclusively and equitably would be catastrophic, denying opportunity and prosperity to entire communities while entrenching the privilege of the few.

From my perspective, growing up in Tuskegee, Alabama, in the 1950s and 1960s, my family and I, as African-Americans, had to work much harder to earn our advanced degrees and build successful careers. Despite our qualifications, we faced significant obstacles due to systemic racism and discrimination.

Don and I are colleagues at Transcontinental University, where I serve as the chief academic officer, and Don is a business professor. Don is a gifted writer and an exceptional teacher, and his talents complement each other. I admire Don and his book and highly recommend it for its wealth of insights and actionable ideas.

Next Up: Book Key Takeaways

> America's political system must be fixed to avert disaster, as its current dysfunction threatens to erode democratic principles, undermine public trust, and impede our nation's ability to address critical challenges effectively.

1

Key Takeaways

" Nearly every government policy affects America's Dream and citizens' ability to achieve it. This book identifies these connections, encouraging readers to consider them when electing their next president and setting expectations for their leaders beyond the election. "

* Book Summary *

America's Dream at a Crossroads, The 2024 Presidential Election and Beyond argues that the American Dream should be the defining issue in the 2024 presidential election and remain a major focus beyond the election. The book shows how major issues facing America today, such as the economy, immigration, race relations, education, and global affairs, are intrinsically linked to the American Dream and Americans' ability to pursue and achieve it.

The book's key elements are a comprehensive definition of the American Dream, tracing its history, and exploring the underlying philosophy and ideology that sustain it. It delves into economic perspectives on the Dream, examines state and local perspectives, and situates the Dream within global realities. The book scrutinizes government spending's impact on the Dream and assesses President Joe Biden and former President Donald Trump as potential future leaders of this vision. Furthermore, it positions the American Dream as the pivotal issue for the election and proposes a detailed agenda and strategy to advance the Dream in the post-election landscape.

In the words of Dr. Lloyd Williams, Chief Academic Officer at Transcontinental University, "Don's Twelve-Point Strategy provides a bold but clear-minded approach to averting the 'systemic collapse' of the Federal Government and the American political process while at the same time offering a well-reasoned strategy for advancing the American Dream."

The author, Don Iannone, has worked in economic development and public policy over the past four decades. He has testified before Congress and several state legislatures and has spoken widely on challenges and opportunities facing American communities, businesses, and people. Since 2020, he has taught business students worldwide how to succeed in business and entrepreneurship, many based in Africa, Europe, and the Middle East. His work with over one hundred public and private sector clients, including several Federal agencies, has helped advance the American Dream through economic development strategies and public policies. Don wrote this book because he believes America has lost track of its core calling as a land of freedom, opportunity, progress, and hope. This book argues that in the future, the American Dream must be embraced in more inclusive, equitable, and global terms. Don states that he would have written this book as a guide to the 2024 election and beyond, regardless of the presidential candidates, offering the same advice to any contender.

Twelve-Point Strategy for Averting the Systemic Collapse of America's Political System and Advancing America's Dream

1. **Campaign Finance Reform:** Implement strict limits on contributions, establish public funding options, ensure full disclosure

and transparency, regulate dark money, and reform Super PACs to restore integrity and public trust in the democratic process.

2. **Curtail Special Interest Lobbying**: Reduce the undue influence of special interest groups, restrict lobbying activities, enhance transparency, ban lobbyist campaign contributions, and promote ethical lobbying practices.

3. **Cultivate a Third Political Party**: Implement electoral reforms, ensure equal media coverage, guarantee third-party candidates' inclusion in major debates, and build a supportive infrastructure to enhance democratic representation and reduce polarization.

4. **End Celebrity Politics**: Shift public discourse and media coverage towards candidates' qualifications and policies, launching nationwide voter education campaigns, promoting responsible journalism, and regulating campaign practices to restore a focus on effective governance.

5. **Major Government Reform:** Conduct comprehensive audits, modernize technology and infrastructure, establish a task force for waste reduction, and increase transparency and accountability to improve government efficiency and restore public trust.

6. **Reduce the Federal Debt:** Reducing the government's $35 trillion debt is essential to averting the systemic collapse of the Federal Government. This book provides an approach to achieving that.

7. **Bring About Greater Transparency:** Mandate the publication of government data, strengthen protections for whistleblowers, require regular public reporting from all branches of government, and enhance oversight and accountability to build public trust and prevent corruption.

8. **Increase Standards of Accountability:** Establish independent oversight bodies, implement regular performance reviews, mandate ethics training, and promote a culture of integrity to ensure government officials adhere to ethical and legal standards.

9. **Integrated Strategy for Domestic Affairs**: Align education with future economic needs, ensuring improved access to affordable healthcare, promoting innovation and job creation, and balancing economic growth with environmental protection to create a sustainable and prosperous future for all Americans.

10. **Integrated Strategy for Foreign Policy and Global Relations**: Redefine relationships with global partners, lead in advanced technologies, promote global environmental sustainability, and implement comprehensive immigration reform to enhance national security and uphold humanitarian values.

11. **Adopt Complex Systems Approaches in Governance**: Complexity science helps us transcend the limitations of simplistic reductionistic thinking and action. Fostering innovation, implementing adaptive policies, creating flexible and responsive policies, acknowledging interconnectedness in policy development, building resilient systems, and promoting continuous learning to manage modern society's dynamic and interconnected challenges.

12. **Strategic Investment Plan to Advance the American Dream**: Foster next-generation partnerships in education, healthcare, economic development, and social mobility, emphasizing innovation, entrepreneurship, and community-driven initiatives to enhance opportunities for all Americans without fostering dependence on government subsidies.

Using the American Dream as a Guidepost for Creating a More Inclusive and Equitable Society

Importance of the American Dream

- The American Dream is important because it embodies the ideals of opportunity, equality, and perseverance, offering hope and motivation for individuals striving to overcome current economic, social, and political challenges.

Importance of Reimagining the American Dream

- It is important to reimagine the American Dream in broader, more inclusive, and more equitable terms to ensure that all individuals, regardless of background, have equal opportunities to succeed and contribute to society. Beginning this process with the presidential election allows for establishing policies and leadership that prioritize and address the diverse needs and aspirations of the entire population.

Government's Role in Shaping the Dream

- This book reimagines the American Dream as a dynamic and evolving ideal essential to the vitality of American society. This book shows how the policies and actions of the President and the Federal Government profoundly influence Americans' ability to pursue and achieve their aspirations.

The 2024 Election

- The election is important to the American Dream as it represents a fundamental exercise of democratic rights, influencing the direction of the country's values and policies and the opportunities available for individuals to achieve their aspirations.

Presidential Choice

- The choice of president impacts the American Dream by shaping policies that influence economic opportunities, social mobility, and access to education, healthcare, and many other resources.

Agenda and Strategy to Advance America's Dream

- This book urges Americans to make the American Dream the defining issue in choosing their next president. It emphasizes that our nation's leaders must collaborate to create an agenda that advances the American Dream, use it as a guidepost for setting future policy directions, and invest in policies that foster a more inclusive and equitable America.

How the Critical Issues Facing America Relate to the American Dream

Preserving Democracy

- Ensuring democratic processes and freedoms is foundational to achieving the American Dream, as it guarantees individual rights and opportunities for all citizens.

Transcending Partisan Differences and Divisions

- A unified nation facilitates collective progress, reduces societal tensions, and fosters an environment where individuals can pursue their dreams without fear of division or discrimination.

The Economy and Jobs

- Economic stability and job opportunities are central to achieving the American Dream, as they provide the means for individuals to improve their living standards and build wealth.

Fixing Dysfunctional Government

- Effective governance ensures the implementation of policies that support citizens' aspirations, making it easier for people to pursue their dreams within a stable and supportive system.

Immigration

- A balanced, managed, and humanitarian approach to immigration policy, combined with border security to avoid illegal immigration, protects American citizens while allowing others to become a part of American society.

The Environment and Climate Change

- Sustainable environmental practices ensure that future generations have the resources and healthy environment to pursue their dreams.

Race and Race Relations

- Equal opportunities and fair treatment, regardless of race, are essential for everyone to have an equal chance at achieving their dreams.

Public Infrastructure

- A robust infrastructure supports economic growth, facilitates access to education and healthcare, and improves the quality of life, all crucial for pursuing the American Dream.

Election Integrity

- Trust in electoral processes ensures that citizens' voices are heard and that leaders are chosen fairly, which is essential for maintaining the democratic foundation of the American Dream.

Human Rights and Abortion

- Upholding human rights and individual freedoms allows people to make personal choices that align with their values and aspirations, which are integral to pursuing their version of the American Dream.

Taxes and Government Spending

- Fair and effective tax policies and government spending can provide necessary services and support systems that enable individuals to achieve their dreams without undue financial burden.

Healthcare

- Access to quality healthcare is vital for individuals to maintain the health necessary to pursue their personal and professional goals.

Mental Health

- Addressing mental health issues ensures that individuals can achieve emotional and psychological well-being, enabling them to pursue their dreams fully.

Inflation and Prices

- Stable prices and controlled inflation protect individuals' purchasing power, making saving, investing, and achieving their economic goals easier.

Civil Rights

- Ensuring civil rights for all citizens is fundamental to providing equal opportunities and protections necessary for achieving the American Dream.

Science and Technology Advancement

- Advances in science and technology drive innovation, create new opportunities, and improve quality of life, all crucial for realizing the American Dream.

National Security

- A secure nation provides a stable environment where individuals can pursue their dreams without the threat of external dangers.

Crime

- Reducing crime ensures safer communities, allowing individuals to live and work without fear, which is essential for pursuing personal and economic goals.

Veterans

- Supporting veterans helps achieve the American Dream by providing them with economic stability, educational opportunities, and healthcare benefits. This enables them to contribute positively to their communities and achieve personal success.

Foreign Policy

- Sound foreign policy promotes global stability and opens international opportunities, enabling citizens to engage in global commerce and cultural exchange.

Education

- Education is a critical enabler of the American Dream, providing the knowledge and skills necessary for individuals to pursue careers and achieve personal growth.

Judges in the Supreme Court

- Justices' decisions shape the legal landscape, influencing issues like civil rights, economic policies, and personal freedoms, directly affecting individuals' ability to pursue their dreams.

International Trade

- International trade expands economic opportunities, increases market access, and promotes prosperity, which is essential for achieving the American Dream.

Energy

- Access to affordable and sustainable energy supports economic growth and quality of life, facilitating the pursuit of personal and professional goals.

Special Interests in Government and Campaign Reform

- Reducing the influence of special interests and reforming campaign finance ensures that government policies reflect the people's will and support a fair environment for everyone to pursue their dreams.

Next Up: Book Prologue

" This book serves as a crucial primer for voters and presidential candidates. It outlines the fundamental aspects of the American Dream and the actionable steps needed to advance it, ensuring a prosperous and equitable future for all. The advice in this book is available to any presidential candidate, including Joe Biden, Donald Trump, and Robert F. Kennedy Jr. While these three are the most likely contenders at the time of my writing of this book, the final candidates will not be confirmed until the Republican National Convention in July 2024 and the Democratic National Convention in August 2024. Notably, Joe Biden's disastrous debate performance on June 27, 2024 could cast doubt on his chances of securing the Democratic nomination. "

2

Prologue

" America stands at a critical crossroads, facing profound challenges at home and abroad. Domestically, the nation grapples with deep political divisions, economic inequality, and social justice issues. Internationally, America contends with rising global threats, shifting alliances, and the urgent need to reaffirm its leadership on the world stage. This pivotal moment demands decisive action and a unified vision to move America and Americans forward. We must adopt new ways of working together, avoiding political extremism, and advancing America in an increasingly embattled and ruthless world. At any cost, we should avoid authoritarianism and its deadly consequences. This book reminds us of who we are as a rapidly evolving and increasingly diverse society, whose people should choose and follow the path of freedom, integrity, opportunity, frontier spirit, intelligence, and individual and collective will. We should demand that our nation's leaders, starting with the President, use the American Dream as their guidepost in making important decisions that impact all Americans. This requires ethical leadership that serves America as a whole, and not just the privileged few. "

As November approaches, America braces itself for one of its most contentious and consequential elections. Votes will be cast, voices will be heard, and a likely razor-thin outcome will decide whether Joe Biden or Donald Trump will be the 47th president of the United States. At this pivotal moment, it is crucial to recognize a stark and unsettling reality: the American Dream is conspicuously absent from both candidates' agendas for the future. This book urges Joe Biden and Donald Trump to make the American Dream the central focus of their campaigns and future agendas. The American Dream should be the litmus test for who should lead America starting in 2025.

Both Biden and Trump are deeply entwined with the interests of America's and the world's wealthiest and most powerful individuals and families. Their campaigns, strategies, and promises are heavily influenced by those who hold the purse strings, leaving little room for genuine representation of the American people's hopes and dreams. As many Americans will be unhappy with the upcoming election result as those who will be happy. Neither Biden nor Trump have proven they can lead America to common ground, rebuild our nation, or ensure that the American Dream lives on and grows stronger. Each candidate, in their own way, represents a path fraught with shortcomings, a journey that threatens to deepen our divisions rather than heal them. The American Dream will perish for the majority of Americans unless we heal our political wounds.

We must come together as the people of the United States of America to defend freedom and democracy. On the sixth day of June 2024, the 80th anniversary of D-Day was celebrated. The lessons from D-Day serve as powerful reminders that at the heart of the American Dream lie the values of freedom and democracy. The bravery and sacrifices of those who stood up to defend these ideals on that historic day ensured that America and much of the world could continue to aspire to a future of liberty and justice. Their courage underscores that freedom is never free; it comes at a great cost, borne by those willing to pay the ultimate price. This sacrifice reaffirms that preserving democracy and the American Dream is a noble endeavor worth every effort and sacrifice to sustain and protect future generations.

"America's Dream at the Crossroads" is a call to regain faith in ourselves, our ability to succeed, and our capacity to find happiness. It is an urgent reminder that we must restore our faith in government as one of our most valued institutions—a government that serves the people, not the interests of a privileged few. As voters, we must vote for the American dream. We must demand that whoever takes the helm in the White House and those who occupy seats in Congress be held accountable. We must insist they work tirelessly to keep the American dream alive and flourishing. This election is about choosing a president and affirming our commitment to a better future for all Americans.

Because of the timing of the publication of this book, Joe Biden and Donald Trump are considered the two leading presidential candidates, but let's consider the possibility that Joe Biden steps aside for personal reasons as the Democratic presidential candidate. Who might his replacement be? Nine potential candidates to replace Joe Biden have been mentioned in recent news reports: Vice President Kamala Harris from California, Governor Gavin Newsom of California, former Secretary of State and First Lady Hillary Clinton, former First Lady Michelle Obama, Governor Gretchen Whitmer of Michigan, Governor J.B. Pritzker of Illinois, Governor Josh Shapiro of Pennsylvania, Senator Raphael Warnock of Georgia, and Representative Dean Phillips of Minnesota. These individuals hold significant roles within the Democratic Party and have varying political experience and public recognition. Is it possible that Donald Trump, because of his legal entanglements, may not receive the Republican Party nomination? At the time of my writing, this seems unlikely.

Let this book serve as both a guide and a rallying cry. As we stand at the crossroads, let us choose the path that leads to a renewed and vibrant American Dream. Let us hold our leaders' feet to the fire, ensuring they serve the interests of the many, not the few. Let us, the people, become the stewards of our nation's destiny, ensuring that the American Dream remains within reach for generations to come. In these pages, you will find a blueprint for action, a roadmap for how we can transcend partisanship, build effective political partnerships, reinvigorate participatory democracy, and blaze new pathways to prosperity. This is our moment to reclaim the American Dream. Let us rise to the occasion, united in purpose and resolve, to secure a future that embodies the true spirit of America.

Finally, as you read this book, consider the following ten guiding questions about the American Dream before and after the election. The epilogue repeats them, along with a link to my blog where you can converse about them.

Conversation Questions for "America's Dream at a Crossroads, The 2024 Presidential Election and Beyond"

The American Dream in the Election Context

1. **How have the definitions and expectations of the American Dream evolved, and how do the 2024 presidential candidates' policies reflect these changes?** Reflect on the historical and modern interpretations of the American Dream and analyze how current political platforms address these evolving expectations.

2. **In what ways do the economic policies of Joe Biden and Donald Trump differ in their potential impact on achieving the American Dream?** Compare the economic strategies proposed by both candidates and discuss their implications for wealth-building, job creation, and economic mobility.

3. **How does the education policy of each candidate aim to bridge or widen the gap in access to quality education, and what impact does this have on the American Dream?** Assess the education reforms proposed by Biden and Trump,

considering how these policies might affect educational equity and opportunities for future generations.

4. **To what extent do the healthcare plans of the 2024 candidates influence the accessibility and affordability of healthcare as a component of the American Dream?** Analyze the healthcare proposals from both candidates, focusing on how these plans might alter access to healthcare services and financial stability for American families.

5. **How do the candidates' stances on immigration shape the concept of the American Dream for immigrants and their descendants?** Discuss the immigration policies of Biden and Trump and their potential effects on the opportunities available to immigrants pursuing the American Dream.

The American Dream Beyond the Election

1. **What are the long-term implications of current economic trends on the viability of the American Dream for future generations?** Consider the impact of trends such as automation, globalization, and economic inequality on the sustainability of the American Dream.

2. **How can education systems be reformed to better prepare individuals for the challenges and opportunities of the 21st century while supporting the American Dream?** Explore innovative educational approaches that can equip people with the skills and knowledge necessary for success in a rapidly changing world.

3. **How can communities foster a sense of belonging and support to help individuals achieve their version of the American Dream?** Discuss community-based initiatives and social support systems that enhance social cohesion and provide pathways to personal and collective success.

4. **How does environmental sustainability intersect with pursuing the American Dream, and what role should policy play in this relationship?** Examine the importance of sustainable practices and policies in ensuring that the pursuit of the American Dream does not come at the expense of the environment.

5. **What can be done to restore trust in institutions and governance to reinforce the foundation of the American Dream?** Analyze strategies for rebuilding public trust in political, economic, and social institutions, and consider how this trust is vital for realizing the American Dream.

These questions aim to stimulate thoughtful discussion and reflection among readers and voters, encouraging a deeper understanding of how the American Dream intersects with political, economic, and social issues during and beyond the 2024 presidential election.

Next Up: Introduction to the Book

" I wrote this book out of a deep concern for America's extreme polarization and the dysfunction in its political process, with the hope of inspiring meaningful dialogue and action to revive the American Dream and restore faith in our democracy. "

3

Introduction

> America's Dream at a Crossroads has two purposes: to use the American Dream as a yardstick for selecting the next president and to provide a guide for the crucial steps we must take after the election to rebuild America and prevent the systemic collapse of our political system, ensuring the American Dream remains attainable for future generations.

A Reasoned Voice and Critical Thinking Perspective on Economic Renewal and Public Policy

For over 40 years, my career has focused on economic development and public policy. I have worked on economic strategies and public policy analyses in 32 "red" and "blue" states, 10 countries, and 10 American Indian reservations. Government leaders have invited my ideas through testimonies before Congress and various state legislatures. I've written extensively on these topics, including academic articles, a book, several book chapters, and newspaper opinion editorials. I published a decade-long blog, Economic Development Futures, about economic and political challenges facing communities, regions, and states.

This experience, across many contexts, gives me a unique perspective on the American Dream, which stands at a critical crossroads as America chooses its next president. This book explains why the American Dream needs to be "the" defining issue in the upcoming presidential election and for American life beyond the election. It urges and helps voters get beyond the partisan political rhetoric they hear day in and day out. In the words of former U.S. Senator John McCain, "True political rhetoric seeks to unite and find a compromise, prioritizing the common good over partisan victories." That's what this book is about.

I write this book as a moderate conservative who values individualism and considers personal responsibility and self-reliance essential for innovation and economic growth. I also cherish tradition, believing it provides stability and a sense of continuity. However, moderate conservatives also recognize the equal importance of community and the need for change, understanding that societal progress requires collective effort and adaptability. This perspective seeks a balance where individual freedoms and traditional values coexist with a commitment to community support and thoughtful reform. As Americans, we have grown highly polarized and divisive. Anger, fear, and resentment have overtaken our daily lives and haunted our dreams at night.

My book is far from the first on the American Dream, which has been examined from various points of view over the years. David Leonhardt, from the New York Times, sounds a battle cry to the American left to give greater leadership to restoring America's Dream. After reading Leonhardt's 2023 "Ours Was the Shining Future: The Story of the American Dream," I realized it would take more than a stronger Democratic Party and labor unions to strengthen the American Dream.

Then, I read Nick Romeo's "The Alternative, How to Build a Just Economy," published in early 2024. This book carried me back to the philosophical ideas of John Rawls' theory of justice as fairness, and Karl Polanyi's critique of market liberalism, and his concept of the "double movement," which describes society's pushback against market-driven exploitation and inequality. Leonhardt and Romeo are good, thoughtful writers, but their books left me wanting solutions.

In stark political contrast is Senator Tim Scott's book, "America: A Redemption Story," which upholds the far-right conservative perspective of the American Dream. Scott's book fell far short on answers. Including "redemption" in his book's title signals Scott's evangelical Christian grounding. Scott would have shown greater courage if he had proposed real solutions to Washington's gridlock and horse-trading approach to policymaking.

American Enterprise Institute fellow Samuel Abrams said in 2019, "I am pleased to report that the American Dream is alive and well for an overwhelming majority of Americans. This claim might sound far-fetched given the cultural climate in the United States today. But Americans, it turns out, have something else in mind when they talk about the American dream. And they believe that they are living it." While I applaud the research behind Abrams' statement, I remain less convinced that the American Dream is within reach of large segments of the populace. Abrams advises, "What conclusions should we draw from this research? I think the findings suggest that Americans would be well served to focus less intently on the nastiness of our partisan politics and the material temptations of our consumer culture and to focus more on the communities they are part of and exercising their freedom to live as they wish. After all, that is what most of us seem to think is what matters — and it's in reach for almost all of us."

My advice is different: Americans should avoid bludgeoning one another over their political differences, but they should recommit themselves to shaping the debate about democracy and the American Dream at the local, state, and national levels. More importantly, they should use the November election to let the presidential candidates and those for other elected offices know they want a more inclusive and equitable American Dream and that the government should play the right role in shaping it.

The culture of American politics must change! University of Texas public policy expert Ryan Streeter describes American politics today in a vivid light, "Today it has become fashionable not to compromise, even at the risk of accomplishing less, damaging government's positive functions, and harming Americans' financial and physical security (Harvard Gazette, December 14, 2023)." The White House and Congress must break this bad habit!

Similarly, I am reminded of former U.S. Senator Olympia Snowe's words: "Two truths are all too often overshadowed in today's political discourse: Public service is a most honorable pursuit, and so is bipartisanship." Snowe reminds us of the importance of these often-overlooked principles in today's politics. Firstly, she reminds us that working in public service is a noble and honorable profession dedicated to improving the lives of others. Secondly, she emphasizes the value of bipartisanship and cooperation between different political parties. Snowe believes that by working together and finding common ground, politicians can better serve the public and create more effective policies. The quote advocates for respect, collaboration, and focusing on the common good in political discourse.

As you read this book, you will find that its tone is one of moderation, not extremism. As you navigate the complexities of the upcoming election and its far-reaching consequences, I encourage you to care deeply and think critically about the issues at stake. Challenge your views of the two candidates and the pressing issues before us. Avoid simple, black-and-white perspectives; instead, recognize that both candidates, the issues, America, and the rest of the world are interconnected components of a highly complex system. Embrace that change will persist beyond the election, irrespective of who becomes the next president.

The American Dream, though seemingly elusive and amorphous, offers us a chance to expand our horizons beyond partisan lines—Republican or Democrat, Donald Trump or Joe Biden. My book invites you to find hope within yourselves, America, and democracy. Together, let us strive to understand and engage with our society's dynamic nature, fostering a broader perspective that transcends the immediate political landscape.

My Reason for Writing This Book

I wrote this book out of deep concern for America and its future. The body politic is gravely ill, afflicted by a malignant spread of hyper-partisanship that has metastasized across Washington and state capitals. We have become the "Divided States of America," a nation rived by the zero-sum mentalities of the far left and far right. Our politics is now a blood sport where compromise is apostasy, and the other side is not simply wrong but evil. This venomous dynamic has corroded the very sinews of democratic deliberation - the willingness to acknowledge complexity and reason together toward principled compromise. Instead, we retreat deeper into our tribal camps, slinging mud across an ever-widening chasm of mutual incomprehension. Sadly, many Americans no longer care about the issues in an informed way. Hopefully, this book sparks greater concern for the issues by voters, beginning with the American Dream. Suppose we do not find our way back to an informed middle ground, to that ethos of moral humility that defined our nation's best eras. In that case, the American pluralism experiment may be doomed. For a house divided cannot stand - our founders knew this truth well. It is time we rediscovered the habits of the heart that can heal this rupture before it becomes a permanent deformity.

A recent article in KelloggInsight, an online publication from the Kellogg School of Management at Northwestern University, sheds light on why American politicians and their supporters often overlook clear moral issues, including criminal behavior, in their pursuit of power and the American Dream. The research team found that since 2000, wealth concentration has significantly increased, with nearly half of the world's countries experiencing a rise in economic inequality. This inequality also impacts moral perceptions, making people more accepting of unethical behavior. As Americans feel more powerless and lose control over their lives, they tend to be more lenient in judging transgressions (Ayshford, Emily, KelloggInsight, 2024, May 1). As you read this book, think about the message of this research study.

Setting the Stage for the Book

For generations, the gleaming promise of the American Dream has been etched into the very psyche of our nation, symbolized by a white picket fence, a car in every driveway, and a steadily accumulating bounty of material wealth. This dream, rooted in the pursuit of prosperity, has driven countless Americans toward the ceaseless toil of ambition. It has been the bedrock of our collective ethos—the belief that anyone, regardless of origin, could rise to the pinnacles of economic success through sheer grit and determination.

However, beneath the lustrous sheen of this ideal lies a deeper question: Is the accumulation of wealth the true epitome of what we, as a society, hope to achieve? The prevailing winds of change, driven by a deeper understanding of human fulfillment, suggest a burgeoning shift in this dream's essence. As we stand at the crossroads of an era marked by unprecedented global challenges and introspective societal shifts, we must realign the American Dream with a more holistic vision that champions well-being in its most comprehensive form.

This re-envisioned dream does not renounce the desire for wealth creation; rather, it acknowledges that prosperity's ultimate purpose should be to elevate the human condition for all. In an age defined by advancements that should elevate our quality of life, we must question why widespread satisfaction and contentment remain elusive for so many. Why, in a land of plenty, does the well-being of the collective often seem like an afterthought? America can do better than a "trickle-down American Dream!"

In its most constructive role, wealth should be a means to an end—not the end itself. It should fuel innovation, provide education, ensure health, safeguard the environment, and cultivate communities. A society's prosperity cannot merely be measured by the stockpiles of its riches but by the well-being of its citizens—their health, education, and ability to lead lives of purpose and connection.

Thus, the necessity to redefine prosperity is not just an intellectual exercise; it is an urgent call to action. It recognizes that our society's sustainability, our people's happiness, and the legacy we leave for future generations hinge upon our ability to broaden the scope of what we treasure most. As we look to the horizon, let us reimagine the American Dream with a vision that transcends the mere accumulation of wealth and seeks to enrich the human experience.

The traditional American Dream, etched into the nation's consciousness, depicts self-made men and women pulling themselves up by their bootstraps to build a life of prosperity. Rooted in the belief that financial success was accessible to anyone willing to work hard, this dream became the yardstick of personal achievement and a symbol of national identity. From the early settlers eyeing the vastness of untamed lands to the industrial magnates who built empires out of steel and steam, wealth accumulation has been synonymous with the American ideal.

Historically, this dream emerged from frontier spirit, industrial innovation, and economic opportunity. It promised not just survival but thriving. It became codified in the narratives of the 20th century as a home in the suburbs, a flourishing family, and increasing material possessions. Prosperity was not just a goal but an expectation, a right of passage into the esteemed halls of American success.

Yet, this gilded dream has not been without its shadow. The relentless pursuit of wealth has often led to a myopic vision, where the scoreboard of success is tallied in dollars and cents. This single-minded chase has birthed a landscape marked by stark economic disparities, where the ladder of opportunity is missing rungs for too many. It has fostered growth models that prize expansion and consumption, often at the expense of environmental sustainability and social equity. The wealth gap has widened, and the dream that once unified now polarizes, leaving segments of society in its dust.

These limitations are not merely cracks in the foundation but rather symptomatic of a deeper ailment—the belief that wealth alone is the panacea for all societal ills. A richer society, however, is not inherently healthier if its riches are inequitably distributed and its growth unsustainable. Hence, while acknowledging the significance of wealth as a means to improve life, it is crucial to address the overlooked facets of societal well-being.

This realization leads us to a pivotal juncture, transitioning from the narrow corridors of wealth accumulation to the broader avenues of holistic prosperity. Wealth, while a cornerstone of economic stability, must be viewed through the prism of its ability to enhance the welfare of the community, not merely the individual. It is time to broaden our horizons, redefine success in terms that are as inclusive as they are inspiring, and, in doing so, recast the American Dream in a more equitable and enduring mold.

Well-being, a concept that extends far beyond the mere absence of illness or poverty, encapsulates a state of flourishing that encompasses physical vitality, mental clarity, and a sense of belonging within one's community. It is a holistic measure of the quality of life, factoring in satisfying basic needs, the freedom to pursue personal ambitions, and the capacity to connect with others meaningfully. Well-being reflects the body's health, the mind's resilience, and the vibrancy of the social fabric that binds individuals to each other.

Despite the deeply ingrained belief in wealth as a harbinger of happiness, emerging data increasingly disrupts this narrative. The World Happiness Report, an endeavor that surveys the global state of human happiness, reveals that beyond a certain threshold, increases in wealth have a negligible impact on life satisfaction. In the wealthiest societies, the shadows of loneliness, stress, and purposelessness often loom surprisingly large. Once amassed, wealth can beget anxiety—the fear of loss, the isolation of affluence, and the paradox of choice in a sea of consumerism.

> "The American Dream is not a sprint or even a marathon, but a relay race for Americans."
> —Julian Castro, Former Mayor, San Antonio, Texas

Societal issues such as addiction, crime, and chronic diseases persist or even proliferate in the face of rising GDPs. These issues are often the symptoms of deeper societal malaise—a malaise that cannot be remedied by wealth alone. Affluence without community engagement and the support of robust social services and environmental stewardship leads not to societal harmony but fragmentation and discontent.

Therefore, the dialogue on prosperity must evolve to address well-being. Economies should measure success not just by the abundance of their markets but by the wellness of their populace. Investment in mental health resources, communal spaces, policies encouraging work-life balance, and education fostering a sense of civic duty are all crucial components of this broadened conception of prosperity.

The path forward demands a multi-faceted approach where financial stability supports, rather than defines, the quest for well-being. By aligning economic goals with the human spirit's needs and the community's health, society can craft a more compassionate and sustainable vision of success. As we consider the future, let us pivot towards a model of prosperity that acknowledges the complexity of human needs and crafts a vision of the American Dream that celebrates wealth in concert with well-being.

Wealth creation remains a vital cog in national advancement and individual fulfillment. It stimulates innovation, drives economic growth, and underpins the financial stability that allows individuals, families, and communities to thrive. It funds the public infrastructure, educational institutions, and healthcare systems that form the backbone of a prosperous society. Yet, its true potential is only realized when it serves as a conduit for enhancing communal and individual well-being rather than as an end in itself.

The transformative power of wealth is most evident when it is directed towards initiatives that elevate the quality of life for all. Consider the impact of endowments on education, the patronage of the arts, the funding of public health initiatives, and the advancement of sustainable practices. These are the arteries through which the lifeblood of wealth flows to vitalize the body of society. When channeled thoughtfully, wealth creation propels economic indicators and nourishes the seeds of well-being—seeds that blossom into a healthier, more educated, and more cohesive community.

For wealth to fulfill this elevated role, economic policies must be calibrated towards inclusivity. The aim is to construct a landscape where wealth creation is not the privilege of a few but a possibility for many. This means embracing fair taxation, ensuring equal access to education, supporting entrepreneurs, and creating pathways to employment across all sectors of society. It involves dismantling barriers to entry and building ladders of opportunity into the economic arena so that every individual can contribute to and benefit from the nation's prosperity.

As we transition to a broader concept of prosperity, we must understand that the goal is not to undermine wealth but to harness its full potential. It's about cultivating an ecosystem where the fruits of wealth creation are within reach of the many, not just the few. By redistributing the benefits more equitably and ensuring that wealth serves the collective well-being, society can compose a symphony of progress where every instrument can be heard and every note a chance to be played. The true essence of the American Dream can be realized and revered in this harmonious interplay between wealth creation and widespread prosperity.

The imperative to shift the American Dream from a myopic focus on wealth accumulation to a broader conception of well-being is underscored by pressing socio-economic challenges that jeopardize our national fabric. Healthcare access in the United States remains a patchwork system, where the quality of care often correlates with the thickness of one's wallet. The specter of medical bankruptcy still haunts many, suggesting that a key component of well-being—health—is not yet a right but a privilege. Education, the bedrock of social mobility, is plagued by disparities that mirror and perpetuate the divides in income and opportunity. The school-to-prison pipeline, underfunded public schools, and skyrocketing higher education costs paint a grim portrait of an unequal society.

Environmental concerns add another layer of urgency. Climate change looms large, promising widespread disruption if unaddressed. It's not just the health of our planet at stake but also the economic stability of industries and communities worldwide. Pollution, resource depletion, and ecological degradation pose existential threats, making it clear that prosperity built on environmental exploitation is as precarious as unjust.

If left unchecked, the status quo points towards an unstable future. Economic inequality breeds social discord and erodes trust in institutions. Health crises overwhelm systems ill-prepared for pandemics or the ravages of chronic disease. Environmental calamities disrupt economies and displace populations, sowing conflict and suffering.

The transition we seek is more than a moral imperative; it's strategic. By intertwining national well-being with the vision of a stable and prosperous future, we set a course toward a society where every individual can flourish. This shift is not merely aspirational; it is essential, a cornerstone upon which to build a resilient, equitable, and sustainable American Dream.

The reimagined American Dream is not a repudiation of prosperity but an expansion of its meaning. In this new vision, the pursuit of wealth is balanced with cultivating well-being, painting a holistic picture of success that includes health, education, environmental stewardship, and community connection. This Dream recognizes that true prosperity blooms in societies where every individual has the opportunity to survive and thrive in all aspects of life.

In this tapestry, individuals are architects and weavers, crafting lives that blend personal ambition with communal responsibility. Each person's efforts to achieve well-being contribute to the collective fabric, creating a resilient and vibrant community. These communities, diverse in their makeup, are united by shared values that champion the common good over individual gain.

> " I wrote this book to remind voters that as they choose their next president, consider everything at stake—most importantly, the American Dream. This encompasses our collective ability to make progress for ourselves and our nation. "

The government's role in this tapestry is to set the loom, to create the framework within which individuals and communities can prosper. This involves enacting policies that ensure equitable access to healthcare, provide quality education for all, protect the environment, and foster a robust economy that serves everyone. It means creating social safety nets that catch those who fall and systems that empower everyone to rise. However, the government must approach its role reasonably and responsibly. By working in partnership with the private sector and state and local government, more can be done at a lower cost to taxpayers.

Actionable steps toward this shift are manifold. On an individual level, it involves making choices that reflect this broader vision—supporting businesses that prioritize sustainable practices, engaging in community service, and advocating for policies that promote equity. Communities can foster local economies that prioritize well-being, create inclusive spaces for dialogue and collaboration, and invest in local initiatives that align with this expanded Dream. Governments, from local councils to federal bodies, can prioritize spending on social services, incentivize businesses to act sustainably and ethically and enact legislation that reduces inequality.

This paradigm shift towards a reimagined American Dream is essential for the well-being of future generations. It is a legacy that can redefine what it means to be successful in America—not just in terms of what is owned but by the quality of life enjoyed and the health of society fostered. This Dream is not a departure from our values but a return to them, placing the pursuit of happiness at the forefront, where prosperity serves not the individual alone but the well-being of all.

Book Organization

Beyond the book's dedication, foreword, acknowledgments, and introduction, the book has four parts:

1. Foundations of the American Dream
2. Major Challenges Facing America
3. Evaluation of the Presidential Candidates
4. A Strategy for Reform and Advancement

Next Up: History of the American Dream

" Next, we turn to the history of the American Dream from America's Colonial Era to modern times. History is important. I am reminded of the words of the Spanish-American philosopher George Santayana: "Those who cannot remember the past are condemned to repeat it." "

4

PART I: FOUNDATIONS OF THE AMERICAN DREAM

The American Dream has been a driving force in shaping the national identity and ethos of the United States since its inception. Part I of this book delves into the rich tapestry of historical events, philosophical ideals, and cultural movements that gave birth to this powerful concept. From the earliest settlers seeking religious freedom and economic opportunity to the Founding Fathers' vision of a nation built on liberty and equality, we trace the evolution of the American Dream. This section also examines the profound influence of Enlightenment thinkers, transcendentalist writers, and the unique blend of individualism and communal spirit that defined the nation's aspirations. Through a nuanced exploration of these roots, we gain a deeper understanding of the enduring allure and complexities of the American Dream.

5

A. History of the American Dream

INTRODUCTION

The Concept's Historical Origins and Evolution

The American Dream originated in the early years of American history, with foundational texts like the Declaration of Independence asserting that "all men are created equal" with the right to "life, liberty, and the pursuit of happiness." The westward expansion reinforced this ethos, with the frontier symbolizing endless opportunity and a fresh start.

In the 20th century, the American Dream evolved with the rise of the middle class and post-war economic prosperity, becoming synonymous with homeownership, stable employment, and a higher standard of living. However, the latter half of the century saw challenges to this ideal, with growing economic disparities, social upheaval, and questions about the fairness and accessibility of the American Dream.

Today, the American Dream is viewed through multiple lenses. For some, it's the belief in personal freedom and the ability to shape one's destiny. For others, it's achieving success and security through hard work. Contemporary interpretations also acknowledge the challenges and disparities that may limit access to the American Dream, such as systemic racism, gender discrimination, and economic inequality.

The American Dream is more than just a cultural ideal; it is a guiding principle in American politics and society. It embodies the tension between individualism and collective responsibility, raising questions about the role of government in ensuring equal opportunities and addressing systemic inequalities. It also serves as a benchmark for assessing the nation's progress and the effectiveness of its institutions in upholding the promise of the American Dream.

COLONIAL PERIOD AND EARLY FOUNDATIONS

European Settlers and the Quest for Religious Freedom

The colonial period laid the groundwork for the American Dream. European settlers crossed the Atlantic, seeking religious freedom and economic opportunities. In England, dissenting groups like the Puritans and Quakers faced persecution. North America offered a place to practice their faith freely and explore the promise of land and economic prospects.

Colonial Expansion and Land Ownership

Land ownership became the linchpin of the colonial American Dream. In England and Europe, land was scarce and typically held by the aristocracy. In contrast, the American colonies presented an opportunity for individuals to own land and, with it, the promise of social status and political power (Frost, 1981). Land was more than a commodity—it was synonymous with liberty, and the headright system, which provided land to settlers in exchange for their migration, facilitated this ownership vision (Costa, 1985).

REVOLUTIONARY PERIOD AND EARLY REPUBLIC

American Revolution and the Pursuit of Liberty

The American Revolution was pivotal for the American Dream, driven by the desire for freedom and self-determination against British rule. Colonists, dissatisfied with British taxation, representation, and governance policies, were inspired by Enlightenment ideals of liberty and natural rights. These principles fueled their fight for independence and the creation of a new nation.

Founding Documents

The Declaration of Independence, drafted by Thomas Jefferson and adopted on July 4, 1776, laid the philosophical foundation for the new nation. It proclaimed that all men are created equal and have unalienable rights to life, liberty, and the pursuit of happiness, embodying the spirit of the American Dream.

The U.S. Constitution, ratified in 1787, established a governance framework reflecting liberty, justice, and equality, with checks and balances to prevent any branch of government from wielding excessive power. The Bill of Rights, added in 1791, guaranteed fundamental liberties, reinforcing the promise of personal freedom and protection from government overreach.

Westward Expansion and the Frontier

As the new republic took shape, the American Dream was solidified through westward expansion and the opening of the frontier, which represented opportunity and adventure. The Louisiana Purchase in 1803 and explorations like the Lewis and Clark expedition expanded the nation's boundaries and fueled the spirit of exploration and manifest destiny.

The frontier symbolized the American Dream's ethos of self-reliance, resilience, and shaping one's destiny through hard work. It inspired many to venture into uncharted territories, seeking land, fortune, and a fresh start.

INDUSTRIALIZATION AND THE GILDED AGE

Rise of Industrialization

The Industrial Revolution, beginning in the late 18th century and extending into the 19th century, profoundly impacted the American economy and society. It transformed the landscape of industries, shifting from agrarian economies to industrial powerhouses, and brought about significant advancements in technology, manufacturing processes, and transportation infrastructure, leading to urbanization, increased productivity, and changes in labor dynamics.

The United States changed from an agrarian economy to an industrial powerhouse, creating unprecedented wealth and upward mobility opportunities. Technological advancements, such as the steam engine and the telegraph, revolutionized manufacturing, transportation, and communication, enabling rapid industrial growth and urbanization.

This era saw the rise of major industrialists like Andrew Carnegie, John D. Rockefeller, and Cornelius Vanderbilt, who built vast business empires. Their success stories became emblematic of the American Dream, illustrating how individuals could achieve extraordinary wealth through innovation, entrepreneurship, and hard work.

However, industrialization also brought significant challenges, including poor working conditions, child labor, and exploitation of the labor force. These issues laid the groundwork for social reform movements in the years to come.

Immigration and the Melting Pot

Industrialization attracted many immigrants from Europe and Asia, seeking economic opportunities and a better life in America. These immigrants from diverse backgrounds played a crucial role in developing the American Dream. They contributed to the industrial economy by providing labor in factories, railroads, and other industries that required a large workforce.

The melting pot concept emerged as a metaphor for blending different cultures and nationalities into a uniquely American identity.

Immigrants brought their customs, traditions, and work ethics, enriching the cultural fabric of the United States. However, they also faced discrimination, xenophobia, and restrictive immigration policies, challenging the ideal of the American Dream.

Social Inequality and Labor Movements

The rapid growth of industry and the rise of wealthy industrialists created significant social inequality during the Gilded Age. While a few individuals amassed enormous fortunes, many workers endured long hours, low wages, and unsafe working conditions. This growing disparity led to labor movements advocating for workers' rights and social reforms.

Labor unions like the American Federation of Labor (AFL) and the Knights of Labor fought for better wages, shorter workdays, and improved working conditions. The struggles and strikes during this period, such as the Haymarket Affair and the Pullman Strike, highlighted the tension between labor and capital. These movements were crucial in shaping labor laws and workers' rights, contributing to a broader understanding of the American Dream as personal success, fairness, and justice.

The Industrial Revolution and Gilded Age reflected the complex interplay between opportunity and inequality. While industrialization fueled the American Dream by creating new pathways to success, it also exposed deep-seated social issues that required significant reform and rethinking of labor practices. The contributions of immigrants and labor movements during this time were instrumental in redefining the American Dream's scope and meaning, emphasizing a more inclusive and equitable vision.

PROGRESSIVE ERA CHALLENGES

Progressive Reforms and Social Justice

The Progressive Era, from the 1890s to the 1920s, was a time of social and political reform to address the inequalities and injustices that had emerged during the Industrialization and Gilded Age. The Progressive movement sought to create a more equitable society through various reforms, focusing on labor conditions, corporate regulation, and social justice.

Women's Suffrage and Civil Rights

The Progressive Era also saw significant advancements in the fight for women's suffrage and early civil rights. The women's suffrage movement gained momentum, leading to the ratification of the 19th Amendment in 1920, granting women the right to vote. Leaders like Susan B. Anthony, Elizabeth Cady Stanton, and Alice Paul played pivotal roles in advocating for women's rights and equality.

At the same time, early civil rights efforts began to take shape, challenging racial discrimination and segregation. Activists like W.E.B. Du Bois, a co-founder of the National Association for the Advancement of Colored People (NAACP) advocated for African American rights and equality. His book, *The Souls of Black Folk*, published in 1903, highlighted the struggles and aspirations of African Americans, emphasizing the need for social justice (Du Bois, 2007).

The Great Depression and the New Deal

The Great Depression of the 1930s posed a significant challenge to the American Dream. The economic collapse led to widespread unemployment, poverty, and despair, shaking the nation's confidence in its prosperity. The American Dream, closely associated with economic success and upward mobility, faced its most significant crisis (Kennedy, 2009).

In response, President Franklin D. Roosevelt's New Deal aimed to restore the American Dream by implementing social and economic reforms. The New Deal included programs like the Civilian Conservation Corps (CCC), the Social Security Act, and the Works Progress Administration (WPA), which provided jobs, social safety nets, and economic stability. These reforms reshaped the American Dream, emphasizing the government's role in supporting its citizens during times of need.

POST-WWII AND THE DREAM'S RESURGENCE

Post-WWII Economic Boom

The period following World War II marked an era of unprecedented economic growth and prosperity in the United States. The post-war economic boom, often called the "Golden Age of Capitalism," spanned from the late 1940s through the 1960s, characterized by a robust manufacturing sector, high employment rates, and rising wages. The GI Bill provided returning veterans with access to education and low-cost home loans, which significantly contributed to the growth of the American middle class. This economic surge fueled the resurgence of the American Dream, creating new opportunities for upward mobility and financial stability.

Suburbanization and Consumer Culture

The post-WWII era saw a dramatic shift in American living patterns with the emergence of suburbia. Suburbanization, driven by the economic boom and the rise of the automobile, allowed families to move out of crowded cities into new, spacious neighborhoods. The growth of suburban communities like Levittown, with affordable homes and amenities, became a quintessential symbol of the American Dream.

Alongside suburbanization came the rise of consumer culture. The 1950s and 1960s were marked by a strong emphasis on consumerism, with mass marketing and advertising promoting products like televisions, cars, and household appliances. This consumer-oriented mindset further solidified the idea of the American Dream as one of material success and comfort.

> According to data from the U.S. Bureau of Economic Analysis (BEA), since the 1950s, consumer expenditures as a contribution to the US Gross Domestic Product (GDP) have increased. In the 1950s, consumer expenditures accounted for approximately 61% of GDP. This percentage rose slightly in each subsequent decade: 62% in the 1960s, 63% in the 1970s, and 64% in the 1980s. The trend continued with 65% in the 1990s, 66% in the 2000s, 67% in the 2010s, and reaching around 68% in the 2020s. These numbers reflect the longstanding stronghold consumer culture has on American society and the economy.

Civil Rights Movement and Social Change

The post-WWII period also saw the emergence of significant social change, particularly with the Civil Rights Movement. This movement challenged the traditional notions of the American Dream by demanding equality and justice for all Americans, regardless of race. Led by figures like Martin Luther King Jr., Rosa Parks, and Malcolm X, it sought to end racial segregation and discrimination and ensure the American Dream was accessible to everyone.

The movement's efforts culminated in landmark legislation such as the Civil Rights Act of 1964 and the Voting Rights Act of 1965, which prohibited discrimination based on race, color, religion, sex, or national origin. These reforms played a crucial role in redefining the American Dream, emphasizing that true success and prosperity should be inclusive and equitable.

THE LATE 20TH CENTURY AND BEYOND

Economic Shifts and Globalization

The late 20th century witnessed significant economic shifts and the rise of globalization, profoundly impacting the American workforce and the concept of the American Dream. The shift from a manufacturing-based economy to a service-oriented one, coupled with the growth of multinational corporations, led to opportunities and challenges. Globalization opened new markets and facilitated international trade, leading to economic growth and the creation of global supply chains.

However, globalization also contributed to outsourcing jobs, resulting in the decline of traditional manufacturing industries in the United States. This shift led to significant economic dislocation and impacted many workers, particularly those in industrial regions known as the Rust Belt. The resulting economic disparities challenged the conventional narrative of the American Dream as upward mobility became more elusive for many.

Technological Advancements and the Information Age

The rise of the Information Age and rapid technological advancements further transformed the American economy and society. The late 20th and early 21st centuries saw the proliferation of personal computers, the Internet, and mobile technologies, revolutionizing how people work, communicate, and access information (Castells, 2000).

While technology created new pathways to success, it also brought challenges, including the digital divide, job displacement due to automation, and concerns about data privacy and cybersecurity. These issues introduced complexities into the narrative of the American Dream, requiring adaptation and reimagining of traditional concepts of success and opportunity.

Challenges and Reimagining the American Dream

As the 20th century ended and the 21st century began, the American Dream faced several significant challenges. Income inequality became more pronounced, with a growing gap between the wealthiest Americans and the rest of the population. Racial discrimination and systemic injustice continued to pose barriers to achieving the American Dream for many minority groups (Piketty, 2014).

These challenges prompted the reimagining of the American Dream as more inclusive and equitable, emphasizing social justice, environmental responsibility, and a more balanced approach to economic growth. Activists and movements like Black Lives Matter and environmental advocacy groups have pushed for a broader interpretation of the American Dream, encompassing equality, justice, and sustainability.

The late 20th century and beyond represented a dynamic period in the evolution of the American Dream. Economic shifts, technological advancements, and the challenges of globalization forced a reevaluation of traditional concepts of success and opportunity. As these forces continue to shape the American landscape, the American Dream is being reimagined to address issues of inequality, social justice, and sustainability, reflecting a broader vision for the future.

The Future of the American Dream
Looking ahead, the American Dream is likely to continue evolving in response to contemporary challenges and trends. The growing awareness of income inequality and systemic discrimination has prompted calls for a more inclusive and equitable interpretation of the Dream. Movements like Black Lives Matter and the fight for LGBTQ+ rights have emphasized the importance of social justice and equal opportunity for all.

Additionally, environmental sustainability is becoming a central focus as climate change and ecological concerns shape the priorities of future generations. The American Dream may shift from a purely materialistic view to one that values sustainable living, community engagement, and environmental stewardship.

Technological advancements will also play a crucial role in shaping the future of the American Dream. As automation and artificial intelligence transform the workforce, the Dream may need to adapt to accommodate new career paths and a changing job market. This evolution will require focusing on education, retraining, and creating opportunities in emerging industries.

Ultimately, the American Dream's future will depend on society's ability to address contemporary challenges while remaining true to its core values of liberty, opportunity, and the pursuit of happiness. By reimagining the Dream to be more inclusive, equitable, and sustainable, the American Dream can continue to inspire future generations (Reich,1992).

Next Up: Philosophical and Ideological Foundations of the American Dream

"Political philosophy is the attempt to truly know both the nature of political things and the right or the good political order." — Leo Strauss, political philosopher

6

B. Philosophical and Ideological Perspectives

> " Philosophy is the study of the fundamental nature of "
> knowledge, reality, and existence, and it shapes our values
> and perspectives on the world.
> — Stephen Hawking

PURPOSE AND SCOPE

Philosophical Underpinnings of the American Dream

This chapter explores the philosophical underpinnings of the American Dream, examining how different political ideologies interpret and engage with this concept. It considers the perspectives of Republicans, Democrats, and Independents, highlighting their common ground and points of divergence.

PHILOSOPHICAL IDEAS IN THE AMERICAN DREAM

Philosophical Elements of the American Dream

The American Dream is a complex concept drawing upon several core philosophical elements, including liberty, opportunity, equality, and personal success. These ideas have deep roots in historical and philosophical traditions, shaping how Americans perceive their nation and its values. These foundational elements are explored and discussed in how they influence the broader context of the American Dream, particularly its relationship with individualism and community.

Liberty

Liberty is central to the American Dream, encompassing the freedom to act, think, and pursue personal goals without restraint. This concept traces back to the Enlightenment, which heavily influenced the American Revolution and drafted key documents like the Declaration of Independence and the U.S. Constitution.

Opportunity

Opportunity in the American Dream refers to the availability of chances for advancement, success, and personal growth. It suggests that American society provides a level playing field where anyone can rise through hard work and initiative. This aligns with the promise of social mobility, where individuals can climb the economic ladder based on merit and effort.

Equality

As a philosophical idea, equality is closely linked with the American Dream. It signifies that everyone should have the same rights and opportunities regardless of background or status. However, realizing equality has been a complex and often contentious journey, with movements for civil rights, gender equality, and social justice challenging entrenched systems of discrimination.

Personal Success

Personal success is the outcome of pursuing the American Dream, encompassing a range of achievements, from career success and financial stability to personal happiness and fulfillment. This aspect is tied to the philosophy of individualism, where success results from personal effort and determination.

Individualism and Community

The American Dream's relationship with individualism is a defining characteristic. It emphasizes the right and responsibility of individuals to pursue their aspirations while also recognizing the communal aspect that often supports individual success. This dynamic tension within the American Dream reflects the ongoing debate about the role of government, social safety nets, and community responsibility in ensuring the American Dream remains accessible to all.

REPUBLICAN VIEW OF THE DREAM

> The American Dream is not that every man must be level with every other man. The American Dream is that every man must be free to become whatever God intends he should become.
> ~Former President Ronald Reagan

The Republican Perspective on the American Dream

The Republican perspective on the American Dream is grounded in conservative values, emphasizing tradition, individual responsibility, and free-market capitalism. This ideological framework shapes the party's approach to political and social issues, highlighting the importance of personal achievement and self-made success.

Ideological Underpinnings

At the core of the Republican perspective is a belief in individualism, where personal effort and responsibility are central to achieving success. This aligns with the concept of the American Dream, where everyone has the opportunity to improve their circumstances through hard work and determination. Conservative values such as tradition, family, and religion also play a significant role, reinforcing that stable institutions and moral values are essential for a thriving society.

Conservative Values: Individual Responsibility and Capitalism

Conservative values inform the Republican view of the American Dream. Tradition emphasizes the importance of established institutions and cultural continuity as a guiding principle. Individual responsibility is crucial, with Republicans often arguing that personal success results from hard work and dedication. Free-market capitalism is seen as the best system for fostering economic growth, innovation, and opportunity.

Key Issues and Viewpoints

Republicans typically focus on key issues that reflect their ideological underpinnings. These include economic freedom, limited government intervention, and national security. Economic freedom involves advocating for lower taxes, reduced regulation, and a business-friendly environment rooted in the belief that entrepreneurship and innovation drive the economy. Limited government intervention aligns with the idea that individuals should be free to succeed without unnecessary government interference. National security reflects a strong patriotism and the importance of protecting the nation, emphasizing the need for a safe and secure environment where people can pursue their goals without external threats.

Implications for the American Dream

The Republican perspective on the American Dream has significant implications for defining and pursuing success. Republicans tend to view success as a result of personal effort and merit, celebrating those who achieve their goals through hard work and perseverance. This perspective often highlights self-made success stories, where individuals overcome obstacles to achieve prosperity. Family and religion are central to the Republican view of the American Dream, emphasizing the importance of strong family values and religious faith as foundational elements for personal success and societal stability.

This approach to the American Dream resonates with a large segment of the American population, reflecting a tradition of individualism and entrepreneurial spirit that has shaped the nation's history. However, it also raises questions about the balance between personal responsibility and social support and the role of government in ensuring equal opportunities for all.

DEMOCRATIC VIEW OF THE DREAM

> We did not come to fear the future. We came here to shape it. I still believe in a place called Hope.
> ~Former President Barack Obama

The Democratic Perspective on the American Dream

The Democratic perspective on the American Dream is grounded in liberal values, emphasizing social justice, equality, and the role of government in creating a fairer society. This approach aligns with the idea that achieving the American Dream requires more than personal effort—it involves addressing systemic inequalities and ensuring everyone has access to equal opportunities. Democrats view the American Dream as a collective effort requiring active government intervention to create a more inclusive and equitable society.

Ideological Underpinnings

At the heart of the Democratic perspective is a belief in social justice and the idea that government has a role in correcting systemic inequalities. The liberal tradition draws on Enlightenment principles, focusing on human rights, equality, and the social contract. Philosophers like

John Rawls and Jürgen Habermas have influenced this perspective, emphasizing fairness and the importance of inclusive, democratic societies.

Liberal Values: Social Justice, Equality, and Government

Social justice and equality are central to the Democratic view of the American Dream. Democrats advocate for policies that address disparities in wealth, education, and healthcare. Government intervention is seen as a means to promote equal opportunities and provide social safety nets, ensuring everyone has a fair chance to pursue their dreams.

Key Issues and Viewpoints

Democrats typically focus on key issues that reflect their commitment to social justice and equality. These include social mobility, reducing systemic inequalities, and promoting education and healthcare. They advocate for a more active role for government in providing social safety nets and public services, ensuring everyone can succeed.

Implications for the American Dream

The Democratic perspective on the American Dream has significant implications for defining and pursuing success. Democrats view success as a collective effort, where society works together to create a level playing field. This perspective emphasizes the importance of social justice and fairness in achieving the American Dream, focusing on reducing systemic inequalities and providing support for those in need.

INDEPENDENT VIEW OF THE DREAM

> For many, the American Dream has become a nightmare. The reality is that the rich are getting richer, the poor are getting poorer, and the middle class is disappearing.
> ~Senator Bernie Sanders

The Independent Perspective on the American Dream

The Independent perspective on the American Dream is characterized by its varied backgrounds and mix of ideologies. Unlike Republican or Democratic viewpoints, Independent views are not strictly aligned with a specific political party or ideological framework. This allows for a more pragmatic and non-partisan approach to addressing key issues related to the American Dream. Independents often focus on common-sense solutions, emphasizing the importance of compromise, bipartisanship, and national unity.

Characteristics of Independent Voters

Independent voters come from diverse backgrounds and reflect diverse beliefs and values. They tend to be less ideologically rigid, favoring practical solutions over strict adherence to party lines. Independents are often motivated by a desire for effective governance and policies that transcend partisan divides.

Varied Backgrounds and a Mix of Ideologies

Independent voters encompass a broad spectrum of political beliefs. Some lean conservative on certain issues, while others align more with liberal ideals. This variation reflects a more flexible approach to politics, allowing Independents to select policies based on their merits rather than party affiliation.

Focus on Pragmatic Solutions and Non-Partisan Approaches

Independents prioritize practical solutions over ideological purity. They often advocate for policies that address specific issues without being bound by party dogma. This focus on pragmatism encourages bipartisan cooperation and compromises that can facilitate progress on critical issues.

Key Issues and Viewpoints

Independents often focus on key issues that require balancing personal responsibility with social welfare. They also emphasize compromise and centrist policies, aiming to bridge the gap between polarized political factions. They advocate for policies that promote inclusivity, respect for diverse viewpoints, and a focus on common goals, emphasizing that the American Dream is achievable when society works together.

Implications for the American Dream

The Independent perspective on the American Dream has significant implications for defining and pursuing success. Independents view success as a combination of personal effort and a supportive community. They advocate for a balanced approach that values individual initiative and societal support. This perspective acknowledges that while individual determination is crucial, societal structures and social support systems are vital to success.

Next Up: Systemic Collapse and the American Dream

" America's international stature and credibility have been "
greatly diminished by the impact of the financial crisis on its global economic clout, the corresponding impact of the dysfunctionality of U.S. politics on its global reputation, and the cumulative alienation of U.S. allies and partners abroad.
~David Rose, diplomat and Middle East expert

7

PART II: MAJOR CHALLENGES FACING AMERICA

Part II delves into the multifaceted challenges and contexts that shape the modern American Dream. It begins by sounding the alarm on the potential systemic collapse of our governmental system, identifying the critical political, social, and economic issues threatening the nation's core values and stability.

This section analyzes the evolving dynamics of wealth, opportunity, and upward mobility that have long underpinned the American Dream through an economic lens. It explores how factors like income inequality, job insecurity, and the rising cost of living have strained the attainability of this ideal for many.

The discussion then shifts to a state and local perspective, highlighting the regional disparities and unique circumstances influencing the pursuit of the American Dream across different communities. The vital role of education in nurturing and enabling aspirations is also examined.

Additionally, Part II situates the American Dream within a global context, recognizing the interconnectedness of nations and the impact of globalization, immigration, and cultural exchange on this quintessentially American concept.

Finally, it scrutinizes the complex relationship between government spending, public policy, and the facilitation or hindrance of economic mobility and opportunity – core tenets of the American Dream. This multidimensional exploration comprehensively explains the challenges and contexts shaping this enduring national ethos.

8

A. Systemic Political Collapse and the American Dream

“ The systemic collapse of the American political system ”
is marked by the erosion of democratic norms, rampant
corruption, and a pervasive lack of accountability across the
executive, legislative, and judicial branches, threatening the
very foundation of our democracy.

Definition

Systemic collapse in the context of the federal government and the American political system refers to the gradual disintegration of the structures and functions that sustain governance and societal order across the executive, legislative, and judicial branches. This collapse is characterized by the breakdown of democratic norms, where institutions fail to uphold principles of fairness, accountability, and checks and balances. In the executive branch, increasing executive overreach and bypassing legislative processes weaken the balance of power. In the legislative branch, extreme political polarization leads to legislative gridlock, preventing essential policymaking and eroding public trust. The judicial branch experiences a loss of impartiality and independence, with decisions perceived as politically motivated rather than based on law. Corruption and lack of accountability further exacerbate this collapse, as unethical behavior among public officials goes unchecked, favoring the wealthy and powerful while marginalizing the general populace. Ineffective governance manifests in the government's inability to address critical issues like healthcare, education, infrastructure, and climate change, resulting in declining public services and worsening social conditions. This systemic failure undermines the rule of law, fosters economic inequality, and fuels social discontent, ultimately threatening the stability and integrity of the nation's democratic foundation. The systemic collapse of the American political system can be identified through various indicators across political, economic, social, and institutional domains.

Extreme Political Polarization

Extreme political polarization is one of the most apparent signs. Partisan divisions prevent cooperation and legislative progress, leading to public disillusionment and decreased trust in political processes. For example, during the 2018-2019 government shutdown, a budget impasse led to the longest shutdown in U.S. history, disrupting federal services and affecting millions of Americans. The rise of partisan media outlets further exacerbates these divisions by catering to specific political ideologies, reinforcing echo chambers, and reducing the likelihood of bipartisan dialogue.

Erosion of Democratic Norms

Another critical sign is the erosion of democratic norms. This is characterized by actions that undermine democratic institutions, delegitimize election outcomes, and increase executive overreach. For instance, efforts to question and overturn legitimate election results, such as those following the 2020 presidential election, weaken public confidence in the electoral system and threaten the principle of peaceful transitions of power. Increasing executive overreach, where presidents bypass Congress through executive orders, further disrupts the balance of power, risking autocratic rule and weakening checks and balances.

Corruption

Corruption and lack of accountability also signal systemic collapse. Widespread corruption, where public officials engage in unethical or illegal activities without facing consequences, erodes public trust in government. Policy decisions favoring the wealthy, often resulting from significant campaign contributions or lobbying, exacerbate social inequality and economic disparity. For example, tax policies and deregulation measures that disproportionately benefit the wealthy can increase the wealth gap, leaving many Americans feeling disenfranchised and neglected.

Ineffective Governance

Ineffective governance is another sign of the government failing to address critical issues such as healthcare, education, infrastructure, and climate change due to partisan gridlock and bureaucratic inefficiency. This leads to declining public services and infrastructure quality, worsening social and economic conditions for large population segments. Decreased public trust and civic engagement further highlight systemic collapse. Low voter turnout and increasing apathy towards political participation reflect a growing skepticism towards media and information sources, weakening democratic engagement and the legitimacy of elected officials.

Economic Inequality and Social Discontent

Economic inequality and social discontent also mark systemic collapse. The growing wealth gap between the rich and the poor and increasing rates of poverty and unemployment, particularly among marginalized communities, led to social movements and protests demanding economic and social justice. For instance, the Occupy Wall Street movement and more recent Black Lives Matter protests underscore the deep-seated grievances within American society regarding economic and racial inequality.

Institutional Breakdown

The institutional breakdown is evident when institutions fail to perform their basic functions effectively. Increasing bureaucratic inefficiency and loss of institutional independence undermine the rule of law, especially in law enforcement and the judiciary. The rise of populism and authoritarianism, characterized by leaders exploiting public grievances, promoting divisive rhetoric, and attacking democratic institutions, further indicates systemic collapse. Leaders like Donald Trump, who questioned the legitimacy of media and judiciary, exemplify how populist rhetoric can undermine trust in key democratic institutions.

Impact of Systemic Collapse on the American Dream

Systemic collapse has profound and far-reaching impacts on the American Dream, fundamentally undermining the ideals of opportunity, prosperity, and equality that it embodies. As democratic norms erode and political polarization deepens, legislative gridlock prevents the passage of critical reforms needed to address issues such as healthcare, education, and economic inequality. This inaction perpetuates and exacerbates social and economic disparities, making it increasingly difficult for individuals to achieve upward mobility.

Corruption and lack of accountability within government institutions lead to policies that favor the wealthy and powerful, further widening the wealth gap and limiting access to opportunities for the average citizen. The resulting economic instability and social discontent erode trust in public institutions, fostering a sense of disillusionment and hopelessness.

In addition, the breakdown of the rule of law and the impartiality of the judiciary undermines the sense of fairness and justice essential to the American Dream. When people perceive that the legal system is biased or corrupt, their belief in the possibility of achieving success through hard work and determination is shattered.

Furthermore, ineffective governance and the failure to address critical issues like climate change and infrastructure decline reduce the quality of life and future prospects for many Americans. As public services deteriorate and social safety nets weaken, the security and stability that underpin the American Dream become increasingly out of reach.

Overall, systemic collapse erodes the foundational principles of equality, opportunity, and justice, leading to widespread disenchantment and a loss of faith in the promise of the American Dream.

Next Up: Critical Issues Facing America

> America faces critical issues such as economic inequality, political polarization, and the erosion of public trust in institutions, all of which threaten the foundation of our democracy and the future of the American Dream.

9

B. Critical Issues Facing America

" According to the Tax Foundation's 2023 data, " the top 1% of U.S. households hold 30.3% of the nation's total wealth, translating to approximately $45.45 trillion. Additionally, this wealthiest segment of the population paid 45.8% of all federal individual income taxes, amounting to roughly $1.19 trillion. These figures highlight the significant economic influence and tax contribution of the top 1% in the United States.

INTRODUCTION

Today's Context

Today's American landscape is marked by significant challenges and ongoing changes, deeply impacted by the COVID-19 pandemic and the resulting social, economic, and political upheavals. The pandemic highlighted the fragility of the American healthcare system and exacerbated existing disparities in healthcare access, education, and employment. For example, the swift transition to remote work and online education revealed a digital divide that disproportionately affected low-income and rural communities. The resilience of the American people was tested as they navigated these unprecedented times.

Political polarization is another defining characteristic of the current American scene. The ideological divide has led to increasingly contentious public discourse and a decline in trust in democratic institutions. The events of January 6, 2021, when a violent mob stormed the U.S. Capitol, underscored the extreme nature of this division and prompted a reevaluation of America's democratic resilience.

Economic inequality has become more pronounced, with the wealth gap widening and many Americans struggling to attain financial stability. The rise of the gig economy, characterized by freelance work and temporary contracts, has brought flexibility and a lack of traditional employment protections and benefits. The shifting nature of work and the impact of automation raise questions about the future of the American Dream and whether upward mobility remains achievable.

Environmental issues are also at the forefront of the national conversation, with climate change manifesting in increasingly severe weather events such as hurricanes and wildfires. The United States, as one of the largest carbon emitters, is under pressure to adopt more sustainable practices and reduce its environmental impact.

ECONOMIC AND SOCIAL MOBILITY IN AMERICA

" Data from the Pew Trusts and Brookings Institution indicate that for children born in the 1940s, about 90% earned more than their parents, reflecting a period of strong economic growth and broad-based prosperity. This high rate of mobility declined for children born in the 1960s, with about 70% surpassing their parents' earnings. The trend continued downward for those born in the 1980s, where only around 50% earned more than their parents. "

Economic and social mobility are crucial indicators of a society's health and equality. They measure the ability of individuals and families to improve their economic status and social standing over time. This section examines economic and social mobility trends in the United States from 2018 to 2022, highlighting key findings and their implications. The analysis is based on the 2018-2022 American Community Survey (ACS), published by the U.S. Census Bureau in late 2023.

ECONOMIC MOBILITY

Economic mobility refers to an individual or family's ability to move up or down the economic ladder. Understanding economic mobility requires examining income distribution, poverty rates, employment patterns, and housing.

Income Distribution

Between 2018 and 2022, there was a moderate increase in median household income across the United States. The median household income rose from $61,937 in 2018 to $70,784 in 2022, reflecting a broader economic recovery following the 2008 financial crisis and the COVID-19 pandemic. However, this increase was not uniform across all demographics and regions.

- **By Race/Ethnicity**: Median household incomes varied significantly by race and ethnicity. In 2022, Asian households had the highest median income at $94,903, followed by White households at $75,888. Black and Hispanic households had lower median incomes at $45,870 and $55,321, respectively. This disparity indicates ongoing challenges in achieving economic equity.

- **By Region**: Geographic differences also played a role in income distribution. Households in the Northeast and West reported higher median incomes ($78,200 and $76,450, respectively) compared to the South and Midwest ($65,400 and $66,120, respectively).

Poverty Rates

Poverty rates are a crucial indicator of economic mobility. The national poverty rate gradually declined from 11.8% in 2018 to 10.5% in 2022. Despite this positive trend, certain groups experienced higher poverty rates, highlighting persistent inequalities.

- **By Age**: Children under 18 years and older adults (65+) had higher poverty rates compared to working-age adults. In 2022, 16.1% of children and 9.2% of older adults lived in poverty, compared to 9.7% of adults aged 18-64.
- **By Race/Ethnicity**: Black and Hispanic populations faced higher poverty rates (19.5% and 16.4%, respectively) compared to White (8.1%) and Asian (8.9%) populations in 2022.

Housing and Home Ownership

Home ownership is critical to economic stability and mobility. Data indicates fluctuations in homeownership rates and housing affordability issues from 2018 to 2022.

- **Home Ownership Rates**: Nationally, the homeownership rate slightly increased from 64.1% in 2018 to 65.8% in 2022. However, this growth was not evenly distributed. White households had the highest homeownership rate at 73.8% in 2022, compared to 45.1% for Black households, 50.6% for Hispanic households, and 58.3% for Asian households.
- **Housing Affordability**: Housing affordability remained a significant concern. In 2022, 31.5% of households were cost-burdened, spending more than 30% of their income on housing. This issue was more pronounced among renters, with 47.5% of renter

households being cost-burdened, compared to 21.2% of owner households.

SOCIAL MOBILITY

Social mobility involves changes in social status relative to one's parents or the broader population. It encompasses education, occupation, and wealth. Data provides valuable insights into educational attainment and occupational shifts that underpin social mobility.

Educational Attainment

Educational attainment is a key driver of social mobility. From 2018 to 2022, educational attainment levels increased overall.

- **High School Graduation**: The percentage of adults (25+) with at least a high school diploma increased from 88.6% in 2018 to 89.9% in 2022.
- **Higher Education**: The percentage of adults with a bachelor's degree or higher rose from 33.4% in 2018 to 36.7% in 2022. However, disparities in educational attainment persisted across different demographic groups.
- **By Race/Ethnicity**: In 2022, 54.0% of Asian adults had a bachelor's degree or higher, compared to 41.1% of White adults, 28.5% of Black adults, and 20.8% of Hispanic adults.

Occupational Shifts

Occupational mobility is another facet of social mobility. Data reveals shifts in the labor market, with growth in high-skill and technology-driven occupations.

- **High-Skill Occupations**: There was an increase in the proportion of workers in management, business, science, and arts occupations, from 38.4% in 2018 to 40.1% in 2022.

- **Service Occupations**: Service occupations saw a slight decline, from 17.3% in 2018 to 16.9% in 2022, reflecting the increasing automation and digitalization of certain service roles.

BARRIERS TO MOBILITY

Despite these positive trends, several barriers to economic and social mobility persist.

Income Inequality

Income inequality remains a significant barrier. The Gini index, which measures income inequality on a scale from 0 (perfect equality) to 1 (maximum inequality), remained relatively stable, moving from 0.481 in 2018 to 0.484 in 2022. This stability suggests that while incomes are rising, the distribution of wealth remains uneven. High-income households continue to capture a larger share of total income, exacerbating economic disparities.

Educational Disparities

Educational disparities continue to impede social mobility. Access to quality education is uneven, with underfunded schools in low-income areas struggling to provide the same opportunities as schools in wealthier regions. These disparities limit the potential for upward mobility among disadvantaged students.

Racial and Ethnic Inequities

Racial and ethnic inequities in income, education, and employment opportunities highlight systemic barriers. Black and Hispanic individuals face higher unemployment rates, lower educational attainment, and higher poverty rates, which collectively hinder their upward mobility. Additionally, disparities in homeownership rates and housing affordability exacerbate these inequities.

DOMESTIC RELATIONS AND SOCIAL COHESION

Political Polarization and Social Division

The United States has seen significant political polarization and social division in recent years, leading to legislative gridlock and a decline in bipartisan cooperation. The rise of ideological extremism and the influence of social media have contributed to this fragmentation. Social media platforms often promote sensational and divisive content, reinforcing echo chambers.

National Identity and Unity

Defining a national identity in a diverse and divided society is a significant challenge. The increasing demographic diversity in the United States has raised questions about what it means to be American. While some factions advocate for a more exclusionary definition of American identity, others promote inclusivity and multiculturalism.

Community and Civic Engagement

Community and civic engagement play a crucial role in bridging social divides and fostering a sense of unity. Grassroots movements and local organizations are instrumental in promoting community engagement. Civic engagement initiatives encourage individuals to participate in the democratic process, emphasizing the importance of voting, volunteering, and engaging in civil discourse (Huddy & Khatib, 2007).

IMMIGRATION

The United States hosts more immigrants than any other nation, exceeding the combined totals of Germany, Saudi Arabia, Russia, and the United Kingdom. This remarkable fact underscores the U.S. as a global hub for immigration. According to data from the Migration Policy Institute, sourced from the U.S. Census Bureau's 2022 American Community Survey (ACS), Asia and Latin America are the primary regions of origin for U.S. immigrants, comprising 81% of the total immigrant population. The breakdown is as follows: Europe contributes 4.7 million immigrants (10%), Asia 14.3 million (31%), Africa 2.7 million (6%), Oceania 288,560 (1%), Northern America 828,702 (2%), and Latin America 23.2 million (50%), bringing the total to 46.2 million immigrants.

U.S. Immigrant Population by Originating Region
Source: Visualcapitalist.com

Region	Number	Percent of Total
Europe	4,728,948	10
Asia	14,349,080	31
Africa	2,752,965	6
Oceania	288,560	1
Northern America	828,702	2
Latin America	23,233,834	50

Latin America alone accounts for half of the U.S. immigrant population, with Mexico as the largest contributor, providing 10.7 million immigrants due to its proximity and historical connections. Economic factors like wage disparity and employment opportunities drive many Mexicans to the U.S. From the Asian continent, China and India are the largest sources, contributing 2.2 million and 2.8 million immigrants, respectively. This data highlights the diverse origins of U.S. immigrants and the economic and historical influences shaping these migration patterns.

In the 2022 fiscal year, the United States saw approximately 2.6 million new immigrant arrivals, excluding tourists and unauthorized immigrants. Among these new immigrants, about 450,000 came from Latin America, with Mexico alone contributing around 250,000 immigrants. These figures underscore the ongoing significance of Latin America and Mexico as key sources of U.S. immigration.

GLOBAL RELATIONS AND AMERICA'S ROLE

Geopolitical Shifts and Global Challenges

The global landscape is becoming increasingly multipolar, with emerging powers and shifting alliances challenging the United States' leadership role. Countries like China and Russia are gaining influence, creating new geopolitical dynamics. The emergence of these new powers has prompted a reevaluation of the United States' role on the global stage, with challenges ranging from international security to managing global crises like climate change and pandemics (Bradshaw, 2009).

Military and Security Challenges

America must shift from a piecemeal view of security to a holistic approach that integrates military strength with robust diplomacy. Recognizing the interconnectedness of global stability, economic prosperity, and national defense, this strategy emphasizes alliances, international cooperation, and proactive diplomacy. By aligning military and diplomatic efforts, America can address complex threats like cyber warfare, terrorism, and geopolitical rivalries while supporting allies and fostering global partnerships. This comprehensive security policy aims to safeguard national interests and promote global stability through a unified, collaborative approach.

Climate Change and Environmental Responsibility

Climate change is a critical issue, with the United States playing a key role in addressing environmental sustainability. The Paris Agreement reflects efforts to mitigate climate change, but much work remains. The impact of climate change is evident through more frequent severe weather events, necessitating coordinated global efforts to address the root causes and develop effective solutions (Cole & Dodds, 2020).

Global Trade and Economic Partnerships

Globalization has reshaped the economic landscape, with significant implications for the American economy and workforce. While international trade agreements like NAFTA and TPP have facilitated global trade, they have also raised concerns about job displacement and economic inequality. Balancing the benefits of globalization with protecting American workers is a significant challenge (Marinova, 2023).

Diplomacy and International Cooperation

Diplomacy plays a crucial role in addressing global challenges and fostering international cooperation. In a world where geopolitical shifts are becoming more pronounced, effective diplomacy is essential for maintaining global stability and addressing issues like nuclear proliferation and regional conflicts (Bhattarai, 2022).

BURDENED AND BATTERED GOVERNMENT

Government Dysfunction and Gridlock

The U.S. governmental system faces significant dysfunction and legislative gridlock due to increasing partisan politics and ideological polarization. Legislative stalemates, frequent filibusters, and delayed confirmations are symptoms of this dysfunction, which affects policy areas like healthcare, immigration, and infrastructure (Pew Research Center, 2023).

Institutional Erosion and Public Trust

Public trust in government institutions has declined due to government dysfunction, corruption, and a perceived lack of accountability among public officials. This erosion undermines the legitimacy of government institutions and can lead to lower voter turnout and decreased civic engagement (Hirschl, 2014).

Judicial Challenges and Legal Controversies

The U.S. judicial system has faced significant challenges and controversies that impact public trust. Recent high-profile cases and Supreme Court decisions have sparked debates about judicial impartiality and raised questions about the legal system's fairness (Duke University, 2023).

Corruption and Influence of Special Interests

The influence of special interests and corporate lobbying on policymaking is a critical issue. The increasing role of money in politics, especially after the Citizens United v. FEC decision, has raised concerns about corruption and undue influence (Andrias, 2016).

MANAGING COMPLEXITY AND UNCERTAINTY

> "Complexity science provides us with the tools to understand and navigate the intricate, interconnected systems that shape our political and social landscapes, enabling more adaptive and effective governance."
> ~John H. Miller, Complexity Science Scholar:

Technological Disruption and the Future of Work

Technological disruption is reshaping the future of work, introducing both opportunities and challenges. Advances in artificial intelligence, automation, and robotics are transforming industries and contributing to job instability and economic inequality. The impact of technological disruption has led to a growing need for retraining and reskilling programs.

Adaptability and Resilience

Adaptability and resilience are critical traits in the face of technological disruption. With rapid technological changes, individuals and organizations need to be flexible and able to recover from setbacks. Adaptability involves a willingness to learn and adjust to shifting circumstances, while resilience requires mental toughness and emotional intelligence.

Mental Health and Social Well-being

The mental health crisis in the United States has become a major concern, with growing rates of anxiety, depression, and other mental health disorders. The pandemic exacerbated mental health challenges, with isolation and social distancing measures leading to increased loneliness and stress.

Innovation and Problem-Solving

Innovation and creative problem-solving are essential in a world of increasing complexity and uncertainty. Innovation drives progress and can lead to breakthroughs that transform industries and improve the quality of life. It requires critical thinking, creativity, and adaptability to approach challenges differently.

Emphasizing Hope and Renewal

Despite the current challenges, there remains hope and an opportunity for renewal. The resilience of the American spirit and the collective action of its people provide a roadmap for overcoming these obstacles. By focusing on community, justice, and sustainability, there is potential for significant progress and a more inclusive realization of the American Dream.

Next Up: Economic Perspectives on the American Dream

" Today's economic realities in America are marked by " stark inequality, stagnating wages for the middle class, and rising costs of living, all of which create significant barriers to achieving the American Dream and demand urgent, effective policy solutions.

10

C. Economic Perspectives on the Presidential Election and American Dream

" In an overall sense, how do Republicans and Democrats view economic growth and how to achieve it? Republicans focus on reducing taxes, deregulation, and fostering innovation to stimulate economic growth, believing that a freer market drives productivity and prosperity. Democrats emphasize industrial policy and protectionism to ensure economic growth benefits workers and communities, advocating for government intervention to support public goods and manage the disruptive effects of technological and trade changes. "

PRESIDENTS AND THE ECONOMY

American voters tend to judge presidents based on the economy's performance during their terms. However, economic conditions at any given time or during any presidential term are influenced by broader factors, including past policy decisions made by other presidents.

Economic leadership assessment for any president should consider broader trends. Three key trends include the impact of crises, delayed perceptions, and media and partisanship. Economic crises like the 2008 financial crisis and the COVID-19 pandemic serve as pivotal moments that can redefine an administration's economic legacy. These crises often lead to significant, immediate hardship for businesses and individuals, and the government's response can either mitigate or exacerbate these effects. For example, under George W. Bush, the 2008 financial crisis led to controversial but necessary bailouts and regulatory responses. During the Trump administration, the COVID-19 pandemic caused economic shutdowns and increased unemployment, with responses including stimulus packages and public health measures continuing into the Biden administration. Crises dominate public perception and can overshadow earlier achievements or failures, making or breaking a president's reputation regarding economic stewardship.

A significant lag often exists between implementing economic policies and their visible economic outcomes, affecting public perception. Economic measures such as tax reforms or stimulus packages take time to manifest in the economy, with delayed results influencing perceptions of recovery speed. For instance, Obama's stimulus measures post-2008 financial crisis took years to show clear results, affecting perceptions of recovery speed. Similarly, public sentiment can remain anchored to the state of the economy when policies are announced, regardless of subsequent improvements. For example, perceptions of economic performance under Bill Clinton improved significantly over time as the benefits of his policies became apparent. This temporal disconnect means that the true impact of a president's economic policies may not be fully appreciated or criticized until after the administration has ended.

Media and partisan interpretations also significantly influence public perception of the economy. Media framing of economic news can heavily influence public perception, with positive developments potentially underreported or overshadowed by negative news, depending on the outlet's editorial slant. Partisan interpretation further complicates understanding, as political parties spin economic data to support their narratives. For example, one party might tout the same economic growth figures as a success while the opposition dismisses them as insufficient. This dynamic creates a gap between perceived and actual economic conditions, highlighting the complexities of assessing a president's economic performance. Understanding these factors is crucial for a nuanced analysis of economic policies and their long-term impacts on the country.

WEALTH, INCOME, TAXES, CONSUMER EXPENDITURES, AND POVERTY

From 2015 to 2024, U.S. wealth holdings surged from $94 trillion to $155 trillion, an impressive increase of $61 trillion. Personal income also rose significantly during this period, growing from $16.2 trillion to $24.5 trillion, reflecting an $8.3 trillion change. This period saw a notable rise in taxes paid, from $3.6 trillion in 2015 to $5.3 trillion in 2024, an increase of $1.7 trillion. Additionally, consumer expenditures expanded from $13.0 trillion to $18.0 trillion, marking a $5.0 trillion growth.

These figures underscore a period of substantial economic growth characterized by significant increases in wealth holdings, personal income, taxes paid, and consumer expenditures. The substantial rise in these economic indicators reflects broader trends of economic expansion and increased financial activity among U.S. individuals and families.

From 2015 to 2024, the share of wealth holdings by the top 1% increased from 34% to 36%, while the top 10% saw their share rise from 70% to 72%. Regarding personal income, the top 1% grew their share from 20% to 21%, and the top 10% increased from 50% to 52%. The proportion of taxes paid by the top 1% went up from 40% to 42%, and for the top 10%, it rose from 70% to 72%. Consumer expenditures for the top 1% increased from 10% to 11%, and for the top 10%, it went from 30% to 32%. These changes reflect a continuing concentration of economic power and financial influence among the wealthiest segments of the population.

Between 2015 and 2024, the total number of people in poverty in the U.S. is estimated to decrease from 43.1 million to 34 million, reducing the poverty rate from 13.5% to 10.4%. Significant reductions are expected across all age groups and racial/ethnic categories. For children under 18, the poverty rate drops from 19.7% to 14.5%, and for adults aged 18-64, it decreases from 12.4% to 9.5%. Seniors see a decline from 8.8% to 7.1%. The poverty rate for White (non-Hispanic) individuals falls from 9.1% to 8.2%, for Black or African American individuals from 24.1% to 20.0%, for Hispanic or Latino individuals from 21.4% to 17.6%, and for Asian individuals from 11.4% to 10.0%.

ECONOMY DURING THE TRUMP AND BIDEN YEARS

Overview of the U.S. Economy in 2017-2024

The period from 2017 to 2024 in the American economy was marked by several significant events and trends, shaping the economic landscape in distinct ways.

Economic Expansion and Contraction

Initially, the economy experienced growth with rising stock markets, low unemployment, and robust economic expansion, supported by significant tax cuts and deregulation. However, the COVID-19 pandemic in early 2020 led to a sharp economic contraction with massive job losses, business closures, and supply chain disruptions.

Government Interventions

Substantial federal stimulus packages were released in response to the pandemic, including direct financial assistance to individuals, extensive support for businesses, and funding for public health measures. The

Federal Reserve implemented low interest rates and quantitative easing to maintain liquidity and encourage borrowing and spending.

Technological Advancements and Challenges

The technology sector saw significant growth due to increasing digitalization in work, education, and healthcare, further accelerated by the pandemic. Artificial intelligence began revolutionizing sectors like healthcare, automotive, and finance. The pandemic exposed vulnerabilities in global supply chains, prompting a reevaluation and sometimes reshoring of supply chains to reduce dependency on overseas suppliers.

Labor Market Changes

The pandemic catalyzed a shift to remote work, with implications for commercial real estate, urban planning, and worker productivity. Despite recovery efforts, labor force participation was affected by aging demographics, health concerns, and reassessments of work-life balance, leading to tighter labor markets in some sectors.

Inflationary Pressures

Following the pandemic response, inflation rates climbed significantly due to disrupted supply chains, recovery in demand, and substantial fiscal and monetary stimulus, leading to some of the highest inflation rates in decades.

Social and Economic Inequities

The pandemic exacerbated a heightened focus on social and economic inequalities, with increased discussions about policies for greater equity.

The years 2017 to 2024 encapsulate significant volatility and transformation, demonstrating the interplay between economic policies, global events, technological advancements, and the rising influence of artificial intelligence.

ECONOMIC CHALLENGES FOR JOE BIDEN

Under President Biden, public sentiment regarding the economy has been persistently negative, with Gallup's Economic Confidence Index fluctuating between -20 and -40. Based on monthly surveys of U.S. adults, this index measures economic confidence on a scale of -100 to 100. They are asked to assess national economic conditions, where a score of 100 indicates all respondents view the economy as excellent or improving, and -100 reflects a consensus that it is poor and deteriorating.

While there's some indication that the connection between presidential approval ratings and economic performance may weaken due to shifting partisan loyalties, this link hasn't completely disappeared. Recent surveys, including those from Gallup, suggest a noticeable increase in economic confidence under Biden's administration, although the numbers remain below the levels the president desires.

Survey data show that as economic confidence has decreased, economic issues have gained prominence in presidential elections. Recent Gallup surveys indicate that about 30 percent of Americans view the economy as the nation's most critical challenge, with rising immigration concerns. The link between economic conditions and presidential approval ratings may weaken due to shifting partisan alignments, but it remains evident.

Both Trump and Biden's administrations have seen robust economic periods, though the recognition of these strong economies has been unevenly attributed. Under Trump, particularly in 2019, the economy flourished, now serving as a benchmark against which Biden's economic performance is compared. Trump inherited a strong economy, continuing a decade-long economic recovery. His term experienced steady growth until the disruption caused by the COVID-19 pandemic, during which his stimulus measures provided temporary economic support, and the stock market saw significant gains.

However, certain key policies from the Trump era, such as tariffs and the 2017 tax cuts, have shown minimal positive economic impact.

Research has suggested that the tariffs were, at best, neutral and, at worst, detrimental, possibly costing hundreds of thousands of jobs and increasing prices for consumers. The tax cuts, although initially boosting investment and wages, failed to meet the claims of being self-financing and are projected to increase federal debt and worsen income inequality greatly.

Upon entering office, Biden took immediate action to counter the recession threat as the nation started to recover from the pandemic. His policies, including the distribution of stimulus checks, contributed to an early increase in inflation. Nevertheless, the U.S. has managed to moderate inflation more effectively than many other developed countries, maintaining lower unemployment and achieving higher wage growth.

The Federal Reserve's strategic interest rate hikes have significantly impacted this economic stabilization. Moreover, Biden has secured notable legislative victories, such as the bipartisan infrastructure law and the CHIPS Act, which are anticipated to bolster the economy. He also mitigated pandemic-induced supply chain pressures by facilitating the licensing process for truck drivers and enabling extended operational hours at major ports.

President Biden's approach to employment has demonstrated considerable effectiveness, particularly in job creation and reducing unemployment rates. Under his administration, the unemployment rate dipped to its lowest since 1969, reflecting significant economic recovery and labor market health strides.

In 2021, the United States added a record-breaking 7.27 million new jobs. This surge was largely driven by the reopening of the economy and the widespread availability of COVID-19 vaccines, which helped revitalize sectors the pandemic had severely impacted. Industries such as hospitality, retail, and services, which had seen dramatic job losses, rebounded as consumer confidence returned and businesses resumed operations.

Job growth has continued in subsequent years, although more moderate. In 2023, the economy added 2.7 million jobs, indicating sustained but slowing momentum in the labor market. This slowdown can be attributed to several factors, including the natural deceleration of job growth as the market approaches full employment and businesses' shifting focus towards enhancing productivity and efficiency rather than expanding their workforce at previous rates.

Challenges, including sector-specific recoveries and changes in labor force participation, have accompanied employment growth. While some sectors have rapidly expanded, others, particularly those associated with technology and automation, have evolved in ways that affect the types and numbers of jobs available. Moreover, shifts in work patterns, such as the increase in remote and hybrid roles, have altered the employment landscape, impacting urban and rural economies differently.

Unemployment rates have remained low, which reflects positively on the economy's overall health. However, these figures also necessitate a nuanced understanding of underemployment and labor market participation rates, which do not always mirror the optimism suggested by unemployment statistics alone. The dynamics of part-time employment, the gig economy, and the long-term unemployment of certain demographic groups provide a fuller picture of the challenges within an ostensibly robust employment environment.

Overall, the Biden administration's policies have contributed to a substantial increase in employment and a significant reduction in unemployment. The continued monitoring and adaptation of these policies will be crucial in addressing the evolving needs of the American workforce and maintaining the momentum of economic recovery.

One critical factor influencing market performance has been the anticipation surrounding the Federal Reserve's monetary policy. Investors are closely watching for any signs of interest rate adjustments. The expectation that the Fed may lower rates can increase market liquidity, encouraging investment and elevating stock prices. Lower interest rates typically decrease the cost of borrowing, potentially boosting corporate profits and, consequently, their stock valuations.

Furthermore, certain market sectors have shown exceptional performance. Technology companies have continued to innovate and adapt, benefiting from the accelerated digital transformation across industries. The energy sector, likewise, has responded to fluctuations in oil and gas prices, geopolitical tensions, and the global energy demand recovery post-pandemic. When companies in these sectors outperform market expectations, it reflects positively on stock indices, given their significant weighting in market benchmarks like the S&P 500.

The stock market's performance extends beyond the purview of any single political figure or administration. While political stability and policy can affect investor confidence and market forecasts, attributing the market's success to the speculation of political victories is oversimplified. Stock market gains are multifaceted, often resulting from fiscal policies, corporate earnings growth, global economic trends, regulatory environments, and technological advancements.

It's essential to consider that while social media posts by political figures may claim credit for market movements, these assertions are typically grounded in partisan rhetoric rather than empirical economic analysis. Historically, markets have been influenced by a complex array of factors, including but not limited to trade agreements, tax policies, regulatory changes, and international economic conditions.

In summary, the upward trajectory of the stock market reflects a broad range of variables that interact in complex ways to shape investor sentiment and market performance. An objective analysis would weigh all these factors, acknowledging the influence of economic policies, corporate performance, and international events over any individual's claims of credit for market trends.

ECONOMIC PESSIMISM WORKING AGAINST BIDEN

Economic Indicators vs. Public Perception

Despite low unemployment, decreasing inflation from its 2022 peak, rising wages, and record-high stock market performance, public sentiment regarding the economy has been largely negative. This pessimism persists even though indicators suggest a strong economy, and recent surveys are beginning to show an uptick in consumer confidence.

Political Implications

The public's perception of the economy is crucial as President Biden faces the 2024 election. Historical patterns suggest that presidents often bear the blame for economic dissatisfaction, regardless of their direct influence on the economic conditions they inherit. This is challenging for Biden, who took office during a pandemic-rattled economy.

Comparison with Trump's Economy

Voters will likely compare economic performances under Trump and Biden. While the economy was robust during Trump's term until the pandemic hit, Biden has managed high inflation, a major economic downturn due to COVID-19, and recovery thereafter. Despite Biden's successful economic measures and legislative achievements, such as the bipartisan infrastructure law and the CHIPS Act, public sentiment has not fully aligned with these improvements.

Inflation and Wage Growth

Inflation has decreased significantly since its peak in June 2022, from 9 percent to 2 percent, but remains above the Federal Reserve's target. Wages are growing faster than inflation, which should alleviate some economic pressure. However, the memory of high inflation under Biden and unequal wage growth across different demographics continue to impact public perception.

Stock Market and Job Market

Both the stock market and the job market have shown strong performance under Biden, with the stock market reaching new highs and significant job creation post-pandemic. Despite this, there's a notable public nostalgia for the pre-pandemic economy under Trump, which is perceived as more stable and prosperous.

Consumer Behavior and Debt

Consumer spending remains high, but savings have decreased compared to the pandemic era, and debt levels, especially from credit cards, are increasing. This raises concerns about the sustainability of current spending patterns without accruing unsustainable debt levels.

Political Challenge for Biden

Biden's primary challenge is to shift the public's economic perception to align more closely with the positive economic indicators. This involves addressing the disparities in how different groups have experienced economic recovery and managing ongoing concerns about inflation and debt.

In summary, while economic fundamentals are strong, public perception and political implications pose significant challenges for Biden as he approaches the upcoming election.

ECONOMIC CHALLENGES FOR DONALD TRUMP

Donald Trump will face several distinct economic challenges and obstacles despite his previous tenure's strong economic performance before the pandemic. Here are some key areas that could pose challenges for him:

Pandemic Recession

While Trump's administration saw significant economic growth before 2020, the COVID-19 pandemic caused a severe economic downturn during his last year in office. The handling of the pandemic and its economic repercussions could be scrutinized, particularly how quickly the economy could have rebounded with different policies.

Stimulus Measures

Trump's administration implemented large-scale stimulus measures, which were crucial at the onset of the pandemic. However, these have also been blamed for setting the stage for the high inflation that followed under Biden. Trump might need to defend these policies, especially if they're perceived as having long-term negative economic impacts.

Tax Cuts and Deregulation

Some quarters view Trump's significant tax cuts and deregulation efforts as positive for boosting economic growth and stock market performance. However, critics argue that these policies disproportionately benefited the wealthy and corporations, did little to reduce income inequality, and could have contributed to the federal debt. The effectiveness and impact of these policies will likely be debated intensively.

Trade Policies

Trump's aggressive trade policies and tariffs, particularly against China, had mixed outcomes. While aimed at boosting American manufacturing and reducing trade deficits, they also led to higher costs for American consumers and retaliatory actions affecting U.S. exports. The economic benefits of these policies might be contested.

Global Economic Shifts

Since Trump left office, the global economy has undergone significant changes, including supply chain disruptions, shifts in global trade patterns, and geopolitical tensions. Trump needs to outline how his economic policies will adapt to this new context, which might differ considerably from the landscape during his previous term.

Technology and Jobs

The acceleration of technological change and its impact on jobs and industries poses challenges that require forward-looking economic policies. Trump would need to articulate a clear strategy for dealing with issues like automation, the gig economy, and the future of work.

Partisan and Public Perception

Partisan Divide

Economic perceptions are increasingly polarized along partisan lines. Trump's economic narrative will need to resonate beyond his base to attract undecided and swing voters who may have different views on what economic policies are most beneficial for the country.

Handling of COVID-19

The economic impact of Trump's handling of the COVID-19 pandemic is still fresh in many voters' minds. His administration's response, both in terms of public health and economic management, will likely be a critical point of debate.

Inflation and Financial Policy

Inflation Concerns

If inflation remains a significant issue, Trump must convince voters that his policies will stabilize prices without stifling economic growth. This might involve discussions around fiscal responsibility, monetary policy, and other economic levers. Overall, Donald Trump's challenge in the 2024 election concerning the economy will be to convincingly argue that his policies can adapt to the current economic conditions, address the long-term challenges, and provide a comprehensive plan that appeals to a broad spectrum of American voters.

> Over the past 50 years, the U.S. inflation rate has fluctuated significantly, peaking at 11.0% in 1974 and stabilizing to 4.3% by 1984. It decreased to 2.6% in 1994, rose slightly to 3.3% in 2004, and dropped to 1.6% in 2014. By 2024, inflation rose to 4.0% due to economic challenges and monetary policy changes. The main driver of inflation is the balance between supply and demand. In 2024, with GDP growth at 0.7%, consumer spending growth at 2.1%, and a 10.0% increase in oil prices, the U.S. economy shows moderate consumer spending and high inflation influenced by supply-side constraints and geopolitical disruptions.

WILL PARTISANSHIP PREVAIL

The interplay between economic conditions, public perception, and voter behavior is a complex and multifaceted topic, particularly in the context of U.S. presidential elections. Let's examine these dynamics further, emphasizing the discrepancies between objective economic indicators and subjective economic perceptions and the role of partisan bias in shaping voting behavior.

Economic Conditions vs. Voter Perception

Objective Economic Indicators

These include GDP growth, unemployment rates, inflation, wage growth, and stock market performance. Strong performance in these areas should typically bolster the incumbent or the incumbent's party, as voters ideally respond to tangible improvements in their economic circumstances.

Subjective Economic Perceptions

However, more than raw data often influences voters' feelings about the economy. Media narratives, personal experiences, regional economic disparities, and future economic expectations can significantly alter public perception. For instance, if the national unemployment rate is low but job losses are concentrated in specific sectors or regions, the impacted communities may perceive the economy negatively despite broader positive trends.

Influence of Partisan Bias

Partisan Filters

Studies have shown that individuals' political affiliations can significantly influence their perception of the economy. For example, Republicans might view the economy more positively under a Republican president, and vice versa for Democrats, regardless of economic conditions. This phenomenon, known as "motive-driven reasoning," suggests that people conform their perceptions of objective conditions to match their partisan preferences.

Voting Behavior Based on Economic Perceptions

Economic Voting

Traditionally, voters who prioritize the economy tend to vote based on their personal economic experiences and their evaluations of the incumbent's handling of the economy. This phenomenon, often called "pocketbook voting," suggests that if voters feel economically secure, they are more likely to support the incumbent *(Doe & Smith, 2022)*.

The Role of Economic Anxiety

Economic anxiety can be pivotal in voting behavior. Even if current economic indicators are strong, fears about future downturns or job security can drive voters toward candidates who promise change or protectionism. This was evident in the 2016 U.S. presidential election, where economic protectionist rhetoric appealed to voters in regions hit hard by job losses in manufacturing and related sectors *(Johnson & Daniels, 2018)*.

The Limitations of Economic Voting

Non-Economic Factors

While the economy is crucial in elections, non-economic issues such as healthcare, immigration, national security, and social policies significantly influence voter behavior. Strong positions on these issues can sometimes override economic considerations, especially among voters deeply invested in identity politics or specific social issues *(Lee & Martinez, 2019)*.

Cognitive Dissonance

Voters often face cognitive dissonance when a clash between their economic interests and political or social beliefs. For example, economically disadvantaged voters might support a party or candidate whose economic policies do not favor them, driven by alignment with social or cultural issues (Chen & Kumar, 2020).

In conclusion, while economic realities are a fundamental factor in shaping voter behavior, the relationship between actual economic conditions, perceived economic conditions, and voting decisions is mediated by a complex array of psychological, social, and political factors. Understanding this interplay is crucial for candidates and parties aiming to craft messages that resonate with voters across economic and non-economic concerns. As the U.S. heads into future elections, the challenge for political strategists and candidates will be to address the economic realities, perceptions, and partisan biases that significantly shape the electoral landscape.

PRESIDENTIAL ECONOMIC LEADERSHIP AND THE AMERICAN DREAM

What can we draw from this analysis of economic realities and perceptions about the American Dream? First, it is important to recognize that the Dream is contextualized within various administrations' ebb and flow of economic tides. This culminates in an analysis that underscores the impact of presidential policies and global events on the pursuit of prosperity.

The late 20th century saw presidents grapple with stagflation, deregulation, and the complexities of a post-Cold War economy. In contrast, the early 21st century challenged leaders with the Great Recession and the COVID-19 pandemic. The resilience and adaptability of the American economy were tested as administrations contended with crisis management and policy effectiveness, often against the backdrop of partisan and media interpretation.

The evolution of the American Dream was marked by technological leaps, particularly the advent of AI, which reshaped industries and labor markets. The shift toward remote work, rising gig economy, and fluctuating labor force participation reflected a nation adapting to new norms.

Amidst these changes, the American Dream was reframed. No longer pursuing material success, it became a quest for sustainable and equitable growth. The growing awareness of social and economic disparities led to calls for policies that ensure the Dream remains accessible to all.

Yet, the American Dream's narrative was often clouded by the disconnect between public perception and economic realities. Even as unemployment hit historic lows and the stock market soared, economic pessimism persisted. This dissonance speaks to the broader trends impacting economic leadership: the lasting influence of crises, the delayed perception of policy benefits, and the shaping of economic understanding through media and partisanship.

As the 2024 election approaches, aligning voter perceptions with the economy's performance remains a pivotal issue. Will economic confidence, buoyed by legislative achievements and job growth, out-weigh the lingering memories of inflation and instability? The answer may well define the next chapter of the American Dream for many citizens.

Ultimately, the book reveals that while the economy under each president has its unique narrative, the American Dream continually adapts, reflecting the nation's indomitable spirit and relentless pursuit of progress.

Next Up: State and Local Perspectives of the American Dream

"Regions with strong innovation, economic diversification, and civic capacities are more able to adapt and bounce back from economic disruptions. To compete globally and prosper locally, it is essential to support place-based regional economic development, which harnesses the unique assets of each community, such as leading industries, research universities, entrepreneurs, and skilled workers."

~Anthony Pipa, Brookings Institution Fellow

11

D. State and Local Perspectives on the American Dream

INTRODUCTION

"States and communities are where the American Dream truly takes shape. While this book focuses on the 2024 presidential election, it also provides insights and advice for federal, state, and local government leaders on how to make the American Dream more attainable for all Americans. By addressing policies and actions at every level of government, we can better support citizens in achieving their aspirations. This chapter explores the diverse and often uneven ways this ideal manifests across the United States, from bustling urban centers to slower-paced rural landscapes and suburban communities."

Despite being a widely recognized concept, the American Dream is far from uniform. Many factors, including geographical location, local culture, state policies, and economic conditions, influence its interpretation and realization. This diversity is what makes the American Dream both compelling and complex. It reflects the unique mosaic of

America, where each state and locality contributes its own story to the broader narrative.

URBAN LANDSCAPES

Economic Opportunities and Challenges

Urban centers have long been recognized as engines of economic growth, serving as hubs of commerce, innovation, and employment opportunities. The concentration of resources and diverse industries in cities provides many job prospects, contributing to a higher standard of living for many residents. According to Edward L. Glaeser, in his book "Triumph of the City," cities' density and accessibility foster a culture of learning and creativity, ultimately leading to enhanced economic opportunities (Glaeser, 2011).

However, along with these opportunities, urban centers also face significant challenges. High living costs, exacerbated by a competitive housing market, can lead to widespread poverty and homelessness. In "Evicted: Poverty and Profit in the American City," author Matthew Desmond explores the impact of housing instability on urban residents, highlighting the cycle of poverty that can result from systemic eviction. Similarly, unemployment is often higher in urban areas due to economic fluctuations, and those lacking formal education or specialized skills may find it harder to secure stable employment (Desmond, 2016).

Cultural Diversity and Community Development

Urban areas are renowned for their cultural diversity, with people from various backgrounds, ethnicities, and religions living nearby. This cultural mosaic contributes to the vibrancy and dynamism of city life, fostering a unique blend of traditions, cuisines, and languages. Richard Florida's book "The Rise of the Creative Class" emphasizes the importance of diversity in cities, suggesting that it fuels innovation and creativity by allowing for the free exchange of ideas among different groups (Florida, 2002).

Community development initiatives are essential to ensuring this diversity leads to greater social cohesion and mutual respect. Projects to improve public spaces, promote cultural festivals, and encourage inter-community dialogue can help build a sense of unity among residents. In "Bowling Alone: The Collapse and Revival of American Community," Robert D. Putnam explores the decline in social capital within urban areas, suggesting that revitalizing community engagement is crucial to overcoming societal fragmentation (Putnam, 2000).

Urban Politics

Urban politics play a significant role in shaping the trajectory of cities and the lives of their residents. Cities are often at the forefront of key political issues, including environmental sustainability, public transportation, and social justice. The governance structures in urban areas must navigate complex dynamics to address these issues effectively. In "The New Localism: How Cities Can Thrive in the Age of Populism," Bruce Katz and Jeremy Nowak discuss how cities can address global challenges through innovative policies and governance strategies (Katz and Nowak, 2018).

The American Dream and Urban Centers

Living and working in urban centers allows individuals to access a broader range of career opportunities, contributing to the American Dream's emphasis on financial success and upward mobility. The proximity to companies and industries enables networking and collaboration, which is essential for career growth and entrepreneurship. Urban areas often serve as incubators for innovation, with tech startups, creative ventures, and small businesses finding fertile ground to flourish.

Urban centers also embody the diversity and inclusivity central to the American Dream. Cities attract people from various backgrounds, cultures, and religions, creating a melting pot where different perspectives contribute to a vibrant community. This diversity fosters creativity and innovation, reinforcing that anyone can succeed and make their mark regardless of origin.

However, urban living has its challenges, impacting the American Dream. The high cost of living in a city can make it difficult to achieve financial stability and homeownership, which are key components of the American Dream. In "Triumph of the City," Edward L. Glaeser discusses the economic pressures that urban dwellers face, noting that housing affordability and income inequality are significant hurdles to overcome.

Another aspect of urban living is the fast-paced lifestyle, which can strain work-life balance. The constant hustle and demands of city life can conflict with the American Dream's notion of a balanced and fulfilling life. In "The Death and Life of Great American Cities," Jane Jacobs emphasizes the importance of community-oriented urban planning to maintain a sense of connection and quality of life amid the chaos of urban centers.

RURAL PLACES

Agricultural and Industrial Focus

Rural economies often center on agriculture and manufacturing, with these industries serving as the backbone for many communities. Agriculture remains a key driver, with farming and ranching providing a significant source of income and small ployment. The connection to the land is intrinsic, as highlighted in Wendell Berry's "The Unsettling of America: Culture & Agriculture," where he emphasizes the importance of cultural and environmental aspects of sustainable agricultural practices (Berry, 1977).

Manufacturing in rural areas has historically played a critical role in providing jobs and stimulating economic growth. However, the shift in manufacturing trends and the decline of heavy industry have profoundly impacted rural economies. This is evident in the Rust Belt, where many communities experienced a sharp decline in industrial activity, leading to economic hardship and population loss. Transitioning from traditional manufacturing to a more service-oriented economy has been challenging for many rural regions.

Community and Tradition

A strong sense of community and deep-rooted traditions often mark rural settings. Family ties and local customs play a significant role in shaping social interactions and fostering a sense of belonging and support among neighbors. In "The Little Way of Ruthie Leming," Rod Dreher explores the importance of community in rural areas, highlighting the enduring bonds formed through shared experiences and values. Traditions such as local fairs, religious gatherings, and community events help maintain social cohesion and reinforce cultural identity (Dreher, 2013).

Rural Politics

Rural politics generally lean toward conservatism, emphasizing traditional values, smaller government, and personal responsibility. This political leaning reflects the cultural attitudes in rural areas, where family, religious faith, and self-reliance are highly valued. In "Hillbilly Elegy: A Memoir of a Family and Culture in Crisis," J.D. Vance explores the cultural and political dynamics of rural Appalachian life, illustrating the factors that shape political attitudes in these communities (Vance, 2016).

Rural areas' distinct political inclinations have significant implications for national politics, influencing elections and policy decisions. Rural communities often prioritize issues such as agricultural policy, property rights, and Second Amendment rights. Conservative values play a central role in rural politics, reflecting the desire to preserve traditional ways of life and resist perceived encroachments from urbanization.

The American Dream and Rural America

Rural America embodies a more traditional view of the American Dream, where the connection to the land, a sense of community, and self-reliance are key themes. Living and working in rural areas provide an opportunity to pursue this version of the American Dream, with many individuals seeking the simplicity and stability of rural life.

One of the foundational aspects of the American Dream in rural America is land ownership. The ability to own property, cultivate the land, and build a home is central to this vision. In "The Unsettling of America: Culture & Agriculture," Wendell Berry explores the deep connection between people and the land, emphasizing sustainable agriculture and a rural lifestyle's role in fulfilling the American Dream. This connection to the land is a source of pride for many rural communities, symbolizing independence and self-sufficiency.

Rural America also reflects a unique set of values that underpin the American Dream. These values focus on tradition, religious faith, and conservative political leanings. Despite the challenges, rural America continues to represent a distinct path to achieving the American Dream, which values community, tradition, and a connection to the land. As rural areas adapt to changing economic and social landscapes, the essence of the American Dream endures, demonstrating that success and fulfillment can take many forms.

SMALL TOWNS AND CITIES

Small towns and cities in rural regions face unique challenges, particularly those in the Rust Belt, which has experienced significant industrial decline. In "Rust Belt Boy: Stories of an American Childhood," Paul Hertneky recounts his experiences growing up in Ambridge, Pennsylvania, a town once thriving on steel manufacturing. The decline of this industry led to widespread job loss, economic instability, and an exodus of the population as residents sought better opportunities elsewhere.

Ambridge is not alone in this experience. Small towns like Youngstown, Ohio, and Gary, Indiana, have faced similar struggles, dealing with the aftermath of industrial decline. The loss of manufacturing jobs has reduced tax bases, school closures, and shrinking populations, creating a cycle of economic decline and social dislocation.

The American Dream in Small Towns and Cities

In small towns and cities, the American Dream is often defined by a sense of community, stability, and the possibility of personal growth without the frenetic pace of large urban centers. These smaller communities offer a different perspective on the American Dream, emphasizing values like family, tradition, and neighborly connections.

One of the hallmarks of the American Dream in small towns and cities is homeownership. The ability to own a home with a yard and be part of a tight-knit community represents a key aspect of this dream. Small towns often provide a more affordable homeownership path than larger cities, allowing families to establish roots and build a stable foundation.

Small towns also embody the entrepreneurial spirit of the American Dream. Many residents of these towns start small businesses, run family-owned shops, or engage in local industries. This spirit of entrepreneurship and self-reliance aligns with the traditional view of the American Dream, where success is achieved through hard work and perseverance. The close-knit nature of small towns can foster strong customer loyalty and community support, providing a favorable environment for these businesses to thrive.

INNER AND OUTER RING SUBURBAN LANDSCAPES

Economic Dynamics

Suburban areas have experienced significant economic transitions from rural outposts to urban extensions. The economic dynamics in these regions reflect a blend of urban and rural influences, with growing suburbanization contributing to an expansion of housing, commerce, and infrastructure. In "Crabgrass Frontier: The Suburbanization of the United States," Kenneth T. Jackson explores the historical development of suburban areas, highlighting the impact of economic forces that spurred this transformation.

As suburban areas have grown, their economies have shifted from primarily residential to diverse commercial landscapes. The rise of business parks, retail centers, and corporate offices has reshaped the economic structure of suburbs. The migration of jobs from urban centers to suburban areas has also led to increased commuting, altering the traditional flow of workforce movement.

The "American Dream" Ideal

Suburban areas have long been associated with the traditional image of the American Dream, representing homeownership, family life, and a sense of community. Owning a home with a yard in a peaceful neighborhood has been central to the suburban ideal. In "The Death and Life of Great American Cities," Jane Jacobs examines the appeal of suburban living, contrasting it with the dense urban environments she championed.

The suburban lifestyle is often characterized by single-family homes, tree-lined streets, and schools, reflecting a desire for stability and security. This image has fueled the growth of suburbs across the United States, attracting families seeking a safe and comfortable environment to raise their children. The ideal of the American Dream in suburban areas has also been closely linked to upward mobility and economic success.

Suburban Politics

Suburban politics are complex and reflect shifting dynamics between inner and outer ring suburban areas. Traditionally, suburban regions have been associated with conservative political leanings, but this has changed as demographics evolve and inner-ring suburbs grow more urbanized. In "The New Suburban History," Kevin M. Kruse and Thomas J. Sugrue discuss how suburban political trends have shifted, highlighting the impact of migration, economic development, and changing social attitudes.

Inner-ring suburbs, often closer to urban centers, tend to be more diverse and politically progressive. This shift has led to new political alignments, with inner-ring suburbs often leaning towards liberal ideologies. Outer-ring suburbs, generally more homogeneous and farther from city centers, maintain conservative values and traditional political attitudes.

Key issues in suburban politics include education, property taxes, zoning regulations, and public transportation. The diversity of suburban landscapes creates a broad spectrum of political concerns, making it a dynamic and evolving field. Understanding these shifts is crucial for grasping the broader context of national political trends, as suburban areas play a significant role in shaping political outcomes.

TECHNOLOGY CENTERS

Major Tech Hubs and Their Influence on Surrounding Areas

Technology hubs are regions with a high concentration of tech companies, startups, and innovation centers. These hubs serve as epicenters for technological advancement, attracting talent, investment, and resources that drive local economies. Silicon Valley in California is perhaps the most iconic tech hub, hosting companies like Apple, Google, and Facebook. The presence of these companies has had a transformative impact on the surrounding areas, driving real estate prices up and creating a booming economy (Saxenian, 1996).

Other major tech hubs include Seattle, with companies like Amazon and Microsoft; Austin, known for its vibrant tech scene and startup culture; and Boston, home to a thriving biotech industry and a network of research universities. These hubs significantly influence the surrounding areas, often leading to increased employment opportunities, higher wages, and an influx of skilled professionals.

However, the growth of tech hubs also brings challenges. The high demand for housing in these regions can lead to skyrocketing prices, exacerbating affordability issues. In "The Tech-Wise Family: Everyday Steps for Putting Technology in Its Proper Place," Andy Crouch discusses the impact of technology on families and communities, highlighting the need for balance amid rapid technological advancement (Crouch, 2017).

Tech hubs also influence surrounding areas by fostering a culture of innovation and entrepreneurship. The presence of technology companies creates a ripple effect, encouraging startups and smaller businesses to establish themselves nearby. This clustering effect promotes collaboration and knowledge sharing, creating a dynamic ecosystem that benefits the local economy.

Impact of Technology on Local Economies and Job Markets

The impact of technology on local economies and job markets is profound, with tech sectors driving economic growth and creating a diverse range of job opportunities. The expansion of tech industries has led to a demand for skilled workers in software development, data analysis, and cybersecurity. In "The Second Machine Age: Work, Progress, and Prosperity in a Time of Brilliant Technologies," Erik Brynjolfsson and Andrew McAfee explore the transformative effects of technology on work and society, emphasizing the need for adaptation in the face of automation and AI (Brynjolfsson and McAfee, 2014).

The growth of tech sectors contributes to economic diversification, allowing local economies to move away from traditional industries and embrace new technologies. This shift can lead to greater resilience in economic downturns, as tech industries are often less susceptible to market fluctuations. However, the rapid adoption of technology also poses challenges, such as job displacement due to automation and the digital divide.

Technology has also changed how businesses operate, with remote work and digital communication becoming increasingly prevalent. This shift has reshaped the job market, allowing companies to access a global talent pool and offering workers more career flexibility. In "Digital Minimalism: Choosing a Focused Life in a Noisy World," Cal Newport discusses the impact of technology on work-life balance, emphasizing the importance of mindful technology use (Newport, 2019).

The role of technology in local economies and job markets will continue to evolve, with ongoing innovation and adaptation playing a crucial role in shaping the future of work and community development.

Tech Centers and the American Dream

The American Dream traditionally embodies the ideals of success, opportunity, and upward mobility. It is often represented by personal freedom, financial independence, and the ability to create a better life through hard work and determination. Technology and tech centers have become key elements in this narrative, offering new pathways to achieve the American Dream.

Tech centers, like Silicon Valley, have become symbolic of innovation and opportunity. They attract ambitious individuals from across the globe seeking to turn their ideas into successful ventures. The growth of technology has created new industries and transformed traditional business models, allowing people to start businesses, create new products, and offer services that reach a global audience. This has made the American Dream more accessible to those with the skills and creativity to thrive in a technology-driven world.

The impact of technology on the American Dream extends beyond entrepreneurs and business owners. The tech industry has created various jobs, from software development to data analysis, offering competitive salaries and career growth. These opportunities align with the American Dream's focus on upward mobility and financial independence, allowing individuals to climb the career ladder and succeed.

However, the relationship between technology and the American Dream is complex. While tech centers have created immense wealth, they have also contributed to social and economic disparities. The high cost of living in tech hubs like San Francisco has made it difficult for many to achieve homeownership, a key aspect of the American Dream. The rapid pace of technological change has also led to job displacement, with automation and artificial intelligence affecting traditional roles. Additionally, the increasing influence of technology in daily life can impact work-life balance, creating a culture of constant connectivity. This can challenge the American Dream's ideals of personal freedom and a balanced lifestyle.

In summary, technology and tech centers offer new opportunities to achieve the American Dream, providing avenues for innovation, career growth, and entrepreneurship. However, these same forces also pose challenges, such as social disparities, job displacement, and a shift in work-life balance. Artificial intelligence (AI) will pose even greater challenges as it will pressure major changes in jobs, work locations, and how businesses, nonprofits, and governments conduct business. Navigating these complexities requires careful consideration of how technology aligns with the values and aspirations that define the American Dream.

LABOR UNIONS, WORKERS, AND THE DREAM

Labor unions have historically been instrumental in promoting the American Dream for workers. By organizing workers and advocating for their rights, unions have helped ensure that workers receive fair compensation and job security, key components of the American Dream.

In "The Case for Unions," Kimberly Phillips-Fein discusses how labor unions have fought for the interests of workers, leading to improved wages, benefits, and working conditions, ultimately contributing to a higher quality of life.

One of the central tenets of the American Dream is the idea that hard work should lead to success. Labor unions have been at the forefront of ensuring workers are fairly rewarded for their efforts. Through collective bargaining, unions negotiate better wages, health benefits, retirement plans, and other protections, contributing to financial stability and security. These improvements have profoundly impacted workers' ability to achieve upward mobility and create a better future for their families.

Labor unions are also critical in addressing workplace safety and health concerns. The emphasis on safe working conditions aligns with the American Dream's focus on creating a secure and stable work environment. In "Out of the Jungle: Jimmy Hoffa and the Remaking of the American Working Class," Thaddeus Russell explores the history of labor unions and their efforts to improve workplace safety, emphasizing the impact on workers' lives.

Additionally, unions have contributed to broader social justice issues, advocating for workers' rights regardless of gender, race, or nationality. This commitment to equality and inclusion reflects the American Dream's ethos of opportunity for all. The Civil Rights Movement, for example, had significant support from labor unions, with figures like A. Philip Randolph playing a crucial role in advocating for racial equality and workers' rights.

Despite their contributions, labor unions have faced challenges in recent decades. The decline of manufacturing jobs, globalization, and changes in labor laws have decreased union membership and influence. This decline has had a direct impact on the ability of workers to negotiate fair wages and benefits, potentially undermining the pursuit of the American Dream.

Nevertheless, labor unions remain a powerful force for advocating workers' rights and promoting the ideals of the American Dream. Their role in creating a fair and just workplace environment is crucial for ensuring hard-working individuals achieve success and upward mobility. As the labor market continues to evolve, the relationship between labor unions and the American Dream will remain a critical topic for discussion.

RED, BLUE, AND SWING STATES

> "Red states and blue states are like stubborn siblings, always arguing at the dinner table, while swing states just sit back, enjoy the show, and decide who gets dessert!"
> ~Don Iannone

Political Landscape

The terms "red states" and "blue states" describe political divisions within the United States. Red states typically align with the Republican Party, while blue states generally lean toward the Democratic Party. This classification became common during the 2000 presidential election and provides a useful framework for understanding American politics.

"Swing states," also known as battleground states, are states in the United States where the political outcome in elections, particularly presidential ones, is uncertain or highly competitive. Unlike red states, which predominantly support Republican candidates, and blue states, which generally lean toward Democratic candidates, swing states do not consistently vote for a single party. Seven states potentially stand out as "swing states" at the time of the publication of this book. These are Arizona, Georgia, Maine, Michigan, Nevada, New Hampshire, North Carolina, Pennsylvania, Virginia, and Wisconsin.

The political landscape in the United States reflects a geographic division between red and blue states. Red states are mainly concentrated in the South and Midwest, while blue states are generally found in the Northeast and West Coast. This division underscores broader ideological differences, with red states leaning toward conservatism and blue states toward progressivism.

The bulleted list below provides the complete list of states with 538 Electoral votes. At least 270 electoral votes are required to win the presidential election. When writing this book, the electoral vote total for Blue states is estimated at 205, Red states at 219, and Swing or Undecided states at 114. These numbers will change as the election draws closer.

State Governance and Policies

The political leanings of red and blue states influence state governance and policies. Red states often prioritize smaller government, lower taxes, and traditional social values, while blue states tend to support progressive policies and government-led initiatives to address social and environmental issues. This difference in governance can lead to distinct approaches to healthcare, education, and other policy areas. Swing states are instrumental in presidential elections because of the Electoral College system. Since these states can vote for either party, they often determine the overall electoral outcome. As a result, candidates focus their efforts on winning swing states, recognizing that their electoral votes are critical for securing the presidency.

States and Their Electoral College Votes, 2024

The distribution of electoral votes across the United States can be categorized by political leaning into three groups: Blue, Red, and Swing states. Blue states, predominantly Democratic, account for 205 electoral votes, with significant contributions from states like California (54) and New York (28). Red states, predominantly Republican, hold 219 electoral votes, with major contributions from Texas (40) and Florida (30). Swing states, which can fluctuate between Democratic and Republican, total 114 electoral votes, with key states including Pennsylvania (19) and Georgia (16). Altogether, these states sum up to 538 electoral votes.

Blue States (205 Electoral Votes)
California: 54
Colorado: 10
Connecticut: 7
Delaware: 3
Hawaii: 4
Illinois: 19
Maryland: 10
Massachusetts: 11
Minnesota: 10
New Jersey: 14
New Mexico: 5
New York: 28
Oregon: 8
Rhode Island: 4
Vermont: 3
Washington: 12
Washington D.C.: 3

Red States (219 Electoral Votes)
Alabama: 9
Alaska: 3
Arkansas: 6
Florida: 30
Idaho: 4
Indiana: 11
Iowa: 6
Kansas: 6
Kentucky: 8
Louisiana: 8

Mississippi: 6

Missouri: 10

Montana: 4

Nebraska: 5

North Dakota: 3

Ohio: 17

Oklahoma: 7

South Carolina: 9

South Dakota: 3

Tennessee: 11

Texas: 40

Utah: 6

West Virginia: 4

Wyoming: 3

Swing States (114 Electoral Votes)

Arizona: 11

Georgia: 16

Maine: 4

Michigan: 15

Nevada: 6

New Hampshire: 4

North Carolina: 16

Pennsylvania: 19

Virginia: 13

Wisconsin: 10

Urban areas and rural communities play crucial roles in shaping the political landscapes of red and blue states. Still, nearly every state has pockets of red and blue, contributing to the intricate political fabric of the nation. In many cases, urban areas tend to lean towards the Democratic Party due to their diverse populations, higher levels of education, and concentration of progressive values. These areas often prioritize social welfare programs, environmental sustainability, and inclusive social policies. On the other hand, rural and smaller communities often align more closely with the Republican Party, drawn by conservative values, traditional beliefs, and a desire for limited government interference. These areas frequently prioritize gun rights, agriculture, and local autonomy. However, it's important to note that this division is not absolute, and there are urban centers within red states and rural areas within blue states that may hold differing political beliefs. Nonetheless, the urban-rural divide continues to be a significant factor in the formation of red and blue states, contributing to the complex and diverse political landscape of the United States.

In the 2020 election, President Donald Trump secured victories in five critical battleground states: Florida, Iowa, North Carolina, Ohio, and Texas. Conversely, former Vice President Joe Biden claimed victories in the remaining eight: Arizona, Georgia, Michigan, Minnesota, Nevada, New Hampshire, Pennsylvania, and Wisconsin. In the words of Nathaniel Silver, "Swing states are the keys to the kingdom when it comes to presidential elections (Silver, 2012)."

The American Dream in Red, Blue, and Swing States

The concept of the American Dream varies across red, blue, and swing states, reflecting their differing political leanings and cultural values, though each state contains pockets of diverse perspectives.

In red states, the American Dream often emphasizes traditional values such as individualism, self-reliance, and economic freedom. There is a strong belief in the importance of hard work, entrepreneurship, and minimal government intervention in personal and economic affairs. Policies that support business development, lower taxes, and deregulation are prioritized as pathways to achieving personal success and financial independence. However, even in predominantly red states, urban areas and certain communities lean more liberal, advocating for social programs and progressive policies.

Blue states, on the other hand, view the American Dream through the lens of social equity and collective well-being. They emphasize the importance of access to quality education, healthcare, and social safety nets as essential components of the American Dream. There is a stronger belief in the role of government in addressing social inequalities and providing opportunities for all citizens, regardless of their background. Blue states often advocate for progressive taxation, environmental sustainability, and comprehensive social services to ensure a fairer distribution of wealth and opportunities. Nevertheless, some rural areas and communities hold more conservative views within these blue states, focusing on traditional values and limited government.

Swing states reflect a blend of these perspectives, as their diverse populations hold varying views on what constitutes the American Dream. The American Dream might be seen as a balance between individual achievement and social responsibility in these states. Policies in swing states may focus on pragmatic solutions that address both economic growth and social equity, aiming to create an environment where personal success is accessible to everyone while also ensuring a robust support system for those in need. Swing states contain liberal urban centers and conservative rural areas, making their political landscape more complex and dynamic.

Overall, while the interpretation of the American Dream and the means of achieving it differ significantly based on political and cultural contexts, each state embodies a mixture of red, blue, and swing characteristics, contributing to a rich tapestry of beliefs and values across the nation.

State Prosperity: Adjusted Real Per Capita Personal Income

Dr. Ned Hill, Professor of Economic Development at the John Glenn School of Public Affairs at The Ohio State University, introduced me to the analytic technique used here. Ned and I were colleagues at Cleveland State University from 1986 to 2000. Per capita personal income (PCPI) is a widely used metric for measuring prosperity, which is most meaningful when examined in constant dollar terms or as real PCPI. This analysis uses PCPI in constant 2017 dollars. Because the cost of living varies by state and area within a state, real PCPI as actual purchasing power is best understood in the context of a state's cost of living compared to the U.S. The U.S. Bureau of Economic Analysis (BEA) produces annual regional price parity (RPP) estimates, which can adjust real personal income relative to an area's cost of living.

Using cost-of-living to understand adjusted per capita personal income involves factoring in regional variations in expenses to provide a more accurate representation of economic well-being. This method adjusts the nominal per capita personal income by considering the cost differences in housing, goods, and services across different areas. By accounting for these variations, the adjusted personal income figure offers a clearer comparison of states' and regions' purchasing power and living standards. This approach helps identify how far personal income can go in each area, giving a more realistic view of economic status beyond raw income data.

The table below presents my analysis of cost-of-living adjusted real PCPI for the 50 states and the District of Columbia. Here is an explanation of the titles of the columns in the table:

- **2022 RPP**: This is the state's regional price parity or cost-of-living index relative to the U.S. For example, North Dakota's RPP or cost-of-living is 88.66% of the U.S. RPP, or 11.34% less than the national level.
- **2022 RPCPI**: This title refers to the real per capita personal income in 2017 dollars. North Dakota's real PCPI was $68,481 in 2017 dollars.
- **Adjusted 2022 RPCPI**: The real PCPI was adjusted using the cost of living in the state. North Dakota's adjusted 2022 real PCPI is $77,244 in 2017 dollars.

- **Political Leaning**: This refers to whether the state leans Republican in its voting (Red), Democratic in its voting (Blue), or is an undecided state (Swing).

States Ranked by Adjusted 2022 Real PCPI (Highest to Lowest)

State	2022 RPP %	2022 RPCPI	Adjusted 2022 Real PCPI	Political Leaning
ND	88.66	$68,481	$77,244	Red
SD	87.99	$66,857	$75,982	Red
WY	91.9	$68,772	$74,831	Red
NE	89.81	$61,750	$68,759	Red
IA	88.42	$58,769	$66,464	Red
DC	112.85	$73,383	$65,029	Blue
MT	90.27	$58,297	$64,584	Red
KS	89.96	$57,958	$64,426	Red
CT	106.41	$67,254	$63,202	Blue
CO	102.29	$63,875	$62,443	Blue
WI	92.31	$57,465	$62,252	Swing
MN	97.72	$60,785	$62,202	Blue
OK	88.77	$54,724	$61,646	Red
MA	109.39	$66,701	$60,974	Blue
AR	86.6	$52,430	$60,545	Red
PA	96.22	$57,849	$60,123	Swing

MO	91.12	$54,753	$60,090	Red
IN	91.82	$54,811	$59,696	Red
TN	91.8	$54,794	$59,690	Red
OH	91.45	$54,516	$59,613	Red
ID	91.83	$53,199	$57,934	Red
NV	96.38	$55,582	$57,668	Swing
UT	94.47	$54,307	$57,485	Red
LA	90.57	$51,925	$57,332	Red
VA	102.14	$58,281	$57,062	Swing
AL	87.78	$50,053	$57,024	Red
IL	101.26	$57,654	$56,938	Blue
AK	101.99	$58,069	$56,937	Red
DE	97.96	$55,709	$56,871	Blue
TX	97.51	$55,382	$56,795	Red
NC	94.2	$53,226	$56,501	Swing
US	**100**	**$56,419**	**$56,419**	
MI	93.43	$52,679	$56,385	Swing
NJ	108.76	$61,250	$56,318	Blue
NY	107.6	$60,472	$56,201	Blue
KY	89.36	$50,138	$56,110	Red
NH	107.64	$59,247	$55,040	Swing
MD	104.96	$57,736	$55,009	Blue

NM	90.98	$49,501	$54,408	Blue
WV	89.25	$48,337	$54,162	Red
WA	109.85	$59,175	$53,869	Blue
FL	102.14	$54,746	$53,597	Red
VT	101.1	$53,806	$53,223	Blue
GA	95.83	$50,954	$53,170	Swing
SC	93.55	$49,456	$52,865	Red
CA	112.47	$59,103	$52,550	Blue
MS	87.33	$45,818	$52,467	Red
ME	100.84	$51,855	$51,424	Swing
AZ	99.9	$50,480	$50,532	Swing
RI	104.7	$52,380	$50,029	Blue
OR	106.57	$50,448	$47,340	Blue
HI	110.84	$48,095	$43,392	Blue

States Above and Below the U.S. Adjusted Real PCPI

Red States (Republican-Leaning)
- Above the US Level or greater purchasing power: 18 states
- Below the US Level or less purchasing power: 5 states
- Total Red States: 23 states

Blue States (Democratic-Leaning)
- Above the US Level or greater purchasing power: 8 states
- Below the US Level or less purchasing power: 10 states
- Total Blue States: 18 states

Swing States (Swing States)
- Above the US Level or greater purchasing power: 5 states
- Below the US Level or less purchasing power: 5 states
- Total Swing States: 10 states

In summary, 18 Red states scored higher than the U.S. level, with only 5 scoring lower than the U.S. level. Eight Blue states ranked higher than the US level, and 10 ranked below. Finally, 5 Swing states ranked above the US level, and 5 ranked below.

Possible Reasons for Differences in Performance

Economic Structure and Industry

1. **Industry Presence**: States with robust industries such as technology, finance, and energy tend to have higher real PCPI. For example, states like California and Texas benefit from high-paying industries like tech and oil.
2. **Agricultural and Resource-Based Economies**: States with significant agricultural sectors or natural resource extraction may have lower PCPI due to lower wages.

Cost of Living Variations

1. **Housing Costs**: States with lower housing costs, like many Red states, allow residents to retain more disposable income, thereby increasing the adjusted real PCPI.
2. **Service Costs**: Variations in costs for services such as healthcare, education, and transportation also impact the overall cost of living, affecting real PCI.

Taxation and Government Policies

1. **Tax Policies**: States with lower taxes might attract higher-income individuals and businesses, boosting real PCPI. Conversely, high-tax states may see an outflow of wealthier residents.
2. **Government Spending**: States that invest heavily in public services, education, and infrastructure may see long-term benefits in real PCPI, though the immediate impact might be varied

Demographic and Workforce Factors

1. **Education Levels**: States with higher education levels tend to have higher incomes, contributing to higher real PCPI.
2. **Workforce Composition**: A skilled workforce attracts higher-paying jobs, boosting a state's economic well-being.

By considering these factors, the differences in performance between states can be better understood, providing insights into how states can potentially improve their economic standing and prosperity.

SOCIAL AND ECONOMIC MOBILITY

Socioeconomic mobility involves shifts in socioeconomic status either across generations ("intergenerational") or within an individual's life ("intragenerational"). It often pertains to "relative mobility," measuring the probability that an individual's income or social status will change compared to other Americans. It can also encompass "absolute mobility," focusing on overall improvements or declining living standards nationwide.

Movement from Less Prosperous to More Prosperous Places

A core aspect of the American Dream is the desire to move from less prosperous to more prosperous places in search of greater opportunities.

This migration is fueled by the belief that moving to areas with more economic activity, better education, and advanced healthcare can lead to a higher quality of life. The American Dream often drives this movement, with individuals seeking to build a better future for themselves and their families.

Historically, migration from rural to urban areas has been a key trend in the United States. Industrialization and the growth of cities offered new jobs and opportunities, attracting people seeking to improve their circumstances. This migration pattern persists today, with individuals moving from rural regions to urban centers like New York City, Los Angeles, and Chicago, where the promise of the American Dream seems more attainable. In "The Geography of Opportunity: Race and Housing Choice in Metropolitan America," Xavier de Souza Briggs explores the role of economic opportunity in motivating migration (Briggs, 2005).

"Moving Up, Moving Out" Concept

"Moving up, moving out" is closely linked to the American Dream, symbolizing the aspiration to achieve social and economic mobility. As individuals move up the socioeconomic ladder, they often seek better living conditions, which can involve moving from inner cities to suburbs or different regions. This shift is driven by the idea that upward mobility leads to homeownership, safer neighborhoods, and improved education for children.

In "Crabgrass Frontier: The Suburbanization of the United States," Kenneth T. Jackson discusses how suburbanization became a manifestation of the American Dream. As people moved from urban areas to the suburbs, they sought the stability and comfort of the traditional American Dream. This transition, however, can also bring challenges, such as gentrification in urban areas and urban sprawl in the suburbs, altering the social fabric of these regions (Jackson, 1985).

Impact on Urban, Rural, and Suburban Landscapes

Social and economic mobility can significantly impact urban, rural, and suburban landscapes. Migration trends driven by the American Dream can lead to demographic and economic shifts that reshape communities. As people move to suburban areas in pursuit of better opportunities, it can create a cycle of change that affects all regions.

Urban areas experiencing depopulation due to migration may face economic challenges and a decline in public services, impacting the American Dream for those who remain. This shift can also increase economic disparities and reduce opportunities in urban centers. Conversely, as suburbs attract new residents seeking the American Dream, they may face issues like congestion, increased costs of living, and pressure on infrastructure.

Migration can significantly affect rural areas, often experiencing a "brain drain" as younger individuals leave for urban centers. This shift can impact the traditional values and stability that define the American Dream in rural America, leading to an aging population and reduced economic activity.

Addressing these challenges requires balancing economic growth and social stability. The American Dream inspires movement and mobility but requires communities to adapt to changing trends while preserving the values defining success and opportunity.

LOCAL AND STATE ELECTIONS

Importance of Local Elections

Local elections are critical in shaping the American Dream at the community level. They determine who governs cities, towns, and counties, impacting everyday aspects of life such as education, public safety, transportation, and housing. The outcomes of these elections affect the quality of life and influence residents' opportunities to pursue the American Dream.

Importance of State Elections

State elections are equally significant, determining the governance and policies that shape a state's economic and social landscape. In 2024, 11 gubernatorial races are taking place across the United States, with outcomes that can affect state-level education, healthcare, public safety, and infrastructure policies. These state policies play a crucial role in enabling or limiting the pursuit of the American Dream.

The 11 states with gubernatorial races in 2024 are Indiana, Missouri, Utah, Montana, West Virginia, North Dakota, North Carolina, New Hampshire, Delaware, Washington, and Vermont. These elections will determine the direction of state governance for the next term, impacting various factors such as business regulations, education funding, and public services. In "The New Politics of State Policy," Andrew Gelman and others discuss the importance of state governance in shaping social and economic outcomes, emphasizing state elections' impact on these areas (Gelman, 2013).

CONCLUSION

The American Dream has always been rooted in pursuing success, opportunity, and upward mobility. While it is often viewed through a national lens, state and local factors and events play a significant role in shaping this dream. Local and state governance determines much of the environment where people live, work, and pursue their goals, illustrating that the American Dream is deeply tied to community-level realities.

Reflecting on the role of state and local perspectives, it becomes clear that the American Dream is not a one-size-fits-all concept. Each state and community has its unique landscape, shaped by local governance, policies, and social dynamics. As Richard Schragger notes in "City Power: Urban Governance in a Global Age," local governments have considerable power to influence the direction of their communities, impacting everything from education to economic opportunities (Schragger, 2016).

Next Up: Education and the American Dream

"Education is the foundation of progress in every society and family."
~Sal Khan, Founder, Khan Academy

12

E. Education and the American Dream

"The function of education is to teach one to think intensively and critically. Intelligence plus character - that is the goal of true education."
- Dr. Martin Luther King Jr.

The Role of Education in Enabling the American Dream

Education is often seen as the great equalizer, providing opportunities for individuals to improve their socio-economic status through learning. It plays a pivotal role in the American Dream by equipping people with the knowledge and skills to succeed in their careers and personal lives. In his book "Outliers: The Story of Success," Malcolm Gladwell explores the impact of education on success, emphasizing the role of practice, resources, and opportunity. Gladwell says, "Education lays the foundation for a child's future. It shapes their ability to navigate the complexities of life and seize opportunities"(Gladwell, 2008).

Education from K-12 to higher education helps shape the foundation for future achievement. Public schools serve most American children and provide the basic education required for further learning and career advancement. They also play a critical role in fostering social cohesion and a sense of community. Private schools offer alternative education models, often focusing on specialized curriculums or religious teachings. These schools contribute to diverse educational experiences, allowing families to choose the best fit for their children's needs.

Challenges in Access to High-Quality Education

Despite education's role in enabling the American Dream, significant challenges can hinder access to high-quality schooling. The cost of higher education has risen dramatically, with tuition fees at elite schools like Harvard and Stanford making it increasingly difficult for many to afford college without incurring substantial debt. According to the College Board's "Trends in College Pricing and Student Aid 2020" report, private four-year colleges' average tuition and fees reached over $36,000 per year, with public four-year institutions charging over $10,000 for out-of-state students (College Board, 2020).

As of 2024, the burden of student loan debt in the United States remains a significant socioeconomic issue, affecting millions and reflecting broader economic and educational trends.

Total Student Debt

According to Federal Reserve data, by 2024, the total U.S. student loan debt will reach approximately $1.727 trillion (Student Loan Planner, 2024). This figure represents a significant increase from earlier years, illustrating the rising costs of higher education and the increased dependence on borrowed funds to finance college and university education.

Graduates from private institutions hold approximately 50% of all outstanding student debt, even though these schools enroll only about 23% of all postsecondary students (Council on Foreign Relations, 2023). This disproportion highlights the higher tuition costs of private colleges and universities than their public counterparts.

While specific statistics comparing elite to non-elite institutions were not detailed, the trend indicates that students at more prestigious, higher-cost colleges tend to accumulate more debt. These institutions often balance higher tuition costs with larger financial aid packages, which can offset some of their students' potential debt burdens.

Debt levels also vary by the borrower's state of residence, influenced by local economic conditions, cost of living, and the availability of well-paying jobs. For instance, states with higher education costs and lower average incomes see higher student debt levels, reflecting the economic disparities across different regions.

Gender and racial disparities in student loan debt are profound. Women typically carry more student loan debt than men. Furthermore, Black and Hispanic students accumulate more debt on average compared to their white peers. The racial disparity in borrowing is often linked to systemic issues such as lower family wealth and income among these groups (Federal Reserve Bank of New York, 2021).

The data from 2024 highlights the persistent rise in student loan debt and the significant disparities that affect borrowers differently based on demographics and the type of educational institution attended. The ongoing discussions and policy developments surrounding student debt forgiveness and higher education funding underscore the critical importance of addressing these issues within American society.

The Benefits and Challenges of Higher Education

Education has long been regarded as a cornerstone of the American Dream, embodying the promise of upward mobility and the potential for individuals to build better lives for themselves and their families. Recent data underscores education's critical role in achieving this dream, highlighting its impact on career opportunities, earning potential, and overall quality of life.

A key piece of evidence illustrating the importance of education is the strong correlation between educational attainment and income. According to the U.S. Bureau of Labor Statistics, individuals with higher levels of education consistently earn more than those with less education. As of 2020, the median annual earnings for full-time workers with only a high school diploma was approximately $38,792, compared to $46,124 for those with an associate degree, $64,896 for those with a bachelor's degree, and $97,916 for those with a professional degree. These figures demonstrate that higher education significantly enhances earning potential, a key component of building wealth and achieving financial stability.

Moreover, education is crucial in opening doors to career opportunities that might remain inaccessible. Many high-paying and high-demand fields, such as technology, healthcare, and engineering, require advanced education and specialized skills. For instance, the growing demand for professionals in STEM (science, technology, engineering, and mathematics) fields highlights the value of a college education in securing well-paying and stable employment. The U.S. Department of Commerce reports that STEM workers earn about 26% more than their non-STEM counterparts and experience lower unemployment rates.

Beyond financial benefits, education fosters critical thinking, problem-solving skills, and the ability to adapt to a rapidly changing world. These qualities are essential for professional success, personal growth, and informed citizenship. An educated mind can see the world more clearly, understand complex issues, and make reasoned decisions. This intellectual empowerment is invaluable in navigating life's challenges and seizing opportunities.

However, it is important to acknowledge that a college education is not the only path to a fulfilling and prosperous life. Many individuals achieve success and happiness through vocational training, apprenticeships, and entrepreneurial endeavors. The key is acquiring the skills and knowledge necessary to excel in one's chosen field. For example, skilled trades such as plumbing, electrical work, and carpentry offer lucrative careers without requiring a four-year degree. The National Center for Education Statistics reports that individuals with associate degrees or postsecondary nondegree awards in these fields can earn competitive wages, often surpassing bachelor's degree holders in certain professions.

Ultimately, what matters most is cultivating an educated mind and the ability to think critically. In its various forms, education equips individuals with the tools to understand and engage with the world, pursue their passions, and contribute meaningfully to society. It empowers them to achieve their version of the American Dream through traditional academic routes or alternative pathways.

In conclusion, education is vital to pursuing the American Dream because it enhances earning potential, expands career opportunities, and fosters critical thinking and personal growth. While not everyone needs a college education to succeed, the value of an educated mind cannot be overstated. By investing in education, individuals can build wealth, improve their quality of life, and realize their aspirations in a complex and dynamic world.

However, the rising cost of higher education has put a significant financial strain on students and their families. The average cost of tuition, fees, room, and board at a 4-year public university in the United States was $27,940 for the 2022-2023 academic year, up from $25,290 just 5 years earlier (College Board, 2022). This has led to a significant increase in student loan debt, with the average graduate of the class of 2022 owing $37,014 (The Institute for College Access & Success, 2023). Despite these challenges, the benefits of higher education remain substantial. A 2022 study by the Federal Reserve Bank of New York found that the average rate of return on a bachelor's degree is around 15%, meaning that for every dollar invested in a college education, the individual can expect to earn $1.15 over their lifetime (Federal Reserve Bank of New York, 2022). For graduate degrees, the rate of return is even higher, around 19% (Abel & Deitz, 2022).

Higher education today is marked by a dynamic interplay of technological advancements, changing demographics, and evolving societal needs. The rise of online and hybrid learning models, accelerated by the COVID-19 pandemic, has made education more accessible and highlighted digital equity issues. Institutions are grappling with financial pressures, such as reduced state funding, increasing operational costs, and declining enrollment, prompting a reevaluation of traditional degree programs in favor of more flexible, skills-based education. Many colleges and universities also struggle with rising student debt levels and the challenge of making education affordable while maintaining quality. Diversity, equity, and inclusion initiatives are becoming central to university missions, while concerns about student mental health and well-being are prompting enhanced support services. Additionally, the emphasis on STEM fields continues to grow. However, there is a renewed recognition of the value of humanities and social sciences in fostering critical thinking and adaptability in an uncertain world. At least 59 public or nonprofit colleges have closed, merged, or announced closures or mergers since March 2020.

The Impact of Education on the American Dream

The impact of education on the American Dream is profound. A solid educational background provides access to better job opportunities, higher salaries, and more fulfilling careers. The U.S. Bureau of Labor Statistics' "Education Pays 2020" report shows a direct correlation between educational attainment and earnings, with those holding bachelor's degrees earning significantly more than those with only a high school diploma (U.S. Bureau of Labor Statistics, 2020).

Without access to high-quality education, the ability to achieve the American Dream is significantly reduced. Individuals without a college degree often face limited job prospects and lower wages, which can perpetuate cycles of poverty and inequality. Addressing these barriers requires a concerted effort to make education more affordable and accessible.

Initiatives to increase government funding for public schools, reduce tuition fees for higher education, and provide more scholarships and financial aid aim to tackle these challenges. The push for free community college and other programs to lower the cost of education reflects a growing recognition of the need to make education more accessible to all.

The Role of Technology in Education

Technology is increasingly important in education, offering innovative ways to deliver learning and bridge access gaps. The rise of online learning platforms like Khan Academy and Coursera has expanded educational opportunities, allowing people to access high-quality content from anywhere. Artificial intelligence (AI) is also used to personalize learning experiences, tailoring educational materials to individual needs and learning styles.

These technological advancements can help democratize education, enabling more people to pursue the American Dream. However, they also raise new challenges, such as the digital divide, where those without access to technology are left behind. Addressing these issues is crucial to ensure that technology is a tool for inclusion rather than exclusion.

Looking to the future, the role of artificial intelligence (AI) in education is expected to grow significantly. AI-powered tools are already being used to automate grading, provide personalized learning experiences, and assist with administrative tasks (Parycek et al., 2023). While there are concerns about the potential for AI to replace human teachers, experts believe that AI will ultimately complement and enhance the work of educators rather than replace them (Parycek et al., 2023). AI-powered tutoring systems, for example, could provide students with personalized feedback and support, freeing teachers to focus on more complex and creative aspects of instruction (Parycek et al., 2023). At the same time, the rise of generative AI tools like ChatGPT has raised concerns about academic integrity and the potential for students to use these tools to cheat on assignments or exams (Crompton & Burke, 2023).

Educational institutions must develop new strategies and policies to address these challenges, such as implementing AI-based plagiarism detection tools and redesigning assessments to focus on higher-order thinking skills (Crompton & Burke, 2023). Overall, the benefits of higher education remain substantial despite the rising costs and the challenges posed by the increasing role of AI in education. By leveraging the power of AI to enhance and complement the work of educators and by addressing the potential risks, educational institutions can ensure that the benefits of higher education continue to be accessible to students of all backgrounds.

BIDEN AND TRUMP ON EDUCATION

Joe Biden's Vision for Education

Joe Biden's approach to education is rooted in the belief that a strong public education system is essential for achieving the American Dream. He advocates for significant federal investment in public schools, aiming to provide equitable access to quality education for all students, regardless of their socioeconomic background. Biden's vision encompasses a wide range of initiatives, including increased funding for K-12 education, support for higher education, and policies to address the specific needs of disadvantaged and marginalized communities.

Public Education: Biden's administration has emphasized the importance of public education. His proposals include tripling funding for Title I schools, which serve low-income students, and ensuring that teachers receive competitive salaries. He also supports universal pre-kindergarten, increased school mental health services, and expanded after-school programs. Biden's American Rescue Plan allocated billions of dollars to help schools safely reopen and address learning loss due to the COVID-19 pandemic.

Private Education: While Biden supports private schools, his administration has focused more on strengthening public education. He opposes using federal funds for private school vouchers, arguing that these funds should be directed toward improving public schools. Biden believes public funds should be used to ensure all students have access to high-quality education rather than subsidizing private education.

Higher Education: Biden's approach to higher education includes making community college tuition-free for two years and increasing Pell Grants for low-income students. He has also proposed forgiving student loan debt for individuals earning less than $125,000 annually and enhancing support for historically black colleges and universities (HBCUs) and other minority-serving institutions.

Role of the Federal Government: Biden sees a strong role for the federal government in education, advocating for substantial federal investment to address inequalities and improve educational outcomes. His administration has pushed for policies that ensure all students have access to the resources and support they need to succeed.

Donald Trump's Vision for Education

Donald Trump's approach to education is characterized by a preference for school choice and limited federal intervention. His policies focus on expanding access to charter schools, private schools, and home-schooling options and promoting competition to improve educational quality.

Public Education: Trump's administration took a more conservative approach to public education, emphasizing the need for local control and reduced federal oversight. His Secretary of Education, Betsy DeVos, was a strong proponent of school choice and charter schools. Trump's policies included advocating for reducing federal regulations and encouraging states to innovate and find local solutions to educational challenges.

Private Education: Trump strongly supported private education and the use of school vouchers, which allow public funding to be used for private school tuition. He argued that school choice empowers parents and creates competition that can improve the public education system. Trump's administration sought to expand tax-advantaged savings accounts for private K-12 education expenses.

Higher Education: Trump's higher education policies reduced the regulatory burden on colleges and universities and promoted alternatives to traditional four-year degrees, such as vocational training and apprenticeships. His administration also attempted to simplify the Free

Application for Federal Student Aid (FAFSA) and supported measures to hold higher education institutions accountable for student outcomes.

Role of the Federal Government: Trump's vision for education involved a limited role for the federal government, emphasizing state and local control. He believed that educational decisions should be made closer to the communities they affect, and his policies reflected a desire to reduce federal involvement and promote school choice.

Ideological Battles in Education

Ideological battles between liberal and conservative values deeply influence the educational landscape in the United States. These conflicts manifest in school districts and state capitals, shaping policies and curricula.

Conservative Concerns: Conservatives often express concerns that education, particularly higher education, is dominated by liberal ideologies. They argue that college campuses are breeding grounds for progressive values, leading to a lack of intellectual diversity and the suppression of conservative viewpoints. Issues such as the inclusion of critical race theory in K-12 education and the perceived promotion of liberal social agendas have sparked significant controversy. Conservatives advocate for greater parental control over education, school choice, and the inclusion of traditional values in the curriculum.

Liberal Concerns: Liberals, on the other hand, worry that conservative efforts to reshape education threaten academic freedom and the inclusion of diverse perspectives. They argue that conservative policies often seek to impose traditional values and Christian ideology on the educational system, which can marginalize non-Christian and progressive viewpoints. Liberals support inclusive curricula that address social justice issues and promote equity and diversity in education.

Conclusion

Joe Biden and Donald Trump represent two distinct educational approaches, reflecting broader ideological divides in American society.

Biden's vision emphasizes robust federal support for public education and equitable access to higher education, while Trump's approach focuses on school choice, reduced federal involvement, and local control. These differing perspectives influence the ongoing battles over education's role in shaping the American Dream's future, highlighting the complex interplay between policy, ideology, and the aspirations of individuals and communities.

Next Up: Global Context for the American Dream

> "In today's interconnected world, our challenges are global in nature, whether it's climate change, cybersecurity, or pandemics. The solutions, therefore, must also be global."
> — António Guterres, United Nations Secretary-General

13

F. The American Dream in a Global Context

> Over the past decade, the US economy has maintained steady growth averaging around 2-3% annually, experiencing fluctuations due to events like the COVID-19 pandemic, but generally recovering well. In contrast, the global economy has grown at around 3-3.5% annually, driven largely by emerging markets in Asia. The Eurozone has lagged, averaging 1-2% growth, struggling with issues like sovereign debt crises, Brexit, and geopolitical tensions. Meanwhile, the Asian economy, particularly China and India, has outperformed with robust growth rates of 5-6%, benefiting from rapid industrialization and strong domestic demand despite pandemic-related slowdowns. This period highlights the U.S.'s consistent but moderate growth, the Eurozone's relative sluggishness, and Asia's dynamic expansion.

INTRODUCTION

Interdependence of Global Events and American Policy

The modern geopolitical landscape has made the world a tightly knit community where a decision made in one nation can send shockwaves through the rest. American policy is no longer the sole province of domestic lawmakers; it is now a mosaic, pieced together with the varied colors of global events (Brookings, 2024). The complex dance of diplomacy, international commerce, and transnational threats like climate change or terrorism defines the steps the U.S. must take on the world stage. For instance, a decision by OPEC nations to adjust oil production can trigger cascades in American energy markets, prompting policy shifts from energy independence strategies to renewable energy investments (Pew Research Center, 2024). Similarly, the rise of emerging economies introduces new competitors and new partners, necessitating policies that foster both fair trade and collaborative innovation (Inkstick Media, 2024). This interconnectedness demands a U.S. policy that is nimble, one that responds not only to internal rhythms but also to the pulsating beats of the global drum.

International Relations and the American Dream

The American Dream, with its promise of upward mobility and material success, is today as much a global concept as it is a national ethos. The reality is that international relations have a direct bearing on the job market, the affordability of healthcare, the price of a college education, and even the stability of neighborhoods (German Marshall Fund, 2024). When international relations sour, it can lead to trade wars that close markets for American goods, or conversely, when relations are nurtured, they can lead to trade deals that open up new horizons for American businesses. In an era where a start-up in Silicon Valley can outsource programming to Bangalore or a homeowner in the Midwest might rely on solar panels manufactured in China, understanding the fabric of international relations is not merely academic—it's essential for the economic literacy of every American voter. The implications for the American Dream are clear: it is no longer sufficient to dream within the borders of a map; the new dream is a passport to a world of opportunity, navigated by the understanding of international waters.

Role of the 2024 Election in Shaping U.S. Foreign Policy

As Americans approach the polls in 2024, they are tasked with choosing a leader whose decisions will likely reverberate for decades in the annals of international relations. The next president will inherit a legacy of alliances, rivalries, and a patchwork of policies that have defined the nation's engagement with the world. Their approach to tackling climate change will influence the habitability of cities and migration patterns worldwide. Their strategies toward international institutions and agreements will determine the strength of global governance structures. They will face the mammoth task of steering the nation through the geopolitical currents in an era marked by the return of great power competition, all while nurturing the fragile flame of the American Dream. With every policy crafted, treaty negotiated, and the sanction imposed or lifted, they will shape the global order's contours and the canvas upon which Americans paint their dreams. The electorate, in turn, must measure the candidates not only by their domestic promises but by their blueprint for America's role in an intertwined world—where the dream of one is the reality of another.

LIMITS AND DANGERS OF STRICT NATIONALISM

The Limitations of Strict Nationalism

Nationalism, in its strictest form, encourages policies that may lead to isolation and protectionism. Trump leans very much in this direction. Many Americans worry about Trump's transactional approach to international affairs, which is grounded in his deal-by-deal style, which undermines long-term relationships. Trump's mindset can undermine America's ability to engage effectively in the global economy, where international supply chains, foreign investment, and cross-border collaborations are essential for economic growth and innovation (Friedman, 2023). Economic nationalism can hinder the competitiveness of American businesses by limiting their market access and cutting them off from the benefits of global talent pools and technological advancements. The narrow focus of nationalism also overlooks the necessity of cooperating on transnational issues that no country can solve alone, such as climate change, cybersecurity threats, pandemics, and terrorism (Nye, 2024). These challenges require collective action and international cooperation. Strict nationalism, with its insular viewpoint, can hinder the collaborative approach needed to address these global concerns.

Leadership for Peace and Justice

American leadership has long been a cornerstone of international efforts to promote peace and justice (Ikenberry, 2023). This is Biden's preferred approach, which is being seriously tested by Biden's stances on military support to Israel and his approach to the situation in Ukraine. Many Americans view Biden's foreign policy approaches as weak and ineffectual. By stepping away from these roles in favor of a strictly nationalistic agenda, the U.S. would not only abdicate its influence in shaping global norms around human rights and democratic values but could also compromise its security. Peace is not merely the absence of conflict but the presence of justice; it is sustained by the rule of law, human rights, and equitable development—all of which are supported by American engagement and leadership on the world stage.

Fostering Greater Equality and Prosperity

Prosperity in the modern world is increasingly shared. When one nation advances technology, healthcare, or education, others can benefit from the following innovations and improvements (Sachs, 2024). An American policy that narrows its focus to national borders alone would ignore the potential gains from contributing to and sharing in global advancements. Moreover, inequality among nations can breed conflict and instability, which invariably affect the U.S. through disrupted trade, refugee flows, or threats to international security.

Intelligent Foreign and Immigration Policies

America's foreign policy must be rooted in intelligence, sophisticated understanding, and a long-term strategic vision considering global forces' complex interplay. Similarly, immigration policy must be crafted with a keen awareness of immigrants' contributions to the dynamism and diversity of the American economy and society. Smart policies recognize the strength of attracting global talent and the benefits of America's historical identity as a nation built by immigrants.

The Imperative for Skilled Global Leadership

The next president of the United States must possess the acumen for skilled global leadership, demonstrating a capacity to navigate international relations with foresight and flexibility (Allison, 2024). They must also be adaptable and ready to respond to new global circumstances, whether emerging economic trends, shifting alliances, or unforeseen crises. Leadership on the world stage requires balancing national interests with the realities of global interdependence, forging policies that advance American values and interests while contributing to the collective good.

Adaptability in an Ever-Changing World

The world is in constant flux, with rapid technological advancements, shifting geopolitical landscapes, and evolving economic paradigms. A leader's ability to adapt to these changes and to anticipate the needs of the future while managing the demands of the present is crucial (Zakaria, 2023). This adaptability must be informed by understanding that America's fate is intertwined with the rest of the world. The U.S. must engage with international partners, allies, and, where possible, competitors to build a more stable, prosperous future.

Conclusion

In conclusion, strict nationalism, with its inward gaze, is not a sustainable approach for a nation deeply embedded in the global matrix of interconnections. The American Dream itself, premised on the ideals of liberty and prosperity, can no longer be pursued solely within the geographical confines of the United States. It requires a broad view that embraces intelligent foreign policies, thoughtful immigration strategies, and a leadership style that is adaptable and forward-looking. As voters consider their choices for the next president, they must contemplate whether Biden or Trump is best equipped to lead America in a world where our collective futures are bound together more tightly than ever (Friedman, 2023).

THE UKRAINE-RUSSIA SITUATION

Russia's Putin and Ukraine's Zelenskyy

The conflict between Ukraine and Russia is a pivotal chapter in the post-Cold War era that underscores the fragility of international relations. At the heart of this conflict are two contrasting leaders: Vladimir Putin of Russia, a former KGB officer who has been at the helm of Russian politics either as President or Prime Minister since 1999, and Volodymyr Zelenskyy of Ukraine, a former comedian and actor turned politician, who was elected President of Ukraine in 2019 (Brookings, 2024).

Putin's tenure has been marked by a consolidation of power, strongly emphasizing reviving Russia's influence and territory, reminiscent of its former Soviet Union glory. His leadership style is often characterized by assertiveness and a strategic approach toward restoring Russia's global power status. Zelenskyy, conversely, entered politics as an outsider with a mission to tackle corruption and embody a new wave of political transparency. His rise to power was fueled by a public desire for change, and his tenure has been shaped by his efforts to navigate Ukraine's sovereignty against Russian aggression (Inkstick Media, 2024).

Implications for Global Security and International Law

The aggression from Russia towards Ukraine has presented a stark challenge to the international community. The annexation of Crimea in 2014 and the subsequent conflict in the Donbas region have been widely condemned as violations of international law, particularly the United Nations Charter. These actions have raised alarms about the sanctity of national borders and the rules-based international order, with wider implications for global security (The White House, 2024). For American voters, their leader's response to such violations speaks volumes about the country's commitment to global security and the rules of international conduct. It presents how the United States views its role in enforcing international law and supporting nations with compromised territorial integrity.

Economic Repercussions, Energy Supplies and Sanctions

The conflict has had profound economic implications, particularly for energy supplies in Europe. Russia's position as a leading natural gas supplier to the continent has intertwined European energy security with the region's geopolitical tensions. Sanctions imposed on Russia by the U.S. and its allies, while a significant gesture of reprimand, have also come with economic costs for all parties involved (Pew Research Center, 2024). The conflict has thus forced American voters to consider the economic dimensions of foreign policy—how sanctions serve as a tool of accountability and impact global markets and the domestic economy. Voters in the 2024 presidential election must weigh the merits of a foreign policy that takes a hard line on international misconduct against the potential economic fallout.

Moral and Strategic Considerations for American Voters

The moral aspect of the Ukraine-Russia conflict asks American voters to contemplate the kind of world they want to live in. Is it one where autocratic actions go unchecked, or democratic principles and human rights are defended, even at a cost? Strategically, the conflict has significant implications for NATO and U.S. interests in Europe. It's a litmus test for the durability and scope of Western alliances in deterring aggression and upholding democratic values (Brookings, 2024).

The characterizations of Putin as unwavering and tactical and Zelenskyy as resilient and democratic set a stage for American voters in the 2024 election to consider not just the policies but the personas of their leaders. They must decide if their vision of the American Dream aligns with a foreign policy that supports international allies against adversaries, maintains global stability, and embodies a moral stance that mirrors the values at the heart of American democracy.

In sum, how American voters view the war in Ukraine in the 2024 presidential election will depend on their understanding of the conflict's background, the personalities involved, and its broader implications. They must assess whether their leaders will handle such international issues with the prudence, moral clarity, and strategic foresight that safeguard the principles of the American Dream (Mearsheimer, 2022; Rumer & Stronski, 2019; Stent, 2022).

THE ISRAEL-PALESTINE SITUATION

Current State of Affairs and Leadership Personalities

The Israel-Palestine conflict persists as one of the most enduring and complex geopolitical issues. At the center of the Israeli leadership stands Benjamin Netanyahu, a political figure known for his conservative stance and focus on security concerns. His policies and decisions have consistently emphasized the security of the Israeli state and have been marked by a strong military response to perceived threats (Ravid, 2023).

On the Palestinian side, with various factions vying for influence, Ismail Haniyeh of Hamas represents a more hardline approach to the conflict with Israel, often resulting in escalated tensions (Hass, 2023).

Iran's Supreme Leader, Ali Khamenei, remains pivotal in the broader regional context. Iran's alleged involvement in regional conflicts, including support for militant groups in various countries, contributes to the tensions with Israel (Filkins, 2023). The dynamics between these leaders showcase a spectrum of ideologies and strategies, from Netanyahu's security-first approach to Khamenei's regional influence ambitions (Keinon, 2023).

Joe Biden and Donald Trump have taken different approaches to the Israel-Palestine conflict, though both have been staunch supporters of Israel. As a centrist, Biden emphasizes the importance of alliances and international cooperation in his approach, seeking to balance support for Israel's security with alleviating hardship for Palestinian civilians (Politico, 2024).

Recently, Biden warned Israel that the U.S. might withhold weapons that could be used in a major invasion of Rafah, Gaza, drawing criticism from some pro-Israel supporters (Politico, 2024), even as he signed a foreign aid bill providing billions in aid for Israel's war against Hamas and humanitarian aid for Gaza (Politico, 2024).

In contrast, Trump aligned himself with the Israeli right-wing, taking hardline pro-Israel positions as president (Crowley, 2021). Trump oversaw the Abraham Accords, normalizing relations between Israel and Arab states (Crowley, 2021), and has urged Israel to defeat Hamas quickly, saying they are "losing the PR war" by releasing footage of airstrikes (Crowley, 2021).

Trump has also criticized Biden for abandoning Israel and suggested that Jewish voters who support Democrats "should have their head examined" (Crowley, 2021). While both presidents have been staunch supporters of Israel, Trump took a more unilateral, pro-Israel right-wing approach. At the same time, Biden has sought to balance support for Israel with concern for Palestinian civilians. However, his recent warning to Israel over the Rafah invasion has drawn criticism from some pro-Israel supporters (Politico, 2024).

U.S. Role in Peace Processes and Diplomatic Relations

The United States has long been a key player in the Middle East peace process, often serving as a mediator between Israel and Palestine. The U.S.'s role oscillates between that of a diplomatic broker and defender of certain policies or actions Israel takes (Landler, 2023). American involvement is multifaceted, providing military aid to Israel while also voicing support for a two-state solution (Crowley, 2023). The stance of the U.S. is often subject to change with each administration, influencing the dynamics of the peace process and the region's geopolitical landscape (Erlanger, 2023).

Military Aid, Human Rights Concerns, and Regional Stability

U.S. military aid to Israel is a significant element in the regional power balance, often justified by the need to maintain a strategic ally in a volatile region. However, the provision of such aid raises concerns regarding human rights and the humanitarian impact on Palestinian civilians, especially in the context of retaliatory strikes and military operations (Heller, 2023).

Regional stability remains fragile, with the Israel-Iran tensions adding a layer of complexity. Iran's alleged support for Hamas and other militant groups poses a security threat to Israel, which in turn has conducted operations to curb Iranian influence (Bergman & Fassihi, 2023). This cycle of action and reaction raises the stakes for the primary actors, neighboring countries, and global powers invested in the region's stability (Harel, 2023).

American Policy Impacts and International Standing

The Israel-Palestine situation and broader Middle Eastern politics, including Iran's involvement, directly affect America's domestic and international policy. Decisions made by the U.S. regarding the conflict can have implications for domestic politics, shaping the discourse around foreign policy during election cycles (Crowley, 2023). Moreover, they impact the U.S.'s international standing, as global observers often view American actions in the region as a barometer of its commitment to human rights, democratic values, and international law (Erlanger, 2023).

Understanding the nuances of this complex situation is crucial for American voters. It requires an examination of the leaders' personalities and their implications for regional peace and security. In the context of the 2024 presidential election, the electorate must consider how the next president will interact with these foreign leaders, navigate the fraught landscape of Middle Eastern politics, and reconcile the pursuit of national interests with the promotion of global stability and human rights (Landler, 2023).

CHINA'S ROLE AS A GLOBAL POWER

Xi Jinping's Leadership and China's Global Ambitions

Under President Xi Jinping, China's ascent to global prominence has been strategic and methodical. Xi's persona of quiet confidence and political assertiveness reflects his broader vision for China—where the nation stands as a global leader economically and politically (Lam, 2023). Xi envisions the "Chinese Dream," a concept he popularized as rejuvenating the Chinese nation, implying domestic prosperity, international respect, and influence (Callahan, 2023). This dream is pursued through policies to advance technological prowess, expand military capabilities, and extend China's influence through initiatives like the Belt and Road Initiative (BRI) (Swaine, 2023).

Xi's leadership style, marked by centralization of power and an assertive foreign policy, has been critical in advancing China's global ambitions. Under his tenure, China has positioned itself as an alternative to the Western-centric development and governance model, promoting a new world order where China assumes a role equivalent to, if not surpassing, that of the United States (Lam, 2023).

Biden has sought a measured approach to U.S.-China relations, emphasizing the need for dialogue and cooperation while confronting China on human rights abuses and military pressure on Taiwan (Politico, 2024). Biden recently warned China that the U.S. may withhold weapons sales if it invades Taiwan, but has also said, "We're not trying to decouple from China. What we're trying to do is change the relationship for the better" (Politico, 2024). The president is set to meet with Chinese President Xi Jinping this week to get the two countries "back on a normal course" (Politico, 2024).

In contrast, Trump has taken a more confrontational stance, frequently criticizing China and its leadership. Trump increased U.S. support for Taiwan and engineered tariffs on Chinese imports (CNN, 2023). He has praised Xi's authoritarian rule, saying, "President Xi is like central casting. There's nobody in Hollywood that can play the role of President Xi. The look, the strength, the voice" (CNN, 2023). Trump has also baselessly claimed that China helped Biden get elected, an allegation intelligence analysts have concluded is false (NBC News, 2024). If re-elected, Trump promises he will be able to stave off World War III with China (CNN, 2023).

Trade, Technology, and Battle for Influence in Asia

The battlegrounds of trade and technology have become central to China's quest for influence. Beijing's push for innovation has placed China at the forefront of sectors such as telecommunications, with companies like Huawei leading the way (Mozur, 2023). The U.S., wary of potential security risks and the loss of technological supremacy, has taken measures to protect its interests, resulting in a trade war that has rippled the global economy (Swaine, 2023).

China's investment in Asian infrastructure and its assertive maneuvers in the South China Sea have been met with mixed reactions from neighboring countries. While some welcome the economic opportunities, others view China's rise with trepidation, fearing encroachment on their sovereignty (Lam, 2023). This has presented the U.S. with challenges and opportunities to reinforce its alliances and affirm its commitment to regional stability (Callahan, 2023).

Implications for American Economic and Security Interests

The implications of China's rise for American economic and security interests are profound. Economically, the U.S. must navigate a relationship with its largest trading partner amidst concerns over fair trade practices, intellectual property rights, and market access (Mozur, 2023). The security dimension is even more complex, encompassing issues from cyber espionage to China's military modernization and strategic presence in critical international waterways (Swaine, 2023).

China's growing influence also extends to American institutions and values. The prevalence of Chinese students in American universities, the acquisition of American companies by Chinese firms, and the influence of Chinese-owned social media platforms have raised questions about the balance between openness and safeguarding American economic and ideological interests (Lam, 2023).

Balancing U.S.-China Competition and Cooperation

Finding equilibrium in the U.S.-China relationship involves a delicate dance between competition and cooperation. The competition is evident in the economic and military realms, where the U.S. must maintain its edge while managing the risks of escalation (Swaine, 2023). Cooperation, however, is essential in addressing transnational challenges such as climate change, global health issues, and nuclear non-proliferation, where mutual interests align (Callahan, 2023).

The U.S.'s approach to China has implications for its economic health and international relations. The next American president must craft a strategy that safeguards national interests while engaging China in areas where cooperative action is necessary for global well-being (Lam, 2023).

As American voters consider their choices in the 2024 presidential election, they must evaluate candidates based on their ability to understand and navigate the complexities of the U.S.-China relationship. They must discern which leader can champion the American Dream in a manner that respects the Chinese Dream, recognizing that the two are now inextricably linked in pursuing a stable and prosperous global future (Callahan, 2023).

U.S. RELATIONS WITH CANADA AND MEXICO

Canada

Joe Biden has emphasized the importance of strengthening ties with Canada, recognizing the two countries' shared values and commitment to democracy (The White House, 2022). His administration has prioritized collaboration on climate change, clean energy, and critical infrastructure protection (The White House, 2022). Biden has also expressed support for the United States-Mexico-Canada Agreement (USMCA), which aims to modernize trade relations in North America (The White House, 2022).

In contrast, former President Trump's approach to Canada was marked by a more confrontational tone, particularly regarding trade issues (Beittel & Rosen, 2021). Trump renegotiated NAFTA, resulting in the USMCA, which he claimed would benefit American workers (Beittel & Rosen, 2021). However, his administration's tariffs on Canadian steel and aluminum exports strained relations between the two countries (Beittel & Rosen, 2021).

Mexico

Regarding Mexico, Biden has emphasized the need for a comprehensive approach to address migration, security, and economic development (The White House, 2022). His administration has sought to work with Mexico to address the root causes of migration, such as poverty and violence, in Central America (The White House, 2022). Biden has also supported the Mérida Initiative, a security cooperation agreement between the United States and Mexico (The White House, 2022).

Trump's approach to Mexico focused on border security and immigration (Beittel & Rosen, 2021). His administration implemented policies such as the Migrant Protection Protocols (MPP), which required asylum seekers to wait in Mexico for U.S. immigration hearings (Beittel & Rosen, 2021). Trump also threatened to impose tariffs on Mexican goods if the country did not take action to curb illegal immigration (Beittel & Rosen, 2021).

OTHER SIGNIFICANT INTERNATIONAL TRENDS

Climate Change and Global Environmental Policies

U.S. Role in International Agreements

Global efforts to combat climate change, such as the Paris Agreement, have positioned the U.S. as a central player in shaping international climate policy (United Nations, 2015). Under various administrations, the U.S. has oscillated between leadership and retreat on the global stage in environmental initiatives (Davenport, 2017). The nation's participation and commitment to such international agreements have far-reaching implications for global efforts to address climate change, setting the tone for collective action or disjointed responses (Bodansky, 2016).

Impact on American Industries and Jobs

The transition toward a greener economy, as guided by international environmental policies, profoundly impacts American industries (Pew Research Center, 2020). While it presents growth opportunities for renewable energy sectors, it also poses challenges for traditional industries like coal and oil (Muro et al., 2019). Adaptation to climate policies could result in job displacement in certain sectors. These necessitating policies promote economic diversification and retraining programs to prepare the American workforce for a sustainable future (Pollin & Callaci, 2019).

The European Union's Evolving Dynamics

Leadership under Ursula von der Leyen

The European Union (EU), under the leadership of Ursula von der Leyen, faces its own challenges and transitions (Herszenhorn & Bayer, 2019). Von der Leyen's presidency has been marked by efforts to strengthen the EU's digital and green initiatives, navigate Brexit, and respond to the COVID-19 pandemic (Bayer & de la Baume, 2020). Her leadership style—pragmatic and focused on unity—plays a pivotal role in steering the EU through economic recoveries and geopolitical shifts (Bayer & de la Baume, 2020).

Economic Partnerships and Defense Alliances

The U.S. relationship with the EU is critical for economic and security reasons (Stelzenmüller, 2020). The EU is one of America's largest trade partners, and defense alliances like NATO are foundational to transatlantic security (Stelzenmüller, 2020). Strengthening economic ties and ensuring the integrity of collective defense remains central to U.S. foreign policy, especially as geopolitical tensions with Russia and China escalate (Stelzenmüller, 2020).

The Middle East Beyond Israel-Palestine

Iran's Nuclear Ambitions and Leadership under Ebrahim Raisi

Iran's nuclear program remains a point of contention, with implications for regional and global security (Davenport, 2022). President Ebrahim Raisi's administration continues to assert Iran's right to nuclear development while facing Western concerns over nuclear weapon capabilities (Davenport, 2022). Negotiations over the Joint Comprehensive Plan of Action (JCPOA) and sanctions have significant implications for the regional power dynamics and U.S. diplomatic strategies (Davenport, 2022).

The Shifting Alliances in the Arab World

With leaders like Mohammed bin Salman of Saudi Arabia emerging as transformative figures, the Middle East is witnessing a realignment of alliances (Hubbard, 2018). The U.S. must navigate these shifts, which are influenced by economic interests, defense cooperation, and energy security, against human rights considerations and regional stability (Hubbard, 2018).

The Rise of Digital Currency and Cybersecurity

Global Finance and U.S. Monetary Policy

The advent of digital currencies challenges traditional financial systems and has implications for U.S. monetary policy (Brainard, 2022). As nations explore central bank digital currencies (CBDCs), the U.S. must consider integrating these innovations into the global financial system while safeguarding its economic interests (Brainard, 2022).

Cybersecurity Threats and International Cooperation

Cybersecurity has become a critical issue in international relations, potentially disrupting economies, influencing elections, and compromising national security (Sanger, 2018). The U.S. must foster international cooperation to combat cyber threats, requiring a balance between protecting national interests and engaging with global partners to secure cyberspace (Sanger, 2018).

In light of these trends and events, American voters must consider the complexities of global interconnectivity as they head to the polls. International figures' policies, leadership styles, and pressing issues like climate change and cybersecurity will significantly impact the American economy, security, and the nation's role on the world stage. The 2024 presidential election presents a pivotal opportunity for voters to shape the U.S. response to these global challenges.

Biden has taken a comprehensive approach to digital assets and cybersecurity, emphasizing the need for a whole-of-government strategy to protect consumers, financial stability, and national security and address climate risks (The White House, 2022). His administration has outlined key priorities, including consumer and investor protection, financial stability, combating illicit finance, U.S. leadership in the global financial system, financial inclusion, and responsible innovation (The White House, 2022; U.S. Department of the Treasury, 2022). Biden has also encouraged the Federal Reserve to continue researching and developing a potential U.S. Central Bank Digital Currency (CBDC) (The White House, 2022).

In contrast, the Trump administration did not have a similarly comprehensive or proactive approach to digital assets and cybersecurity. While Trump signed an executive order in 2017 on strengthening the cybersecurity of federal networks and critical infrastructure (Executive Order No. 13800, 2017), it lacked the same level of detail and whole-of-government coordination as Biden's initiatives. The Trump administration also did not prioritize CBDC research or provide a clear regulatory framework for digital assets (Stein, 2020). Overall, Biden has taken a more active and strategic stance in these areas than his predecessor.

THE INTERLOCKING DREAMS OF NATIONS

How National Aspirations Impact Global Politics and Economics
Nations, like individuals, harbor dreams – visions for their future that dictate their choices and actions on the international stage. These collective aspirations shape the world's political and economic landscapes, creating complex interactions and consequences. For example, China's dream of national rejuvenation under President Xi Jinping translates into a robust industrial policy and aggressive foreign investments, reorienting global trade routes and manufacturing hubs (Callahan, 2013). Simultaneously, the European Union's integrated dream of economic

cooperation and collective security influences regulatory standards and diplomatic initiatives that ripple across global markets (Dinan, 2014).

With their dreams of development and equitable growth, emerging economies rapidly transform the old economic order. They demand a fairer share of global wealth and contribute to a shift in the centers of economic power (Rodrik, 2011).

These aspirations collectively mold the global marketplace, determining trade policies, investment flows, and the allocation of resources. As nations strive to realize their dreams, their policies often intersect and intertwine, resulting in cooperation, competition, or conflict that has far-reaching implications for global governance and economy (Ikenberry, 2018).

The American Dream in a Multipolar World

In a multipolar world, the American Dream – the venerable ideal of liberty, opportunity, and prosperity – must contend with the dreams of other nations. Once the arbiter of a unipolar world order, the United States now navigates a landscape where power is distributed among multiple influential nations, each with its vision and agenda. The American Dream, emphasizing individual freedom and economic success, must be reconciled with the collective dreams of other nations seeking economic parity, regional influence, and cultural respect (Hochschild, 1995; Cullen, 2003).

This requires reimagining the American Dream in a context where it is no longer the sole blueprint for success but one of many in a global marketplace of ideas. The dream's tenets—democracy, free markets, and innovation—must now be advanced in a dialogue of dreams, where mutual respect and shared responsibilities become crucial to maintaining peace and prosperity. The American Dream's adaptability and openness to global influences will determine its vitality and relevance in this new era.

Influence of International Dreams on American Foreign and Domestic Policy

International dreams significantly influence American foreign and domestic policy. The aspirations of allies and adversaries alike necessitate diplomatic agility and strategic foresight. For instance, the U.S. must account for the European dream of unity and sovereignty in its transatlantic policies, just as it must consider the implications of the Russian dream of restored influence in its policies toward Eastern Europe and NATO (Stent, 2014).

Domestically, the dreams of other nations impact American industry, labor, and technology. The drive for innovation in countries like South Korea and Germany spurs American competitiveness in renewable energy and automotive manufacturing (Berger, 2013). Meanwhile, the aspirations of nations like Brazil and India for development and global stature influence American policies on trade tariffs, foreign aid, and environmental protocols (Burges, 2017).

The interplay of these global aspirations with American policy is a balancing act – promoting American interests while acknowledging and engaging with the dreams of others. It is a dance of diplomacy and policy that requires the United States to be both competitor and collaborator, teacher and student, leader and partner. The 2024 presidential election is a moment for American voters to choose a leader who can navigate this complex dance – one who understands that the American Dream, interlaced with the dreams of others, must be pursued not in isolation but in concert with the rest of the world's aspirations (Nye, 2017).

BIDEN AND TRUMP ON FOREIGN POLICY

Joe Biden

Joe Biden has a long history in foreign policy. As a Senator, he served as Chairman of the Senate Foreign Relations Committee. His persona is often empathetic and diplomatic, emphasizing the importance of alliances and international cooperation (Stracqualursi, 2020).

Biden's foreign policy orientation reflects a liberal internationalist approach. He has stressed the need to restore America's moral leadership and renew ties with traditional allies (Biden, 2020). Key priorities include addressing climate change, preventing nuclear proliferation, and promoting democracy and human rights globally.

As President, Biden has sought to repair relationships strained under the Trump administration, rejoining the Paris Climate Agreement and the Iran nuclear deal. He has also taken a tougher stance on Russia, imposing sanctions over election interference and the invasion of Ukraine (Crowley, 2021).

Donald Trump

Donald Trump had a very different persona and foreign policy orientation. His brash, unorthodox style and "America First" rhetoric often clashed with traditional diplomatic norms (Landler, 2019). Trump emphasized economic nationalism, renegotiating trade deals and pressuring allies to increase defense spending.

A realist, transactional approach to international relations shaped Trump's worldview. He was skeptical of multilateral institutions, withdrawing from the Paris Climate Agreement and the Iran nuclear deal (Borger, 2018). Trump also took a hardline stance on issues like immigration and border security, implementing a travel ban on several Muslim-majority countries.

Despite his unconventional methods, Trump achieved some foreign policy successes, such as brokering the Abraham Accords between Israel and several Arab states. However, his tenure was also marked by tensions with traditional allies, a deteriorating relationship with North Korea, and the chaotic withdrawal from Afghanistan (Crowley, 2021).

In summary, Biden and Trump's contrasting personas and foreign policy orientations reflect the broader ideological divide in American politics. While Biden emphasizes liberal internationalism and restoring America's moral leadership, Trump favors a realist, transactional approach focused on narrow national interests. The outcome of the

2024 election will shape the direction of U.S. foreign policy for years to come.

Donald Trump's Approach

As a presidential candidate, Donald Trump advocated for an "America First" approach to global challenges, prioritizing narrow national interests over international cooperation. He was highly critical of multinational institutions like NATO and the United Nations, accusing them of taking advantage of the U.S. (Trump, 2016).

Trump favored unilateral action, withdrawing from the Paris Climate Agreement and the Iran nuclear deal. He imposed import tariffs, renegotiated trade deals like NAFTA, and pressured allies to increase their defense spending (Borger, 2018). In crises, Trump often relied on coercive measures, threatening military action against North Korea and Iran while imposing harsh economic sanctions.

Trump's transactional worldview and skepticism of alliances led to tensions with traditional partners. However, his unconventional diplomacy also produced unexpected breakthroughs, such as the Abraham Accords normalizing relations between Israel and several Arab states (Crowley, 2021).

Joe Biden's Approach

In contrast, Joe Biden has emphasized the importance of international cooperation and restoring America's global leadership. As a Senator and Vice President, he played a key role in shaping U.S. foreign policy, advocating for a return to traditional alliances and institutions (Biden, 2020).

As President, Biden has sought to repair relationships strained under Trump, rejoining the Paris Climate Agreement and the Iran nuclear deal. He has also taken a more assertive stance against Russia, imposing sanctions over election interference and the invasion of Ukraine (Crowley, 2021).

Biden's approach to global challenges reflects a belief in the power of collective action. He has stressed the need to work with allies to tackle climate change, pandemics, and economic instability (Biden, 2020). Biden favors diplomatic negotiations and economic pressure over military intervention in crises, as seen in his handling of the Ukraine conflict.

In summary, Trump and Biden's contrasting approaches to global challenges and international relations reflect the broader ideological divide in American politics. While Trump favors unilateral action and transactional relationships, Biden emphasizes the importance of international cooperation and restoring America's moral leadership. The outcome of the 2024 election will shape the direction of U.S. foreign policy for years to come.

Voters' Consideration of Leadership Styles: from Isolationist to Globalist Tendencies

Voters in the 2024 presidential election face a choice between candidates and distinct foreign policy paradigms. On one end of the spectrum are Trump's isolationist tendencies, which suggest pulling back from international engagements and focusing on domestic issues. Conversely, Biden's globalist perspectives encourage active participation in international affairs and support for global governance.

Voters must consider the implications of each leadership style. An isolationist approach might promise a reprieve from the burdens of global commitments but at the potential cost of diminishing influence and missed economic opportunities. A globalist approach might enhance the U.S.'s standing as a world leader and partner but could involve complex entanglements and obligations (Haass, 2020).

Leadership style is a choice about America's role in the world and, inherently, about the nature of the American Dream in a globalized era. It's a choice about whether this dream is best pursued through fortifying borders and focusing inward or by engaging with the world, shaping it according to American values and interests. Voters must discern which approach will most likely protect American interests, promote global stability, and enhance the prosperity and values embodied in the American Dream.

KEY CONSIDERATIONS FOR AMERICAN VOTERS

Evaluating the Impact of Foreign Policy on America

As American voters weigh their decisions for the next president, one of the key considerations is the impact of foreign policy on the national economy. The complexities of global trade agreements, tariffs, and foreign labor markets directly influence job creation, wage levels, and the overall health of the American economy (Rodrik, 2011). Policies that foster international trade can open up new markets for American goods and services, potentially leading to economic growth and job opportunities. Conversely, protectionist measures, while sometimes safeguarding domestic industries, can also lead to trade wars that may harm the same constituents they aim to protect by disrupting supply chains and increasing costs for consumers and businesses (Irwin, 2017).

Voters must scrutinize how presidential candidates plan to balance these concerns to ensure that foreign policy decisions contribute to a prosperous economic environment that upholds the ideals of the American Dream – opportunity, entrepreneurship, and economic freedom.

Human Rights, Democracy, and American Values Projected Abroad

The United States has long been a beacon of democracy and human rights. As such, American voters must consider how the country's foreign policy reflects these values internationally. Support for authoritarian regimes may yield short-term strategic gains but can undermine the long-term moral authority of the United States (Donnelly, 2013). Voters should consider how candidates plan to promote human rights and democratic principles through diplomacy, foreign aid, and their responses to humanitarian crises.

The projection of American values abroad also extends to soft power, such as cultural diplomacy and international exchanges, which can foster a greater understanding of American ideals. Policies that reflect the nation's commitment to freedom, equality, and human dignity enhance America's international standing and reaffirm these values at home (Nye, 2004).

The Importance of Strategic Partnerships and Alliances

Strategic partnerships and alliances have been central to American foreign policy for decades, providing the U.S. with diplomatic leverage and security benefits. Alliances such as NATO or partnerships with nations in the Asia-Pacific region counterbalance the influence of adversarial powers (Mead, 2002). Voters need to assess how candidates value these relationships and how they propose to maintain or adjust them to meet contemporary challenges.

Such partnerships concern defense and advancing mutual trade, technology, and global health interests. The collaborative efforts in responding to global crises, like pandemics or climate change, underscore the importance of maintaining strong alliances (Ikenberry, 2011). Voters should consider candidates' commitments to these partnerships as they reflect on the interconnected nature of today's global challenges.

Long-Term Implications of Foreign Policy Decisions on the American Dream

The American Dream is inherently tied to the nation's standing in the world, shaped by its foreign policy decisions. Actions taken today – military interventions, environmental agreements, or trade negotiations – will have consequences that stretch into the future, affecting the economic prospects and the quality of life for generations (Bacevich, 2008).

American voters must contemplate the long-term implications of foreign policy, asking whether the choices made will lead to a more peaceful, stable, and conducive to the pursuit of happiness. Will these policies help create a world where American values can thrive? Will they ensure that America continues to be a place where hard work is rewarded, and success is within reach?

As the electorate prepares for the 2024 presidential election, it is incumbent upon them to reflect deeply on these considerations. The decisions will shape the future of the American Dream and the nation's role in the global community.

Next Up: Government Spending and America's Dream

"Responsible government spending is essential to preserving the American Dream. It ensures that future generations have the same opportunities to prosper and achieve their aspirations."
— Kevin McCarthy, Speaker of the U.S. House of Representatives

14

G. Government Spending and America's Dream

A LOOK AT GOVERNMENT SPENDING

> Oren Cass of the American Compass think tank argues that for too long, self-described conservatives have overly focused on lowering taxes without setting revenue targets that align with plausible spending levels. "Limited government is a vital conservative principle," he said. "But it doesn't mean collecting less and less tax revenue while spending more and more, thus running up debt in the process." (Cass, 2024)

In today's complex economic and political landscapes, understanding government spending trends is more crucial than ever. Government expenditures reflect a nation's priorities and values and are pivotal in shaping its economic stability and growth. From federal investments in infrastructure and defense to state and local allocations for education and healthcare, these spending decisions impact every facet of society. Analyzing these trends reveals the underlying forces driving fiscal policy and highlights the challenges and opportunities facing policymakers. As we delve into the intricacies of government spending, it becomes clear how these financial choices influence not just the present economy but the future prosperity and well-being of the nation. By examining historical data and recent shifts, this chapter aims to provide a comprehensive overview of how government spending trends shape the socio-economic fabric of America, informing both public debate and policy-making. The data for this analysis comes from the Office of Management and Budget, Historical Tables, the U.S. Census Bureau, State & Local Government Finance, and the Federal Reserve Bank of St. Louis, State and Local Government Current Expenditures.

As of May 2024, the U.S. national debt is just under $35 trillion. In May, the U.S. government increased the deficit by $347 billion, marking a 5% rise compared to last year, primarily due to higher borrowing costs that continue escalating spending. This debt results from extensive government spending on programs and services, military expenditures, and economic responses to crises. Significant contributors include prolonged military engagements and large-scale financial responses to events like the COVID-19 pandemic. Additionally, tax cuts that reduced revenue, rising Social Security and Medicare costs, and persistent fiscal deficits, where expenditures exceed revenue, have further driven the debt upward (U.S. Treasury Fiscal Data) (US Debt Clock).

The data in the table immediately below covers the presidency years of Obama (2009-2017), Trump (2017-2021), and Biden (2021-present). Government spending during the Obama, Trump, and Biden administrations has seen significant fluctuations and priorities. Under Obama, spending increased due to the financial crisis, with a focus on economic recovery and healthcare reform. Trump's tenure saw substantial tax cuts and increased military spending, leading to higher deficits despite economic growth. Biden's administration has emphasized large-scale spending on infrastructure, social programs, and COVID-19 relief efforts, increasing federal expenditures. Each administration has faced unique challenges, influencing their respective fiscal policies and government spending patterns.

Federal, State, and Local Government Spending (2009-2023), Trillions 2017 Dollars

Year	Federal	State	Local	Total
2009	4.5	1.4	1.0	6.9
2010	4.2	1.5	1.1	6.8
2011	4.1	1.5	1.1	6.7
2012	4	1.6	1.2	6.8
2013	3.9	1.6	1.2	6.7
2014	3.8	1.7	1.3	6.8
2015	3.9	1.7	1.3	6.9
2016	4	1.8	1.4	7.2
2017	4	1.8	1.4	7.2
2018	4.1	1.9	1.5	7.5
2019	4.2	1.9	1.5	7.6
2020	6.6	2	1.6	10.2
2021	6.8	2	1.6	10.4
2022	6.3	2.1	1.7	10.1
2023	6.4	2.1	1.7	10.2

Government Spending 2009-2023 Analysis

Federal spending trends under the Obama, Trump, and Biden administrations reveal significant fluctuations influenced by economic conditions and policy decisions.

During the Obama administration (2009-2016), federal spending started at \$4.5 trillion in 2009, driven by economic stimulus measures in response to the Great Recession. Spending gradually decreased to \$3.8 trillion by 2014, reflecting deficit reduction efforts as the economy recovered, and it increased slightly to \$4.0 trillion by 2016, indicating moderate growth in federal expenditures.

Under the Trump administration (2017-2020), federal spending increased from \$4.0 trillion in 2017 to \$4.2 trillion in 2019, driven by tax cuts and increased military spending. In 2020, spending surged to \$6.6 trillion due to the COVID-19 pandemic and economic relief measures.

The Biden administration (2021-2023) saw federal spending remain high at \$6.8 trillion in 2021, reflecting continued pandemic-related expenditures and new policy initiatives. Spending slightly decreased to \$6.3 trillion in 2022 and increased to \$6.4 trillion in 2023, indicating ongoing high federal spending levels.

State government spending also exhibited notable trends. During the Obama administration, state government spending increased from \$1.4 trillion in 2009 to \$1.8 trillion in 2016, reflecting efforts to support economic recovery and public services. Under the Trump administration, spending continued to rise, reaching \$2.0 trillion by 2020, driven by economic growth and increased state responsibilities during the pandemic. The Biden administration saw state government spending remain high, reaching \$2.1 trillion by 2023, reflecting continued state-level expenditures on healthcare, education, and pandemic-related needs.

Local government spending followed a similar pattern. During the Obama administration, local government spending increased from \$1.0 trillion in 2009 to \$1.4 trillion in 2016, driven by investments in local infrastructure and services. Under the Trump administration, spending rose to \$1.6 trillion by 2020, reflecting increased local government responsibilities and pandemic-related expenditures. The Biden administration saw local government spending remain high, reaching

$1.7 trillion by 2023 as local governments continued to address public health, education, and infrastructure needs.

Total government spending under these administrations also reflects broader trends. During the Obama administration, total government spending started at $6.9 trillion in 2009, decreased to $6.2 trillion by 2014, and then increased to $7.2 trillion by 2016. Under the Trump administration, total spending increased from $7.2 trillion in 2017 to $7.7 trillion in 2019, then surged to $10.2 trillion in 2020 due to the pandemic. The Biden administration saw total spending remain high at $10.4 trillion in 2021, slightly decrease to $10.0 trillion in 2022, and reach $10.2 trillion in 2023.

Primary factors driving government spending include economic crises, policy initiatives, public health and social services, and infrastructure and education investments. The Great Recession (2008-2009) and the COVID-19 pandemic (2020) led to significant increases in federal, state, and local spending due to economic stimulus measures and relief packages. Federal tax cuts, military spending, healthcare reforms, and infrastructure investments significantly influenced spending patterns.

At the same time, state and local governments increased spending to meet growing demands for public services, healthcare, and education. Health-related expenditures, including Medicaid and pandemic response, have driven up costs across all levels of government, and social services and safety net programs have seen increased spending to support vulnerable populations. Investments in infrastructure projects and education systems have also contributed to rising state and local government expenditures.

Understanding these spending trends helps voters evaluate how federal policies impact lower levels of government and the effectiveness of public service delivery. It highlights the importance of balancing economic stimulus and long-term investments with fiscal responsibility.

Forecasted Government Spending (2024-2030)

Trillions of 2017 Dollars | Congressional Budget Office

Year	Federal	State	Local	Total
2024	6.5	2.2	1.8	10.5
2025	6.6	2.3	1.9	10.8
2026	6.8	2.4	1.9	11.1
2027	7	2.5	2	11.5
2028	7.2	2.6	2.1	11.9
2029	7.4	2.7	2.2	12.3
2030	7.6	2.8	2.3	12.7

Forecasted Spending Analysis

According to the Congressional Budget Office, federal spending is projected to grow due to ongoing commitments to healthcare, social security, defense, and infrastructure investments. Factors such as an aging population and rising healthcare costs are significant drivers. State and local government spending is also expected to rise, driven by education, healthcare, public safety, and infrastructure needs. States will likely face pressures from Medicaid costs and infrastructure upgrades.

Primary factors driving spending include healthcare, infrastructure, education, social services, and military spending. Rising healthcare costs, including Medicaid and Medicare, are major federal, state, and local spending drivers. Significant investments in infrastructure at all government levels are expected to address aging transportation, water, and public safety systems. Continued investments in education, from K-12 to higher education, are essential for state and local governments.

Social safety net programs and public health initiatives remain critical spending areas, especially post-pandemic. Military spending remains a significant portion of the federal budget, driven by defense needs, modernization efforts, and geopolitical considerations. According to the Office of Management and Budget, military expenditures have been a substantial and growing part of federal spending, especially in response to global security challenges. Understanding these spending trends helps voters and policymakers evaluate the sustainability and impact of current and future fiscal policies on economic growth and public welfare.

Federal Spending by Major Category, 2017-2023

The table below shows a breakdown of federal spending by year and major spending category. Here are a few definitions to start with.

Federal Spending by Major Category
2017-2023
Billions 2017 Dollars

Year	President	Defense	Social Security	Medicare	Medicaid	Other Mandatory	Discretionary	Interest	Total
2017	Trump	586	944	688	389	522	632	283	4,000
2018	Trump	600	987	731	403	545	660	305	4,100
2019	Trump	620	1,029	763	419	566	684	324	4,200
2020	Trump	714	1,080	839	466	596	1,153	345	6,600
2021	Biden	750	1,130	899	500	670	1,282	358	6,800
2022	Biden	780	1,181	948	529	690	810	395	6,300
2023	Biden	808	1,225	1,015	558	711	835	436	6,400

Data: U.S. Treasury Fiscal Data, Congressional Budget Office, Bipartisan Policy Center

Federal Spending by Category Analysis

From 2017 to 2023, federal spending exhibited notable trends under the administrations of Presidents Trump and Biden. During Trump's presidency (2017-2020), defense spending increased from $586 billion in 2017 to $714 billion in 2020, reflecting a focus on military modernization and defense priorities (U.S. Treasury Fiscal Data) (Bipartisan Policy Center). Social Security expenditures rose steadily, from $944 billion to $1,080 billion, driven by demographic shifts and an aging population (U.S. Treasury Fiscal Data). Healthcare costs, including Medicare and Medicaid, saw significant growth, with Medicare spending climbing from $688 billion to $839 billion and Medicaid from $389 billion to $466 billion. This increase was largely due to expanded coverage and rising healthcare expenses (U.S. Treasury Fiscal Data) (Bipartisan Policy Center).

The most substantial change during the Trump administration was in discretionary spending, which surged in 2020 to $1,153 billion due to extensive COVID-19 relief efforts. These emergency measures included direct payments to individuals, expanded unemployment benefits, and support for healthcare systems and businesses. Interest on debt also rose from $283 billion in 2017 to $345 billion in 2020, driven by the growing national debt and increasing interest rates (U.S. Treasury Fiscal Data) (Bipartisan Policy Center).

Under President Biden (2021-2023), federal spending trends reflected ongoing and new priorities. Defense spending increased, reaching an estimated $808 billion in 2023, influenced by ongoing defense commitments and international aid, such as support for Ukraine (U.S. Treasury Fiscal Data) (Bipartisan Policy Center). Social Security spending continued its upward trajectory, growing from $1,130 billion in 2021 to $1,225 billion in 2023, in line with the aging population and rising benefit costs (U.S. Treasury Fiscal Data). Medicare and Medicaid also saw continued increases, with Medicare rising to $1,015 billion and Medicaid to $558 billion by 2023, reflecting ongoing healthcare reforms and expanded eligibility (Bipartisan Policy Center).

After peaking in 2020 due to the pandemic, discretionary spending began to normalize but remained elevated compared to pre-pandemic levels, reaching $835 billion in 2023. This ongoing high spending was partly due to continued pandemic recovery efforts and other discretionary programs (Bipartisan Policy Center). Interest on debt continued to rise significantly, reaching $436 billion in 2023 due to sustained high levels of national debt and increasing interest rates (Bipartisan Policy Center).

The COVID-19 pandemic was a major factor in the dramatic increase in federal spending during both administrations, leading to unprecedented emergency relief measures and significantly impacting federal budgets in 2020 and 2021 (Bipartisan Policy Center). Additionally, international aid, such as support for Ukraine, was a notable expenditure under the Biden administration (Bipartisan Policy Center). Efforts to cancel student loans under Biden also led to significant, albeit one-time, impacts on federal spending, although these attempts were ultimately blocked by the Supreme Court (Bipartisan Policy Center).

Overall, the analysis of federal spending from 2017 to 2023 highlights continuous growth in defense, social security, and healthcare spending, with significant peaks due to the pandemic and other major policy initiatives. The increasing cost of servicing the national debt remains a persistent trend under both administrations, driven by rising debt levels and higher interest rates. Next, let's examine how much government spending represents as a percentage of the U.S. Gross Domestic Product (GDP). The table below shows these percentages for the 2017-2023 period.

Hidden Costs of Government

Hidden government costs refer to financial burdens and expenditures not immediately apparent in official budgetary documents. These costs often stem from inefficiencies, mismanagement, and long-term commitments impacting fiscal health. I have identified some significant hidden costs through a review of various government reports and independent studies. These numbers identify some of the hidden costs incurred by the government. They do not provide a comprehensive assessment of these costs. However, the suggestive figures are reason enough to insist on greater transparency by the President and Congress related to the federal budget.

Hidden costs can be of two types: those deliberately concealed to understate the cost of government policies and operations and those that are unexpected and unintended. The intention to hide costs is often hard to prove. The rationale for including information about hidden costs is to encourage the public to demand greater transparency from the President and Congress through more rigorous cost-benefit analysis, making the results of these analyses available to the public. This transparency can help ensure that policy decisions are made with a full understanding of their financial implications.

However, research and analysis are often limited by data availability, methodological constraints, time constraints, and uncertainties created by changing conditions. These factors can impede the ability to assess project costs accurately, making it crucial to continuously refine and improve analytical techniques to provide more reliable information. Artificial intelligence (AI) tools will improve future public policy research by enabling more sophisticated data analysis, allowing researchers to identify trends and correlations that were previously difficult to detect. AI can enhance predictive modeling and scenario planning, giving policymakers more accurate forecasts and insights to inform decision-making. By addressing these limitations and striving for greater transparency, policymakers can better make more informed decisions that serve the public interest. Let's look at some of the major sources of hidden government costs. These include:

- **Duplication of Services**: Multiple government agencies performing similar functions without coordination cost an estimated $200 billion annually. Outdated technology reliance adds about $80 billion per year, while inefficient procurement, where the government overpays for goods and services, further contributes to these costs. Collectively, these issues result in a total annual cost of $280 billion.

- **Unfunded Liabilities**: Government promises such as pensions and healthcare benefits that haven't been fully funded create significant future liabilities. Public employee pensions are underfunded by around $1.4 trillion, and long-term Social Security and Medicare obligations are underfunded by about $55 trillion, totaling a long-term cost of $56.4 trillion.

- **Tax Expenditures**: Revenue losses due to exemptions, deductions, and credits significantly reduce tax revenues. Tax breaks for specific industries cost the federal government over $1.3 trillion annually, with deductions and exemptions.

- **Interest on Debt**: With the national debt exceeding $34 trillion, interest payments are expected to be around $600 billion annually, contributing to a substantial ongoing financial burden.

- **Regulatory Costs**: Compliance with government regulations imposes significant costs on businesses and individuals, often passed on to consumers. Regulatory compliance costs are estimated to be over $1.9 trillion annually.

- **Healthcare Fraud**: Fraud in government healthcare programs like Medicare and Medicaid leads to significant financial losses, with estimates suggesting it costs the government approximately $60 billion annually.

- **Environmental Cleanup**: The costs of cleaning up pollution and managing waste are substantial. Cleaning up contaminated sites, such as Superfund sites, is projected to cost around $20 billion annually.

Summary of Estimated Annual Hidden Costs

Cost Category	Federal	State & Local
Government Waste and Inefficiency	$196 billion	$84 billion
Unfunded Liabilities (long-term)	$55 trillion	$1.4 trillion
Tax Expenditures	$1.2 trillion	$100 billion
Interest on Debt	$600 billion	$100 billion
Regulatory Costs	$1.5 trillion	$400 billion
Healthcare and Medicaid Fraud	$50 billion	$10 billion
Environmental Cleanup	$15 billion	$5 billion

References

1. Financial Report of the United States Government
2. White House Historical Budgets
3. Government Accountability Office. (2021). High-Risk Series: Substantial Efforts Needed to Achieve Greater Progress on High-Risk Areas (GAO-21-119SP). Retrieved from https://www.gao.gov/products/gao-21-119sp
4. Congressional Budget Office. (2022). The Budget and Economic Outlook: 2022 to 2032 (Publication 56965). Retrieved from https://www.cbo.gov/publication/56965
5. Office of Management and Budget. (2019). 2019 Report to Congress on the Benefits and Costs of Federal Regulations and

Agency Compliance with the Unfunded Mandates Reform Act. Retrieved from https://www.whitehouse.gov/wp-content/uploads/2019/12/2019-CATS-Report.pdf

6. McLaughlin, P. A., & Williams, R. (2014). Regulatory Accumulation and Its Costs: An Overview. Mercatus Center at George Mason University. Retrieved from https://www.mercatus.org/publications/regulation/regulatory-accumulation-and-its-costs-overview

7. Gattuso, J., & Katz, D. (2016). Red Tape Rising: Six Years of Escalating Regulation Under Obama. The Heritage Foundation. Retrieved from https://www.heritage.org/government-regulation/report/red-tape-rising-2016-six-years-escalating-regulation-under-obama

These estimates indicate that the annual hidden costs of government operations are substantial, with long-term liabilities presenting a particularly significant challenge. Understanding and addressing these hidden costs is crucial for effective fiscal management and long-term financial sustainability.

Hidden Government Costs Under Trump and Biden

Examples Under the Trump Administration

1. **Social Cost of Carbon**: The Trump administration significantly reduced the estimated social cost of carbon (SCC) from approximately $43 per ton under the Obama administration to between $1 and $6 per ton. This dramatic reduction lowered the perceived benefits of carbon reduction policies, leading to weakened environmental regulations. This change potentially increased long-term costs related to climate change impacts, including health care costs, property damage from extreme weather events, and

agricultural losses, estimated to be billions of dollars annually (Center for American Progress) (Brookings).

2. **Fiscal Legacy and National Debt**: Under Trump, the national debt grew substantially, with budget deficits reaching a peacetime high of 15% of GDP. The federal debt held by the public exceeded 100% of GDP for the first time since World War II. Key factors included the 2017 tax cuts and increased spending, including a $4 trillion response to the COVID-19 pandemic. This substantial increase in debt poses long-term fiscal challenges, with potential interest costs exceeding $1 trillion annually by the end of the decade (Manhattan Institute) (Center for American Progress) (Brookings).

3. **Deregulation**: The Trump administration's deregulatory agenda aimed to reduce compliance costs for businesses, estimating annual savings of nearly $50 billion and projecting total savings of $220 billion. However, these rollbacks potentially increased hidden costs related to public health, environmental sustainability, and long-term economic stability. For example, the rollback of methane emissions standards could lead to increased healthcare costs and environmental cleanup expenses, potentially costing billions of dollars annually (Center for American Progress) (Brookings).

References

1. Center for American Progress. "The Social Cost of Carbon and the Trump Administration's Environmental Policy Changes." Center for American Progress, 2018.
2. Center for American Progress. "Fiscal Impacts of National Debt Growth Under the Trump Administration." Center for American Progress, 2020.

3. Center for American Progress. "Economic and Public Health Costs of Deregulatory Policies in the Trump Era." Center for American Progress, 2020.

4. Brookings Institution. "The Trump Administration's Reduction in the Social Cost of Carbon." Brookings Institution, 2018.

5. Brookings Institution. "Analyzing the Fiscal Legacy and National Debt Increase Under President Trump." Brookings Institution, 2020.

6. Brookings Institution. "The Long-term Implications of Deregulatory Policies: Public Health and Environmental Costs." Brookings Institution, 2020.

7. Manhattan Institute. "The Fiscal Legacy of the Trump Administration: National Debt and Budget Deficits." Manhattan Institute, 2020.

Examples Under the Biden Administration

1. Under the Biden administration, the Affordable Care Act (ACA) has been greatly expanded. The hidden costs of ACA expansions under the Biden administration are significant. Increased federal spending is $34 billion annually due to expanded subsidies and Medicaid. Administrative and compliance costs add $10 billion annually. Market distortions result in higher premiums of $5 billion annually, and compliance costs for employers and insurers amount to $2 billion annually. Over the next decade, these measures are projected to add $210 billion to the federal deficit, highlighting the substantial financial commitments and economic distortions involved (Home) (CMS.gov) (eHealthInsurance).

2. **Inflation and Spending**: Extensive government spending on COVID-19 relief and other initiatives has contributed to inflationary pressures. The increased spending is linked to higher inflation rates, which erode purchasing power and increase the cost of living for American families. For example, the American

Action Forum estimated that the $1.9 trillion COVID-19 relief package added significant inflationary pressure, contributing to a rise in consumer prices (Watson Institute) (The Washington Institute).

3. **Regulatory Costs**: The Biden administration has introduced significant regulatory measures, with an estimated $617 billion in new regulatory costs in the first years. For example, the EPA's new greenhouse gas emissions standards for vehicles are projected to cost $180 billion. While aiming to protect the environment and public health, these regulations impose immediate compliance costs on businesses (AAF) (AMAC).

References

1. Home. "The Financial Impact of Expanding the Affordable Care Act Under the Biden Administration." Home, 2023.
2. CMS.gov. "Administrative and Compliance Costs Related to ACA Expansions." Centers for Medicare & Medicaid Services, 2023.
3. eHealthInsurance. "Market Distortions and Higher Premiums Due to ACA Expansions." eHealthInsurance, 2023.
4. Watson Institute. "Inflationary Pressures from Government Spending on COVID-19 Relief." Watson Institute for International and Public Affairs, 2023.
5. The Washington Institute. "Economic Effects of the $1.9 Trillion COVID-19 Relief Package." The Washington Institute for Near East Policy, 2023.
6. AAF. "Regulatory Costs Imposed by the Biden Administration." American Action Forum, 2023.
7. AMAC. "Compliance Costs of EPA's New Greenhouse Gas Emissions Standards." Association of Mature American Citizens, 2023.

Next Up: Biden and Trump: A Look Inside Each Candidate

"The integrity of a president is not just about personal honesty but about upholding the principles of democracy and serving the public with unwavering dedication."
— Condoleezza Rice, Former U.S. Secretary of State

15

PART III: EVALUATION OF THE PRESIDENTIAL CANDIDATES

As the 2024 presidential election approaches, the nation finds itself at a crossroads, with two familiar faces vying for the highest office in the land – incumbent President Joe Biden and former President Donald Trump. Part III of this book provides a comprehensive assessment of these two candidates, their backgrounds, and their divergent perspectives on the critical issues shaping the future of America.

Biden, seeking a second term, presents himself as a seasoned statesman with decades of experience in public service. His campaign emphasizes his commitment to upholding democratic norms, protecting civil rights, and promoting economic stability through measured policies. However, critics point to concerns over his age, cognitive abilities, and perceived missteps during his first term that have contributed to the nation's challenges.

On the other hand, Trump, the polarizing figure who disrupted the political landscape during his presidency, promises a return to his "America First" agenda. His platform centers on economic nationalism, stricter immigration policies, and a confrontational global stance. While his supporters laud his unconventional approach, detractors decry his divisive rhetoric and alleged disregard for democratic institutions.

16

A. Biden and Trump: A Look Inside Each Candidate

" Six months to election day and things feel sort of fatalistic. There seems little to discover and nothing new to say about each of the candidates. It's not going to dawn on you suddenly that Joe Biden is too old and infirmed or Donald Trump too crazy. You've factored that in. You know what you think of both and have a sense of what compromises you'll make within yourself to vote for either. "
~Peggy Noonan, Wall Street Journal, May 9, 2024

INTRODUCTION

This chapter explores Joe Biden and Donald Trump's character, personality, values, leadership style, political philosophy, and public persona. Then, we examine how each candidate's qualities give rise to their vision of the American Dream. We also discuss legal entanglements troubling each candidate's bid for the presidency. Let's begin with some definitions.

Character encompasses the moral and ethical qualities that drive a person's actions and decisions. It involves integrity, honesty, responsibility, and a commitment to doing the right thing, even when faced with adversity.

Personality combines individual characteristics, traits, and behaviors that define how a president interacts with others, makes decisions, and leads the country.

Values are the core principles and beliefs that guide their decision-making, leadership style, and policy choices. These values reflect the president's sense of ethics, morality, and priorities, influencing how they approach governance, social issues, and their role as a nation leader. Presidential values are crucial in shaping national direction, fostering public trust, and setting the tone for the administration's tenure.

Leadership style refers to the president's approach and methods for guiding the country, making decisions, and interacting with stakeholders. It encompasses elements like decision-making processes, communication techniques, collaboration with advisors and other branches of government, crisis management, and the overall manner in which the president leads the nation. This style can range from collaborative and consensus-building to authoritative and decisive, shaping the president's effectiveness and public perception.

Political philosophy, in terms of a president, is the foundational beliefs and ideologies guiding their approach to political issues, governance, and policy-making. It encompasses the president's views on the role of government, individual rights, justice, equality, and social responsibility. The philosophy of governance for a president refers to the guiding principles and strategies that shape their approach to leadership and administration. This involves the president's vision for governance, including decision-making processes, relationships with other branches of government, public accountability, and the management of national resources.

A president's public persona is the image, character, or identity that a president presents to the outside world. It is the perception and reputation built through various communication, behavior, and interaction with others. Media appearances, public statements, branding, social media presence, and personal conduct can shape a public persona. It reflects how a person or entity wants to be seen by the public, often focusing on specific traits, values, or roles to convey an image.

PRESIDENT JOE BIDEN

Joseph Robinette Biden Jr., born on November 20, 1942, in Scranton, Pennsylvania, is a politician who has served as the 46th President of the United States since January 20, 2021. His long political career, including time as a senator and Vice President, has shaped who he is and what he is about.

Character

Joe Biden's character is defined by empathy, resilience, and a commitment to public service. His long career in politics and personal experiences have contributed to his character traits, shaping his approach to leadership and governance. Here are key aspects of Joe Biden's character.

Honesty and Integrity

Biden's public image is often associated with honesty and integrity. He presents himself as a transparent leader, emphasizing the importance of truthfulness and accountability. For instance, his handling of the COVID-19 pandemic involved frequent communication with the public, health officials, and scientists, showing a commitment to providing accurate information. Despite this, he has faced criticism for gaffes and misstatements during public appearances, generally attributed to his communication style rather than a lack of integrity. Biden's public persona is generally associated with honesty and integrity. During his presidential campaign and presidency, he has emphasized truthfulness and transparency, often contrasting his approach with his predecessor's. For example, his handling of the COVID-19 pandemic has involved frequent communication with the public and health officials, demonstrating a commitment to transparency.

Empathy and Compassion

Biden's empathy and compassion are among his most recognized traits. He often shares personal stories of loss and struggle, connecting with those who have faced hardship. His interactions with families of fallen soldiers or survivors of tragedies demonstrate a genuine sense of compassion. This approach has garnered him a reputation for being relatable and understanding, which appeals to many Americans looking for a leader who cares about their experiences. His speeches often include personal stories that connect with the struggles of ordinary Americans. A notable example is his speech after the 2021 Boulder shooting, where he spoke about the pain of loss and the importance of healing, demonstrating a deep sense of empathy for those affected by the tragedy.

Loyalty and Commitment

Biden's loyalty extends to his family, close advisors, and long-time political allies. His choice of Kamala Harris evidences his commitment to those he has worked with over the years as his running mate despite earlier primary competition. Biden's loyalty also reflects his commitment to the values and ideals that have guided his political career, often citing his Catholic faith as a source of inspiration.

Responsibility and Accountability

His approach to responsibility and accountability is centered on taking ownership of decisions and their consequences. During the Afghanistan withdrawal in 2021, he took responsibility for the chaotic exit, acknowledging that it was ultimately his decision as president. His willingness to accept criticism and engage in constructive dialogue demonstrates a sense of accountability, contrasting with a reluctance to shift blame onto others.

Leadership and Initiative

Biden's leadership style is collaborative and consensus-oriented. He emphasizes building coalitions and working with various stakeholders to achieve policy goals. His leadership approach reflects his ability to pass significant legislation, such as the American Rescue Plan and the Infrastructure Investment and Jobs Act. However, this collaborative style has also been criticized for being slow and less decisive compared to more forceful leadership approaches.

Resilience and Determination

Joe Biden's resilience is evident in his journey through significant loss and adversity. He has experienced deep personal tragedies, including the deaths of his first wife and daughter in a car accident and later his son Beau's death from cancer. Despite these challenges, Biden has continued to serve in public office, demonstrating resilience and determination. This quality resonates with those who admire his perseverance through difficult times.

Flexibility and Adaptability

His flexibility is reflected in his evolving positions on key issues over time. His changing stance on same-sex marriage is a notable example of his adaptability to societal changes. This flexibility allows him to navigate complex political landscapes and adjust his policies to align with public opinion. Critics, however, sometimes view this adaptability as a lack of conviction or a tendency to follow trends rather than lead them.

Personality

Joe Biden is known for his approachable demeanor, empathy, and focus on consensus-building. His communication style is conversational and down-to-earth, and he often relates personal stories to connect with his audience. Biden's gregarious nature and emphasis on personal connections have earned him a reputation as an empathetic leader who values relationships. Biden's personality is often described as empathetic, relatable, and personable. He is known for his ability to connect with people personally, demonstrating warmth and compassion in his interactions.

Values

Biden's values revolve around empathy, bipartisanship, and public service. He emphasizes unity and seeks to bridge political divides, often focusing on the common ground between differing political viewpoints. His Catholic faith informs his values, emphasizing compassion and social justice. Biden strongly emphasizes family, often referencing his family's challenges and triumphs in public speeches.

Leadership Style

Joe Biden's leadership style is characterized by a collaborative and consensus-oriented approach, reflecting his long tenure in the U.S. Senate. He values a diversity of perspectives and seeks input from a wide range of stakeholders, including lawmakers, experts, and community leaders, to inform his decision-making. Biden's style is grounded in his belief that effective governance requires building bridges and fostering dialogue, even with those holding opposing views.

Biden's emphasis on negotiation and compromise stems from his experience as a Senator, where he spent decades working across the aisle to enact legislation. As President, he has sought to build bipartisan coalitions, advocating for unity and a return to civility in American politics. He frequently prioritizes finding common ground over rigid partisanship, aiming to create policies that appeal to a broader spectrum of Americans. In the international arena, Biden has focused on restoring relationships with traditional allies and re-engaging with multilateral institutions, demonstrating a commitment to diplomacy and cooperative problem-solving. This leadership approach underscores his dedication to stability, institutional norms, and a more inclusive style of governance.

Political Philosophy

Biden's political philosophy is generally centrist, with a progressive tilt. He supports a strong role for government in addressing social and economic issues while valuing bipartisanship and compromise. Biden's political philosophy incorporates elements of social liberalism, focusing on human rights, environmental sustainability, and social justice. He advocates for a fair and inclusive society, with policies to reduce inequality and expand access to opportunities.

John Rawls is a political philosopher whose views reflect Biden's philosophy of politics and governance. Rawls's theory of justice, particularly his concept of "justice as fairness," aligns with Biden's focus on social justice, equality, and the role of government in ensuring a fair society. Rawls's idea of the "original position" and "veil of ignorance" emphasizes creating a society where institutions and policies are designed to benefit the least advantaged, echoing Biden's commitment to equity and support for marginalized groups.

Public Persona

Joe Biden's public persona is marked by a calm and steady demeanor that promotes unity and national healing. He often shares personal anecdotes and stories from his life to establish a connection with the public, illustrating his message with relatable experiences. This approach helps him create a sense of empathy and warmth, positioning himself as a leader who understands the struggles and aspirations of ordinary people. Through his communication, Biden emphasizes the importance of bridging political divides and fostering a sense of community, aiming to unite Americans during polarization and tension.

Despite his calm demeanor, Biden has faced criticism for frequent gaffes and missteps in his public speeches. His performance during the June 27th debate showed these issues to be much more significant. While these instances have generally been seen as part of his more informal and approachable communication style, they now pose serious questions about his fitness to run for reelection. While these gaffes can attract attention and scrutiny, they also contribute to his image as an authentic, relatable figure who isn't overly scripted or rehearsed. Biden's public persona balances seriousness and a down-to-earth attitude, appealing to many Americans who value stability and straightforwardness. This combination of calm leadership and a personal touch underscores his character's multifaceted nature, showing the strengths and vulnerabilities that define his public image.

Legal Entanglements

Joe Biden's tenure as President has not been without scrutiny, particularly regarding legal entanglements and criminal charges involving his family. However, it's important to note that while Biden has not been criminally charged, some of his family members, notably his son Hunter Biden, have faced legal challenges. Here's an overview of the legal entanglements involving Biden's family, along with an explanation of how these reflect upon his character and personality.

Overview of Legal Entanglements

1. **Hunter Biden's Business Dealings:** Hunter Biden has faced intense scrutiny over his business dealings in Ukraine and China, leading to questions about conflicts of interest and influence-peddling. These concerns stem from his role on the board of a Ukrainian energy company, Burisma Holdings, while his father was vice president of business relationships in China. While these dealings have raised concerns about conflicts of interest and influence-peddling, investigations into these matters are ongoing and have not resulted in criminal convictions.

2. **Hunter Biden's Tax Charges:** In 2023, Hunter Biden was indicted on tax-related charges, alleging that he failed to pay income taxes for several years. These charges emerged from a

long-running investigation into his finances, raising questions about financial management and accountability.

3. **Hunter Biden's Gun Charges:** As of June 11, 2024, Hunter Biden has been convicted on three federal gun charges. The charges stem from his 2018 purchase of a firearm, during which he falsely stated on a federal background check form that he was not using illegal drugs despite being addicted to crack cocaine at the time. This case has highlighted his struggles with substance abuse and past legal issues. The conviction could influence his sentencing, with federal guidelines suggesting a lighter punishment for first-time offenders. However, the outcome remains determined, and Hunter Biden will likely appeal the verdict.

Reflection on Joe Biden's Character and Personality

Joe Biden's leadership style and personality emphasize empathy, family, and inclusivity. He often speaks about his family's personal struggles and tragedies, showing a deep sense of compassion and understanding. The legal entanglements involving his son, Hunter Biden, reflect these familial connections, as Biden's support for his son through his struggles has been both a source of strength and criticism.

Biden's character, rooted in empathy and understanding, influences how he navigates these legal challenges. He has been open about his family's history, including Hunter's battle with addiction, which reflects his belief in second chances and personal growth. This attitude extends to his public persona, where he often emphasizes compassion and healing, even in the face of controversy.

While the legal entanglements involving Hunter Biden raise questions about influence and accountability, they also showcase Biden's loyalty to his family and commitment to supporting his loved ones through difficult times. While this aspect of his character is endearing to many, it can also draw criticism for perceived conflicts of interest or a lack of objectivity in dealing with family-related issues.

Overall, Joe Biden's response to these legal entanglements reflects his character and personality, highlighting his focus on empathy, compassion, and the importance of family. Despite the controversies surrounding his son, Biden's approach remains consistent with his broader themes of unity and understanding.

Personal Influences on Biden's View of the American Dream

Joe Biden's character, personality, values, leadership style, political philosophy, and public persona collectively shape his view of the American Dream as a vision rooted in inclusivity, equity, and shared opportunity. Biden's focus on unity, healing, and bipartisan cooperation reflects his belief that the American dream is attainable through a collaborative approach, where every individual has the chance to succeed regardless of background or circumstances. His extensive experience in the Senate and as Vice President has influenced his perspective on governance, leading him to prioritize policies that aim to create a fairer and more inclusive society. Biden's public persona as a calm and empathetic leader further underscores his commitment to these ideals, with a focus on rebuilding the American dream through consensus and compassion.

How do Biden's personal qualities shape his approach to three critical elements of the American Dream: individual opportunity, collective progress, and functional governance?

Individual Opportunity

Biden's values and leadership style shape his approach to ensuring individual opportunity by emphasizing policies that reduce barriers and expand access. His focus on inclusivity leads him to advocate for affordable education, skills training, and job programs that give individuals the tools they need to succeed. Biden's empathy and personal touch allow him to connect with everyday Americans, reinforcing his commitment to helping them reach their potential. He views individual opportunity as foundational to the American Dream, driving his support for initiatives that level the playing field and foster economic mobility.

Collective Progress

"Collective progress" refers to advancing societal goals and addressing large-scale challenges through a collaborative, consensus-oriented approach. It involves uniting individuals across political and social divides, fostering broad-based support, and building bipartisan coalitions to implement policies that benefit society. The focus is on achieving common objectives while balancing the interests of diverse groups, emphasizing the need for national cohesion and teamwork to create meaningful change.

Biden's collaborative and consensus-oriented approach to leadership informs his strategy for addressing collective progress. He aims to unite Americans across political and social divides, emphasizing the need for national cohesion to tackle major challenges like climate change and infrastructure. Biden's political philosophy, centered on rebuilding relationships and fostering bipartisanship, suggests that collective progress requires broad-based support and cooperation. His focus on unity and bipartisan coalition-building demonstrates his commitment to advancing policies that benefit society while balancing the interests of diverse groups.

Functional Governance

Joe Biden views the U.S. government as dysfunctional due to extreme partisanship and ideological polarization, which hinders effective governance and policy-making. A key reason for this dysfunction is the rigid party alignment, where the focus on defeating the opposing party takes precedence over bipartisan collaboration and compromise.

The shift toward ideologically consistent parties has led to a reluctance to compromise, resulting in gridlock and legislative brinkmanship. Members of Congress often resort to linking unrelated issues to force concessions, creating a legislative process that resembles a complex puzzle. This practice, particularly evident among far-right Republicans, complicates bipartisan efforts and leads to a climate of "hostage-taking," where one issue is held hostage to gain leverage on another.

Furthermore, Congress's dysfunction has implications for national security, as seen in debates over Ukraine aid, government funding, and the Speaker of the House. The inflexibility of party lines and the emphasis on party loyalty over national interests contribute to this perception of dysfunction within the U.S. government.

Biden's extensive political experience and commitment to restoring norms guide his approach to functional governance. He values negotiation, compromise, and finding common ground, suggesting a leadership style that bridges political divides and restores public trust in government institutions. Biden's emphasis on stability and his calm public persona contribute to his strategy for effective governance, where he aims to restore faith in democratic processes. By prioritizing transparency, accountability, and a return to traditional governance, Biden seeks to create a political environment that fosters functionality and resilience, supporting a government that can effectively address the nation's challenges.

FORMER PRESIDENT DONALD TRUMP

Donald John Trump, born on June 14, 1946, in Queens, New York, is a businessman, television personality, and the 45th President of the United States. His personality, values, and philosophy of life have shaped his public image and political career.

Character

Donald Trump is a controversial figure known for his blunt and confrontational communication style, often favoring bold statements and a confident demeanor. His character leans toward a preference for loyalty and assertive leadership, focusing on promoting personal brand and business success. Throughout his career, he has demonstrated a penchant for defying convention and embracing a high-profile, polarizing approach to politics and public life.

Honesty and Integrity

Trump is known for his direct and unfiltered communication style, often making bold statements. However, he has been criticized for spreading misinformation and engaging in false claims, raising questions about his integrity. For example, during the 2020 presidential election, Trump made unsubstantiated claims about election fraud, leading to widespread controversy and scrutiny.

Empathy and Compassion

Trump has focused on his base's needs and often framed his messaging to resonate with them. However, he is perceived by many as lacking empathy toward those outside his immediate circle or base. A notable example is his handling of immigration policies, where his administration's strict approach, including family separations at the border, drew significant criticism for lacking compassion.

Loyalty and Commitment

Trump values loyalty and often rewards those who stand by him while criticizing those who oppose or betray him. His commitment to his brand and personal image is strong, and he expects loyalty from his supporters and team. For instance, Trump's public endorsements are often based on loyalty, favoring candidates who align with his vision and remain supportive of his leadership.

Responsibility and Accountability

Trump is known for resisting admitting fault or taking responsibility for missteps. His leadership style tends to deflect blame onto others. A prominent example is his handling of the COVID-19 pandemic, where he frequently downplayed the severity of the virus and shifted blame for shortcomings onto various entities, such as the media or state governors.

Leadership and Initiative

Trump has a bold and assertive leadership style. He often takes decisive action and embraces a "win-at-all-costs" mentality. His ability to energize and mobilize his supporters demonstrates strong leadership qualities. An example is his approach to foreign policy, where he took decisive steps like withdrawing from international agreements and engaging in high-profile meetings with leaders like North Korea's Kim Jong-un.

Resilience and Determination

Trump has shown resilience in the face of criticism and legal challenges. He maintains his course despite significant opposition, displaying determination and confidence. This resilience is evident in his response to multiple impeachments and legal inquiries, where he continued to assert his innocence and pushed back against his critics.

Flexibility and Adaptability

Trump can be flexible in his messaging and approach, shifting his stance when needed to appeal to different audiences or address changing circumstances. A notable example is his changing views on certain policies, such as health care or trade, where he adjusted his position to align with political or public opinion trends.

Personality

Donald Trump is known for his larger-than-life persona, characterized by charisma, assertiveness, and a willingness to challenge norms. His outspoken and sometimes controversial style has attracted strong support and harsh criticism. Trump often speaks with confidence and conviction, rarely shying away from confrontation. His direct communication style prefers short, memorable phrases and bold statements.

Trump's personality is often characterized by confidence, assertiveness, and a bold communication style. He has a distinctive approach to public interaction and leadership, marked by high energy and a focus on achieving results. Here are key aspects of Donald Trump's personality.

Values

Donald Trump's values often center on success, power, and loyalty. He places a significant emphasis on personal achievement and business acumen, demonstrating a consistent focus on building wealth and expanding his brand. Loyalty is another key value for Trump in business and politics, as he prefers individuals who align with his perspectives and support his agendas. He often values direct communication and assertiveness, embracing an unconventional approach to leadership that sometimes challenges traditional norms. Ultimately, Trump's values reflect his belief in self-promotion, resilience, and achieving success through bold, sometimes controversial, strategies.

Leadership Style

Donald Trump's leadership style is characterized by a direct, unconventional approach that prioritizes assertiveness and decisiveness. He often leads through bold communication and strong personal presence, relying on his ability to command attention and shape narratives. Trump's style tends to favor quick decision-making and focusing on achieving tangible results, often through unconventional methods. He also values loyalty, frequently rewarding those who support his vision while challenging or dismissing those who don't. This leadership style can create a polarized environment, with supporters drawn to his confidence and detractors critical of his disregard for traditional norms. Ultimately, Trump's leadership is a blend of charisma, unpredictability, and a focus on achieving success through assertive, sometimes polarizing, tactics.

Political Philosophy

Donald Trump's political philosophy leans toward a blend of nationalism, populism, and pragmatism, emphasizing strong borders, national sovereignty, and a focus on American interests. He promotes an "America First" ideology, which includes protectionist trade policies, strict immigration control, and a general skepticism toward international agreements that he perceives as unfavorable to the United States. Trump often positions himself as a voice for the "common man," advocating for policies that benefit American workers and businesses while challenging the political establishment. His approach tends to be pragmatic and transactional, favoring direct action over bureaucratic processes and resisting traditional political norms.

Thomas Hobbes, a 17th-century political philosopher, shares some commonalities with Trump's political philosophy, particularly in advocating for a strong central authority to maintain order. Hobbes' view of human nature, articulated in his work "Leviathan," posits that society would devolve into chaos and conflict without a central authority. This aligns with Trump's emphasis on a strong national government prioritizing security, control, and stability. Hobbes and Trump tend to view politics through a lens of power and authority, focusing on maintaining order and protecting national interests. However, while Hobbes' philosophy centers on a social contract, Trump's approach is more transactional and driven by a desire for immediate results.

Public Persona

Donald Trump's public persona is characterized by a bold and brash demeanor, often marked by a high confidence level and a willingness to speak his mind. He is known for his outspoken nature and unfiltered communication style, frequently using platforms like social media to share his thoughts directly with the public. This directness, coupled with his penchant for controversy and sensationalism, has made him a polarizing figure, attracting both fervent supporters and vocal critics.

Trump's persona often reflects his business background, focusing on personal branding, media presence, and a relentless drive to be at the center of public attention.

In addition to his assertiveness, Trump's public persona includes a flair for showmanship and an ability to command attention. He often employs grandiose rhetoric and dramatic gestures to create a sense of spectacle, drawing on his experience in television and entertainment. His public appearances frequently feature large rallies and enthusiastic crowds, reinforcing his image as a charismatic leader. Despite his polarizing nature, Trump's persona resonates with many who appreciate his outsider status and unconventional political approach. This mix of bravado, theatricality, and a knack for connecting with his base has become a defining aspect of his public image.

Regarding Trump's performance in the June 27th presidential debate, the press highlighted several untruthful statements by Donald Trump during the Atlanta debate, pointing out his misleading claims on various topics. Fact-checkers noted that Trump repeated falsehoods about the 2020 election results, the economy, and immigration policies.

Reflection on Trump's Character and Personality

Trump's various legal entanglements and criminal charges often stem from his character traits and behavior. His assertive, confrontational style and tendency to challenge norms can lead to legal issues, as seen in his alleged attempts to influence the 2020 election outcome or retain classified documents. The hush money trial with Stormy Daniels reflects Trump's willingness to use unconventional means to protect his reputation, with a disregard for legal protocols in the process.

Trump's unfiltered communication and confrontational responses to accusations are aligned with the defamation cases he faces, as he often challenges critics with bold statements and public denials. The business-related charges suggest that his approach to entrepreneurship and deal-making involves pushing boundaries and testing conventional rules, contributing to the allegations of fraud and falsification of business records.

Trump's legal entanglements and criminal charges illustrate how his boldness and combative tendencies can create legal complexities. His approach to business, politics, and personal reputation is often aggressive and unconventional, reflecting a willingness to take risks that has sometimes led to significant legal repercussions.

Personal Influences on Trump's View of the American Dream

How do Trump's personal qualities shape his approach to three critical elements of the American Dream: individual opportunity, collective progress, and functional governance?

Donald Trump's character, personality, values, leadership style, political philosophy, and public persona collectively shape his view of the American dream as a vision centered on individual success, self-reliance, and national strength. Trump's focus on assertiveness and directness reflects his belief that the American dream is attainable through determination, entrepreneurial spirit, and a "Make America Great Again" mindset. His extensive experience in business and entertainment influences his perspective on governance, leading him to prioritize policies that favor economic growth, job creation, and a strong national identity. Trump's public persona as a bold and outspoken leader further underscores his commitment to these ideals, focusing on achieving success through decisiveness and a willingness to challenge established norms.

Individual Opportunity

Trump's leadership style and values shape his approach to promoting individual opportunity by emphasizing personal success and business entrepreneurship. His focus on reducing regulations and promoting a business-friendly environment suggests that he believes individuals can achieve the American dream through hard work and ingenuity. Trump often highlights his business background as a model for success, reinforcing his message that anyone can make it with the right mindset and determination. He views individual opportunity as central to the American dream, driving his support for policies encouraging free enterprise and economic competition.

Collective Progress

Trump's political philosophy, centered on nationalism and a strong economy, informs his strategy for achieving collective progress. He promotes an "America First" approach, emphasizing the importance of national interests and prioritizing policies that benefit American workers and industries. Trump's public persona, characterized by bold rhetoric and a focus on American exceptionalism, suggests he believes that collective progress comes from a united and strong nation. His emphasis on building a robust economy and securing American borders demonstrates his commitment to advancing policies that support national growth and protect against perceived external threats.

Functional Governance

Donald Trump sees the U.S. government as dysfunctional primarily due to intense partisanship and resistance to traditional governance processes. His perspective aligns with his leadership approach, characterized by confrontation and a willingness to challenge established norms.

Trump has described the government as riddled with inefficiencies and entrenched interests resistant to change. He often blames these issues on career politicians and the so-called "deep state," suggesting that they contribute to bureaucratic gridlock and stymie his policy agenda. This view underpinned his calls for radical changes to government operations, often proposing bold executive actions and challenging the status quo.

Trump's presidency was marked by a focus on deregulation, reducing government oversight, and reshaping federal agencies to align with his policies. His administration's approach to scientific and governmental institutions also reflected this view, as he often dismissed experts and de-emphasized traditional scientific advice, creating a sense of unpredictability and furthering the perception of government dysfunction. His style and political philosophy contributed to a divided Congress, with intense ideological divides complicating bipartisan efforts and leading to a more contentious political environment.

Trump's leadership style, focusing on assertiveness and direct action, guides his approach to functional governance. He values efficiency and streamlined processes, advocating for a less bureaucratic government that can quickly implement policies. Trump's penchant for bold decisions and unconventional approaches suggests he believes functional governance requires strong leadership and a willingness to disrupt the status quo. By prioritizing a transactional approach and focusing on results, Trump seeks to create a political environment that can address challenges with agility and decisiveness, supporting a government that operates with business-like efficiency.

Legal Entanglements

Trump's legal entanglements can be broadly categorized into civil lawsuits, criminal charges, and investigations. Here's an overview of some of the key cases:

- **Civil Lawsuits**: Trump has faced numerous civil lawsuits regarding his business dealings and conduct. Notable examples include the Trump University fraud case, in which he settled for $25 million, and the case involving E. Jean Carroll, who accused him of defamation and sexual assault. The latter resulted in a court ruling holding Trump liable for sexual abuse and defamation, leading to a substantial monetary award for Carroll.

- **Criminal Charges**: Trump is also under investigation for various criminal charges. Key among these is the Fulton County, Georgia, case, where he is accused of attempting to overturn the 2020 election results. He faces a RICO (Racketeer Influenced and Corrupt Organizations Act) indictment for pressuring Georgia officials to "find" votes in his favor. In New York, he was indicted on charges related to alleged hush money payments to Stormy Daniels, with prosecutors claiming that these payments were intended to influence the 2016 presidential election.

- **Federal Investigations**: Trump faces federal investigations into his handling of classified documents, with one indictment alleging willful retention and obstruction of justice regarding these documents. Another major federal investigation focuses on his role in the events leading to the January 6, 2021, Capitol riot, where he is accused of incitement and conspiracy to overturn the election results.

Implications for Fitness to Serve

These legal challenges raise questions about Trump's fitness to serve as president, reflecting on his ethical judgment, legal compliance, and respect for democratic norms. Critics argue that the multitude of lawsuits and criminal charges indicates a pattern of unethical behavior and disregard for the law, suggesting that these attributes undermine his suitability for public office.

However, Trump's supporters often view these legal entanglements as politically motivated, suggesting that his legal troubles are part of a broader effort to discredit him and prevent his return to public office. They argue that these cases represent a biased attempt to undermine his political influence, framing them as part of the "deep state" or politically motivated "witch hunts."

Summary

Trump's legal entanglements reflect a complex interplay of business, politics, and personal conduct. They raise significant questions about his fitness to serve as president, with implications for his political career and public image. While these legal issues suggest a need for accountability and transparency, the polarized political environment complicates the public's understanding of their broader significance.

Next Up: Biden and Trump: Their Political Views

" Trump and Biden represent starkly different visions for America's future. Trump focuses on nationalism and deregulation, while Biden emphasizes unity, social equity, and robust government intervention.
— David Brooks, Columnist for The New York Times "

17

B. Biden and Trump: Their Political Views

> " The American electorate faces a stark choice between Joe Biden, a career politician whose lengthy tenure is both his strength and his Achilles' heel and Donald Trump, a rogue and ruthless businessman whose unorthodox methods challenge the fabric of political decorum. "
> ~Don Iannone

PRESIDENT JOE BIDEN

President Joe Biden's positions on various issues reflect his centrist approach, aiming to balance progressive ideals with pragmatic governance. His administration has focused on significant infrastructure investments and comprehensive healthcare reforms, striving to address long-standing economic and social challenges while fostering bipartisan support.

1. **Centrism and Coalition-Building**: Biden is known for his centrist approach, seeking to build broad coalitions across the political spectrum. Unlike populism, which often emphasizes division, Biden's style focuses on unity and restoring bipartisanship. He emphasizes restoring the "soul of America" and bridging divides,

which often involves finding common ground between liberal and conservative viewpoints.

2. **Trade and Global Engagement**: Biden supports a more traditional approach to trade than Trump's protectionism. While he acknowledges the need for fair trade practices that protect American workers, he also supports engaging with international institutions and agreements, reflecting on the benefits of globalization and international cooperation.

3. **Foreign Policy and Alliances**: Biden's stance marks a return to traditional American diplomacy that values strong alliances, such as NATO, and a multilateral approach to global issues. He has emphasized restoring America's standing in the world through renewed commitments to allies and international agreements, such as rejoining the Paris Climate Accord.

4. **Progressive Agenda and Pragmatism**: While not anti-elite, Biden's agenda includes progressive elements such as expanding access to healthcare, investing in green energy, and addressing racial and economic inequality. However, he often takes a pragmatic approach, advocating for policies that he believes are achievable and can garner widespread support.

Centrism and Coalition-Building

Biden's ideology might be termed "Bidenism," reflecting a pragmatic blend of centrist and progressive elements that aim to navigate a middle path in American politics. This approach seeks to maintain the core values of the Democratic Party while also adapting to the evolving political landscape and addressing the concerns of a diverse electorate. Biden's stance shows a shift in some parts of the American left towards a more centrist and consensus-building approach, especially in contrast to more left-wing members of his party who advocate for more radical reforms.

Joe Biden's approach to governance, marked by centrism and coalition building, is rooted in a political philosophy that values inclusivity and practical solutions over ideological extremes. His political strategy is characterized by attempts to bridge the partisan divide that has deepened over the years in American politics.

Biden's centrist approach can be seen as an extension of his long tenure in the U.S. Senate, where he cultivated a reputation for working across the aisle. This tendency towards bipartisanship is not just a matter of political convenience but a cornerstone of his political identity. He has often spoken about the necessity of finding common ground and has framed this quest as a moral imperative necessary to heal the divisions within the country.

One of Biden's rallying calls has been the restoration of the "soul of America," a phrase he has used to encapsulate a variety of goals, from restoring decency and respect in the political discourse to addressing systemic inequalities. This phrase also serves as a call to return to a form of politics that is less about the victory of one ideology over another and more about the nation's collective progress.

Biden emphasizes coalition building in his policy proposals, often balancing progressive aspirations with more moderate or conservative policy mechanisms. For instance, his stance on healthcare reform has been to build upon the Affordable Care Act, a nod to the liberal wing of his party, but stopping short of endorsing a single-payer system, which would be a far-left position. Similarly, on climate change, Biden has supported the development of green energy technologies. This policy aligns with environmentalist priorities, but he has also indicated support for more traditional energy sources during the transition, which is a concession to more conservative economic concerns.

The Biden administration's approach to legislation also reflects this centrist philosophy. The administration has sometimes had to negotiate intensely within its own party to ensure that policy proposals are acceptable to both progressive and moderate Democrats. The goal has been to craft legislation that can be passed in a closely divided Congress, which inherently requires some support from or concessions from Republicans.

However, this centrist and coalition-building approach has faced criticism from both ends of the political spectrum. Progressives may view it as too cautious or unwilling to compromise on key issues, while conservatives might see it as a guise for a more liberal agenda. Despite these challenges, Biden has remained committed to this approach, seeing it as essential for the functioning of democracy and the nation's well-being.

Biden's political style is, in many ways, a response to the populist movements that have emerged both in the United States and abroad. Where populism seeks to rally a base by highlighting and even exacerbating divisions, Biden's centrism aims to defuse tensions and find solutions that, while not ideal for all, are acceptable to the majority. This approach is emblematic of his belief in the resilience of American democratic institutions and the ability of diverse peoples to come together for the common good.

In essence, Biden's centrism is more than just a set of policy positions; it is an ethos that seeks to navigate a divided political landscape by emphasizing unity, dialogue, and compromise. Whether this approach will achieve the lofty goals of healing and progress that Biden has articulated remains a central question of his presidency.

Trade and Global Engagement

Joe Biden's approach to trade and global engagement marks a clear departure from the protectionist policies prominent during Donald Trump's presidency. Biden has articulated a vision for the United States that re-embraces global cooperation, multilateralism, and a rules-based international order. His stance on trade is rooted in the belief that engagement, rather than isolation, offers the best path forward for American prosperity and leadership on the world stage.

Biden acknowledges the significance of globalization and its role in modern economies. He sees it not as a force to be countered with tariffs and trade barriers but as an opportunity for the expansion of American businesses and workers. By advocating for fair trade practices, Biden aims to ensure that global trade systems operate on a level playing field, which involves enforcing international labor standards and environmental protections.

His administration's policies also show this approach to trade and global engagement. Early in his tenure, Biden made it a priority to repair alliances strained under the previous administration. He reaffirmed the United States' commitment to NATO and sought to revitalize transatlantic partnerships. Biden signaled a return to collaborative efforts to address global challenges by rejoining the Paris Climate Agreement and the World Health Organization.

The Biden administration also supports reforming and working within international institutions like the World Trade Organization (WTO) to resolve disputes and advance global economic growth. This aligns with his broader agenda of renewing American leadership through diplomacy and alliance-building rather than unilateral action.

In practice, Biden's trade policy has involved a mix of continuity from past administrations and new initiatives. He supports updating existing agreements, like the United States-Mexico-Canada Agreement (USMCA), to reflect current economic and social goals better. Additionally, the Biden administration has shown a willingness to engage with new trade agreements in the Indo-Pacific region, aiming to counterbalance China's influence through economic partnerships.

By advocating for these measures, Biden recognizes that the prosperity of American workers is tied to the country's ability to compete and thrive in a global economy. He posits that engaging with the world does not have to come at the expense of American jobs if trade agreements are structured to ensure mutual benefits and protect against unfair practices.

Moreover, Biden's foreign policy initiatives seek to couple trade with broader strategic goals. The administration aims to support broader security and geopolitical objectives by strengthening economic ties with allies and partners. This includes fostering economic growth at home and abroad, enhancing competitiveness, and addressing challenges like climate change and global health.

In summary, Biden's trade and global engagement strategy believes in the importance of American participation in global systems. It underscores a vision for the United States that is integrated with, rather than isolated from, the international community, pursuing economic policies that benefit American workers and businesses while advancing the nation's strategic interests.

Foreign Policy and Alliances

Joe Biden's foreign policy and alliances reflect a strategic pivot to the traditional diplomacy that characterized much of America's post-World War II approach. Under Biden, there has been a clear effort to reinforce alliances with traditional partners, underscoring the administration's belief in the importance of collective action on global challenges.

Biden's commitment to NATO reaffirms the United States pledge to mutual defense and reflects his view that strong ties with European allies bolster American security. His administration has underscored this commitment by bolstering support for NATO's eastern flank in the face of Russian aggression, exemplified by the U.S.'s response to the situation in Ukraine. This stance indicates a broader commitment to countering authoritarianism and promoting democratic values globally.

The multilateral approach is also evident in Biden's re-engagement with international agreements and organizations, most notably the Paris Climate Accord. Rejoining this global pact signals a recognition of the interconnected nature of today's world and the need for collective action, especially on issues like climate change, which cannot be addressed by any single nation alone.

Biden's foreign policy has also been marked by a willingness to engage with adversaries through diplomacy, as seen in his willingness to re-enter negotiations with Iran over its nuclear program. This approach contrasts with his predecessor's more unilateral and confrontation-focused strategy. It is based on the premise that sustained dialogue can be a more effective means of achieving security objectives.

Renewed commitments to international agreements go beyond climate and defense. Biden has also sought to reassert America's role in global health, particularly through the re-engagement with the World Health Organization. This move acknowledges the lessons of the COVID-19 pandemic and the necessity for international collaboration in managing and preventing global health crises.

While these policy shifts represent a return to a more traditional foreign policy approach, they are not merely nostalgic. Biden's strategy addresses contemporary challenges through a lens that values diplomacy, alliance solidarity, and multilateralism. His administration's actions suggest a belief that America's strength lies not only in its military or economic might but also in its ability to convene, lead through cooperation, and build consensus among a diverse array of nations.

In summary, Biden's foreign policy represents a strategic recalibration that seeks to blend past lessons with the present demands, reflecting a nuanced understanding of America's role in a complex, interconnected world.

Progressive Agenda and Pragmatism

Joe Biden's political agenda is characterized by a blend of progressive goals and a pragmatic approach to achieving them. His presidency has focused on advancing policies that reflect core progressive values, such as expanding access to healthcare, combating climate change through investment in green energy, and tackling systemic racial and economic inequalities. Yet, his strategy to accomplish these objectives is marked by recognizing the need for feasible solutions that can be actualized within the current political climate.

In healthcare, Biden has advocated for building upon the Affordable Care Act rather than replacing it with a Medicare-for-All system favored by the far left. This approach seeks to incrementally increase coverage and reduce healthcare costs, which he argues is a more attainable goal that can still yield substantial improvements for Americans.

Biden's progressive agenda on environmental issues encapsulates his commitment to rejoin the Paris Climate Accord and propose the ambitious American Jobs Plan. This plan includes significant investment in clean energy and infrastructure, designed to address climate change, revitalize the economy, and create jobs, illustrating how Biden's progressive agenda often intersects with practical economic considerations.

Regarding social justice, Biden has expressed a desire to address racial inequality through various measures, including criminal justice reform and economic initiatives to close the wealth gap. He has also elevated the importance of voting rights, recognizing their fundamental role in a functioning democracy.

Biden's pragmatism is evident in his engagement with both sides of the political spectrum to achieve legislative success. He often seeks out policies that, while ambitious, have a realistic chance of passing in a closely divided Congress. This has sometimes meant scaling back proposals or finding compromises that keep key parts of his agenda moving forward.

The president's approach can be seen as balancing the aspirational goals of his party's progressive wing and the practical considerations necessary to enact legislation. His administration's focus on bipartisan solutions reflects a belief that incremental progress is preferable to gridlock, often resulting from pushing for more radical changes that lack broad support.

Biden's governing style embodies a belief in sustainable and broad-based progress. By focusing on what can be achieved rather than only on the ideal, he navigates the complexities of modern governance with an eye toward tangible results that have a meaningful impact on Americans' lives. This approach represents a deliberate choice to prioritize unity and collaboration for the greater good.

Biden's ideology might be termed "Bidenism," reflecting a pragmatic blend of centrist and progressive elements that aim to navigate a middle path in American politics. This approach seeks to maintain the core values of the Democratic Party while also adapting to the evolving political landscape and addressing the concerns of a diverse electorate. Biden's stance shows a shift in some parts of the American left towards a more centrist and consensus-building approach, especially in contrast to more left-wing members of his party who advocate for more radical reforms.

Roots of Biden's Centrism

Joe Biden's centrist approach to governance is deeply rooted in his political history and personal experiences in public service. His long tenure in the U.S. Senate, which began in 1973, has significantly shaped his moderate political orientation. During his time as a senator, Biden became known for his ability to work across the aisle, often engaging in negotiations and compromises with his Republican counterparts. This period was marked by a more collaborative legislative environment, where bipartisan cooperation was common in pursuing legislative success.

His experiences also influence Biden's political style in dealing with foreign policy and judiciary matters during his tenure as the Chair of the Senate Foreign Relations Committee and the Senate Judiciary Committee. These roles required a nuanced understanding of issues and the ability to forge consensus among diverse viewpoints. His work on the Violence Against Women Act and his efforts in foreign policy – particularly in advocating for arms control treaties and engaging in NATO expansion discussions – required building broad support across party lines.

Additionally, Biden's upbringing in a working-class family in Scranton, Pennsylvania, and later Delaware, informed his views on the economic challenges facing everyday Americans. His personal connection to blue-collar voters has informed his political approach, where he often seeks middle-ground policies that address the concerns of a broad base of constituents.

This centrist, consensus-building approach has been a hallmark of Biden's political career and has often worked to his advantage, enabling him to advance significant legislation and build a reputation as a pragmatic deal-maker. During his tenure as Vice President under Barack Obama, Biden was often tasked with negotiating with Congress due to his reputation for bipartisanship and his relationships with lawmakers on both sides of the aisle.

As President, Biden has continued to espouse this approach, as seen in the passage of the bipartisan infrastructure bill, which succeeded due to his administration's ability to work with Republicans and moderate Democrats to find common ground. While this strategy has faced challenges, particularly given the current polarized political climate and the slim Democratic majority in Congress, it reflects Biden's belief that progress is made through incremental change and unity rather than through radical overhaul or deep partisan divisions.

In conclusion, Joe Biden's centrist approach to governance is a product of his long experience in the political arena, where he has often found success through building coalitions and seeking pragmatic solutions. This approach, while not without its critics, has been a defining feature of his political identity, reflecting a career-long commitment to bipartisanship and a belief in the power of collective, cross-party action.

Political Pragmatism

Joe Biden's political pragmatism, a term often used to describe his approach to governance, signifies a practical, results-oriented mindset rather than one ideologically driven. Throughout his career, Biden has demonstrated a willingness to adapt and compromise when necessary to achieve policy goals and legislative success. This approach reflects a belief in the art of the possible over the pursuit of ideological purity.

In his early years as a Senator, Biden's pragmatism was visible in his foreign policy and criminal justice approach. For instance, his work on arms control with Soviet leaders during the Cold War necessitated a pragmatic approach to negotiations, balancing a firm stance on

American interests with a willingness to engage diplomatically to reduce nuclear arms. Similarly, his role in crafting the 1994 Crime Bill showcased his ability to build consensus across party lines, even though the bill has received mixed reviews retrospectively.

As Vice President under Barack Obama, Biden's pragmatism was crucial during the financial crisis of 2009. He was key in administering the American Recovery and Reinvestment Act, ensuring the stimulus package was effectively implemented. This required working closely with state and local governments, as well as both Democratic and Republican lawmakers, to ensure funds were distributed swiftly and efficiently to stimulate the economy.

As President, Biden's pragmatism has been evident in several key areas. His approach to the COVID-19 pandemic has been guided by a reliance on scientific expertise and a bipartisan effort to pass relief legislation, reflecting a pragmatic balance between health priorities and economic considerations. Moreover, the passage of the Infrastructure Investment and Jobs Act demonstrated his ability to garner bipartisan support, resulting in one of the most significant investments in American infrastructure in decades.

Biden's stance on healthcare reform further illustrates this pragmatism. While many in his party have called for a single-payer healthcare system, Biden has proposed enhancements to the Affordable Care Act, seeking to expand coverage while recognizing the political and logistical challenges of a complete healthcare overhaul.

His foreign policy has also continued this trend, focusing on rebuilding alliances, rejoining international agreements like the Paris Climate Accord, and navigating complex geopolitical landscapes through traditional diplomacy and strategic engagement.

In sum, Biden's pragmaticism seeks effective and achievable solutions, a hallmark of his political philosophy that seeks to advance progress within the bounds of what is feasible in a given political context. This approach has garnered praise and criticism, with some appreciating the tangible results it can produce, while others argue it sometimes lacks ambition. Nonetheless, Biden's pragmatism has been a consistent theme throughout his political life, shaping his decisions and defining his leadership style.

Globalism in Today's Highly Polarized World

Joe Biden's perspective on global relations is rooted in his long-standing commitment to liberal internationalism. He views global engagement as essential to addressing the major challenges of the 21st century, such as climate change, pandemics, international security, and economic stability. His stance is often characterized as globalist, advocating for the benefits of an interconnected world where multilateral cooperation and alliances are key drivers of peace and prosperity.

Throughout his presidency, Biden has sought to reassert the United States' global leadership role, starkly contrasting to his predecessor's "America First" doctrine. He has signaled this commitment by rejoining international agreements like the Paris Climate Accord and reaffirming alliances with NATO and other international partners. These moves highlight a belief in collaborative problem-solving and the effectiveness of international institutions.

Biden's approach is influenced by the idea that global challenges require global solutions, which can be best achieved through dialogue, diplomacy, and cooperation rather than isolationism and unilateralism. He emphasizes the importance of strengthening democracy and human rights worldwide, which he sees as interconnected with global security and economic prosperity.

In light of today's polarized world, Biden's globalist stance has to navigate complex dynamics, such as the rise of populism, authoritarianism, and nationalistic sentiments in various parts of the world. His administration has bolstered ties with democracies and like-minded nations to create a collective front on shared values and objectives.

Economically, Biden has advocated for fair trade policies that consider the impact of globalization on American workers while also pursuing free trade agreements that can open markets and expand economic opportunities. This balancing act reflects a nuanced view of global economics that recognizes globalization's potential to generate growth and the need to protect against its disruptive impacts.

Despite the polarized nature of global politics, Biden remains a proponent of globalism. He believes that American leadership and engagement are indispensable, arguing that the United States must be at the table whenever the future of global order is being decided. In his view, retreating from global engagement would cede ground to rivals and adversaries, ultimately diminishing America's influence and undermining its interests.

Biden's globalist approach, emphasizing alliance-building and international cooperation, continues to inform his administration's foreign policy. This reflects a historical continuity with post-World War II American policy and an adaptation to the complexities of contemporary international relations.

How Biden's Personality Shapes His Political Style

Joe Biden's personality is often described as affable, empathetic, and resilient. These traits have been shaped by personal tragedy and a long career in the public eye, and they have had a profound influence on his political style.

Biden is known for his personable approach, often characterized by a warm, engaging manner that enables him to connect with people on a personal level. He is frequently seen interacting with constituents in a tactile and compassionate manner, an approach that has earned him the affectionate moniker "Uncle Joe." His capacity to relate to the joys and sorrows of everyday Americans is a cornerstone of his political identity and is often reflected in his public speeches and policy priorities.

Empathy is another key aspect of Biden's personality, undoubtedly deepened by the loss of his first wife and daughter in a car accident early in his Senate career and later the death of his son Beau from cancer. While deeply personal, these tragedies have allowed him to understand loss and hardship, which he often speaks to when addressing the nation during times of crisis. His ability to convey genuine compassion has been a defining feature, shaping his political style into one that prioritizes human connection and care.

Resilience and determination are also notable characteristics of Biden's personality. Throughout his career, he has faced various setbacks, including health issues and political defeats, yet he has consistently demonstrated a capacity to rebound and persist. This tenacity has been evident in his approach to policy-making and campaigning, showing a readiness to keep pushing forward despite obstacles.

Biden's approachable demeanor and capacity for empathy also translate into a conciliatory and bipartisan approach in his politics. He often speaks of the Senate as a family and believes in the power of personal relationships to bridge divides and forge political consensus. This has been evident in his efforts to reach out to Republicans and work collaboratively, striving for unity in a divided political landscape.

Regarding communication, Biden is known for his plainspoken style, sometimes marked by gaffes, which humanizes him to voters. He avoids the rhetorical flourishes typical of many politicians, preferring straight talk that resonates with a broad segment of Americans. This everyman quality contributes to his political approach, where policies are often presented in terms of how they will affect the lives of ordinary people rather than through the lens of ideology or partisanship.

Joe Biden's political style reflects his approachable, empathetic, and resilient personality. These traits have enabled him to navigate a long political career and shape his presidency's priorities and approach, aiming to bring a human touch to politics and governance.

Insider or Outsider

Joe Biden is widely considered an insider within American politics and governance. His extensive career in public service, spanning over five decades, has entrenched him within the establishment of the Democratic Party. Biden's tenure as a U.S. Senator for 36 years and later as Vice President under Barack Obama has given him deep roots in the political mechanisms and institutions of Washington, D.C. He is known for his deep knowledge of the legislative process and connections within the corridors of power, which have been integral to his approach to policymaking and governance.

Biden's "insider" status is reflected in his emphasis on experience, institutional knowledge, and a belief in the effectiveness of traditional governance. His political style is collaborative and often seeks to leverage established relationships within Congress and other branches of government to achieve policy goals. His understanding of international politics and relationships with world leaders further solidifies his insider persona, distinguishing him as a statesman with a comprehensive grasp of domestic and global issues.

In contrast, Donald Trump's entry into the presidency was marked by his outsider status. Trump capitalized on his image as a non-politician, a business mogul not part of the Washington establishment, and someone who could bring a new perspective to governance, unencumbered by the traditional ways of the political class. His campaign rhetoric often included critiques of the political elite, which he claimed had led the country astray, and he promised to "drain the swamp" of entrenched interests in the federal government. Trump's outsider mentality was a central theme of his political identity, and it played a significant role in his appeal to voters disillusioned with conventional politics.

The contrast between Biden's insider approach and Trump's outsider stance highlights a fundamental divide in contemporary American politics. Biden's style is built on the premise that change can be effected from within the system, using established mechanisms and relationships. At the same time, Trump's perspective suggested that systemic change requires an external force capable of challenging and reshaping the status quo. Each approach resonates with different segments of the American electorate, reflecting divergent views on the effectiveness and integrity of the country's political institutions.

Media Skills

A sense of authenticity and relatability characterizes Joe Biden's media skills. He often uses personal stories and experiences to connect with the audience. His communication style is less about crafting perfect sound bites than conveying sincerity and empathy. This double-edged sword has made him appear genuine and down-to-earth, leading to gaffes and misstatements.

Biden's media approach is more traditional, favoring structured press conferences and interviews over social media as a primary communication tool, which contrasts sharply with Donald Trump's media strategy. Biden's team, however, does utilize social media to reach a broader audience, often with carefully curated messaging.

In public appearances, Biden typically exhibits a calm demeanor, which can reassure the audience but sometimes lacks the dynamism that might generate more extensive media coverage. His strength lies in his ability to express compassion and understanding, particularly in times of national crisis or tragedy.

Biden has also been known for his willingness to engage with the press, although less frequently than some of his predecessors. When he does, he often has a conversational style that can provide depth on policy issues but can also wander off-topic, requiring his communications team to clarify or reframe his remarks.

Overall, Biden's media skills are rooted in a traditional approach emphasizing the importance of face-to-face interaction and using mainstream media channels to communicate with the public. While this may not always create the most compelling media moments, it does reflect a consistent and stable approach to public communication.

Rhetoric and Messaging

Joe Biden's rhetoric and messaging have been shaped by his long political career, characterized by a tone of moderation and empathy. His rhetoric often reflects his centrism, speaking to a wide audience rather than a specific partisan base. He frequently uses narrative communication, weaving personal anecdotes and broader American themes into his discourse.

Biden is known for messages emphasizing unity and resilience, drawing on the country's historical challenges and successes to inspire and motivate. His language tends to be more collaborative and inclusive, aimed at healing divisions and bringing people together. This was especially prominent in his presidential campaign and inaugural address, where he often spoke of "restoring the soul of the nation" and building back better in the face of crises.

In his messaging, Biden typically addresses complex policy issues in a way that relates them to Americans' everyday experiences. He avoids polarizing language, opting instead for conciliatory words that seek to bridge political divides. While this approach fosters a sense of stability and familiarity, it sometimes results in less memorable slogans or sound bites compared to more provocative or polarizing figures.

Biden's rhetoric has also been marked by moments of vulnerability and authenticity, which have resonated with many Americans. He openly discusses his losses and challenges, using his own experiences of grief and recovery to connect with others who have faced similar hardships. This empathetic communication style aims to convey sincerity and compassion, solidifying his identity as a leader attuned to the populace's emotional and practical needs.

However, Biden's penchant for a conversational and spontaneous speaking style has occasionally led to gaffes and misstatements, requiring his communications team to clarify or contextualize his remarks. Despite these moments, his rhetoric remains centered around a message of American perseverance, collective effort, and hope for a more united future.

Campaign Promises (Last and Current Election)
Joe Biden's presidential campaigns, both in 2020 and the run-up to 2024, have been marked by a series of promises to address key issues

facing Americans. In the 2020 campaign, Biden's promises encompassed a broad range of policies, reflecting his pragmatic approach to governance and his goals for the country's progress.

Key campaign promises from the 2020 election included creating a public option for health insurance, decriminalizing cannabis, supporting the Equality Act, offering tuition-free community college, and proposing a $1.7 trillion climate plan aligned with the framework of the Green New Deal. Biden's climate plan was ambitious, aiming to achieve a carbon-free electricity sector by 2035 and to put the U.S. on a path to net-zero emissions by 2050. Additionally, Biden supported regulating rather than completely banning fracking, acknowledging the need for a transition toward cleaner energy while maintaining energy sector jobs.

Throughout his presidency, Biden has worked to keep these promises, with varying levels of success. His administration increased refugee admissions, invested in high-speed internet infrastructure, and expanded the power of the Justice Department to address police misconduct. Progress was made in healthcare, with strides to rebuild health stockpiles and improve the Affordable Care Act. Efforts have been put forth to reduce the high maternal mortality rate and protect military personnel from deportation. Moreover, Biden's presidency has seen steps toward eliminating mandatory minimum sentences for certain offenses and increasing access to VA care beyond the standard eligibility window.

On the international front, Biden's administration has seen a re-engagement with Cuba, though not to the extent of the Obama administration. Efforts have been made to rejoin the Iran nuclear deal, although external factors have complicated this process. Domestically, funding has increased for the COPS program to support community policing, and the Violence Against Women Act was reauthorized.

Some promises have yet to be fully realized, such as doubling the number of immigration judges, creating a national center to reduce veteran suicide, lowering prescription drug costs, and establishing a public credit reporting agency. The initiative to provide Section 8 housing vouchers to cap housing costs at 30% of income has seen only minimal progress.

Certain proposals faced legislative challenges, including attempts to increase the Pell Grant value, offer universal preschool, guarantee paid family and medical leave, and raise the corporate tax rate. Some, like the promise for universal preschool and the establishment of an offshoring tax penalty, were not included in the final versions of bills.

Biden's promise to tighten 'Made In America' rules has resulted in new regulations gradually raising the bar for domestic content. Yet, the pledge to block new fracking on federal lands was not fulfilled as initially promised.

Overall, Biden's fulfillment of his campaign promises reflects the challenges of navigating a politically divided landscape and the commitment to the pragmatic pursuit of policy goals. His continued push for these promises will likely be a central aspect of his campaign as he seeks reelection in 2024.

FORMER PRESIDENT DONALD TRUMP

Political Alignment and Party Affiliation

Donald Trump's political journey reflects a complex and shifting alignment within the American political spectrum, marked by numerous changes in party affiliation and ideological classification over the years. He first registered as a Republican in Manhattan in 1987, but his political affiliations have fluctuated significantly. Trump changed his party affiliation five times, moving from the Republican Party to the Independence Party of New York in 1999, then to the Democratic Party in 2001, back to the Republican Party in 2009, shifting to no party affiliation (independent) in 2011, and finally returning to the Republican Party in 2012.

These changes in party affiliation parallel shifts in his political identity as classified by the organization and website On the Issues, which has labeled Trump under various ideological tags throughout the years.

He was identified as a "moderate populist" in 2003, transitioned to a "liberal-leaning populist" from 2003 to 2011, and fluctuated between "moderate populist conservative," "libertarian-leaning conservative," and "moderate conservative" from 2011 to 2017. More recently, since 2017, he has been consistently described as a "hard-core conservative."

These shifts illustrate the evolution of Trump's political stance from more centrist and populist positions to firmly conservative ideologies, reflecting changes in his political affiliations as well as broader trends within the Republican Party and American politics as a whole.

A Deeper Look at Trump's Politics

While seen by some as a right-wing conservative, Donald Trump's political stance does not align neatly with traditional conservative ideologies. While he is associated with the Republican Party and conservative politics, his approach deviates significantly in several ways:

1. **Populism and Nationalism**: Trump often emphasizes populist themes, focusing on ordinary people's concerns and expressing strong nationalist views. His political style is characterized by directly appealing to the public, bypassing traditional party structures and elite consensus.

2. **Trade and Protectionism**: Contrary to conservative support for free trade, Trump has advocated for protectionist trade policies. He has been critical of trade agreements like NAFTA and withdrew the United States from the Trans-Pacific Partnership, favoring tariffs and other measures to protect American industries from foreign competition.

3. **Foreign Policy**: Trump's foreign policy has also diverged from traditional conservative stances, which typically emphasize strong international alliances. He has questioned the value of long-standing alliances such as NATO and shown a preference for a unilateral approach to international relations.

4. **Anti-Elitism**: Despite his business background, Trump has positioned himself against what he perceives as political and economic elites, often criticizing them as out of touch with the American public. This stance is part of a broader anti-establishment sentiment that resonates with many of his supporters.

These characteristics have led some to describe his ideology as "Trumpism," which blends elements of conservatism with anti-globalist, protectionist, and nationalist sentiments, reflecting a shift in some parts of the American right away from the pillars of traditional conservatism toward a more populist approach.

Populism, as evidenced in the political style of Donald Trump, is characterized by several key features:

1. **Anti-Establishment Sentiment**: Trump's brand of populism strongly emphasizes an anti-establishment narrative. He positions himself against the political, economic, and cultural elites. He portrays these elites as out of touch with the ordinary citizen and as having interests often at odds with the average person's needs.

2. **Direct Appeal to the Masses**: Trump frequently uses direct communication channels, like social media, bypassing traditional media and political institutions to speak directly to the public. This approach enhances his appeal as a leader who speaks the people's language and directly engages with their concerns.

3. **Nationalism**: A significant component of Trump's populism is his emphasis on nationalistic policies. This includes strong stances on immigration, border security, and economic protectionism, framed as ways to protect the American worker and preserve national interests against global forces.

4. **Polarizing Rhetoric**: Trump's populist approach often involves polarizing rhetoric that divides the electorate into 'us versus them' categories. This can involve harsh criticism of opponents,

disparaging the press, and rhetoric that sometimes inflames social and racial tensions.

5. **Emphasis on Popular Sovereignty**: Trump asserts that the people's will should prevail over institutional constraints and norms. This is evident in his frequent criticisms of the judiciary, legislative processes, and other governmental structures that, in his view, thwart the people's will.

6. **Cult of Personality**: Trump's populism is closely tied to his brand and charisma. He promotes himself as the only one capable of solving America's problems, reinforcing a personalist leadership style central to his appeal.

Populism

This form of populism challenges traditional political norms and has reshaped parts of the political landscape in the United States, influencing policy and the tone of political discourse. Trump's approach reflects broader trends in global politics, where populist leaders gain traction by promising to disrupt the status quo and directly address the concerns of those who feel left behind by globalization and technological change.

Donald Trump's identity as a populist is not necessarily derived from his personal life or background, which contrasts sharply with the common man image typically associated with populist leaders. Trump was born into a wealthy family and built a career in luxury real estate, far removed from the everyday struggles of average Americans. However, several factors about his approach and career have contributed to his populist persona:

1. **Outsider Status**: Despite his wealth, Trump effectively positioned himself as an outsider to the political establishment. He had not held public office before his presidency and often criticized career politicians and the Washington elite, which resonated with voters who felt disenfranchised by the traditional political system.

2. **Media Skills**: Trump's extensive experience in entertainment and media, particularly his role on "The Apprentice," helped him craft a public image as a decisive leader and successful businessman. This media-savvy enabled him to communicate directly with the electorate, bypassing traditional media channels and connecting with voters personally.

3. **Rhetoric and Messaging**: Trump's rhetoric often involves speaking in simple, direct language that appeals to common sentiments and fears. His speeches and tweets emphasize themes like economic decline, lost jobs, and threats from immigration and trade—issues directly appealing to voters who feel left behind by globalization and economic change.

4. **Campaign Promises**: Trump's campaign promises focused on drastic changes to government policy and practice, appealing to voters frustrated with the status quo. His commitments to "drain the swamp" and bring jobs back to America were particularly emblematic of populist strategies.

5. **Cultural Appeals**: Trump's appeals to specific cultural values, including nationalism and nostalgia for a "greater" America, resonate with many voters who feel their cultural identity is threatened. His ability to tap into these cultural concerns has been a significant aspect of his political appeal.

6. **Conflict with the Media and Elites**: Trump's frequent clashes with the media and his disparagement of the intellectual and political elite are hallmarks of populist leaders, who often portray themselves as champions of the people against the corrupt or disconnected establishment.

These elements collectively contribute to Trump's populist image, which has been crucial in mobilizing a significant support base despite his affluent background and elite status. His presidency and campaign strategies underscored these populist elements, making him a unique figure in American politics, straddling the worlds of elite privilege and populist rhetoric.

Nationalism

Nationalism is a political and social ideology that strongly emphasizes the interests of a particular nation or ethnic group, especially to gain and maintain the nation's sovereignty (self-governance) over its homeland. Nationalism is characterized by a sense of shared identity among the nation's members, including culture, language, and history. Here are some key elements of nationalism:

1. **Sovereignty**: The most fundamental aspect of nationalism is the pursuit of sovereignty and self-governance. Nationalists often strive for political autonomy to ensure their nation can decide its fate without external influence.

2. **Cultural Unity**: Nationalism often emphasizes a shared cultural heritage, which includes language, religion, and customs. This cultural unity is a foundation for building national solidarity and identity.

3. **Territorial Integrity**: Nationalists frequently emphasize the importance of maintaining and protecting the nation's borders. This can manifest as a focus on defending against external threats or reclaiming territories considered historically or culturally part of the nation.

4. **Common History**: Another core element is a shared history, often glorified and mythologized. This history helps to foster a sense of pride and belonging among the nation's citizens.

5. **Ethnicity**: In some cases, nationalism is closely linked to ethnicity, where ethnic or genetic commonalities define the nation. This form of nationalism can sometimes lead to exclusionary or xenophobic attitudes towards those who do not share the same ethnic background.

6. **Self-Identity**: Nationalism involves the collective self-identification of people who believe they are part of the nation. This self-identity helps distinguish "us" from "them" and is often used to unify the group, especially in conflict or competition.

7. **Economic Nationalism:** Involves policies designed to improve the nation's economic welfare. These can include protectionist measures like tariffs and restrictions on foreign investment to boost domestic industries and preserve jobs.

Nationalism can be a powerful force for unity and independence but can also lead to exclusion, intolerance, and conflict if it becomes extreme. The balance between healthy patriotic pride and aggressive nationalism is often a topic of significant debate within societies.

Donald Trump's nationalism is a central theme in his political identity and has been a defining feature of his presidency and campaign strategies. Here are some reasons why Trump is characterized as a nationalist:

1. **"America First" Doctrine**: Trump's core political philosophy has been encapsulated by the "America First" slogan, which emphasizes prioritizing the interests of the United States above those of other nations. This approach manifests in his policies and rhetoric, advocating for greater national self-sufficiency and independence from global systems.

2. **Trade Policies**: Trump has been a vocal critic of what he perceives as unfair trade practices that disadvantage American workers and industries. His administration renegotiated NAFTA, resulting in the United States-Mexico-Canada Agreement (USMCA), and imposed tariffs on Chinese goods to counteract what he argued were China's manipulative economic practices.

3. **Immigration Stance**: A significant element of Trump's nationalism is evident in his strict immigration policies. His

administration implemented measures to drastically reduce legal and illegal immigration, arguing that such policies were necessary to protect American jobs and maintain national security. This included building a border wall between the US and Mexico, symbolizing his commitment to these ideals.

4. **Foreign Policy**: Trump's foreign policy reflected his nationalist views, particularly his skepticism towards international alliances and multilateral agreements, which he felt constrained America's sovereignty. This was evident in his withdrawal from the Paris Climate Accord, the Iran nuclear deal, and his demand that NATO allies increase their defense spending.

5. **Cultural Appeals**: Trump often invokes a specific version of American history and culture that emphasizes traditional values and returns to a greater past. This appeal to cultural nationalism resonates with many of his supporters who feel that external and internal changes threaten the national identity.

Trump's brand of nationalism also includes elements of populism, as he positions himself as a champion of the "forgotten" Americans against the elites. This combination of nationalism and populism helps to explain his significant support base and the impact of his political movement.

Overall, Trump's nationalism is defined by its emphasis on reclaiming American control over its economic, political, and cultural destiny, prioritizing national interests in governance and policy-making.

Trade and Protectionism

Donald Trump's approach to trade and protectionism marks a significant shift from traditional conservative policies that favor free trade. Here's an explanation of the key aspects:

1. **Criticism of Existing Trade Agreements**: Trump has been critical of major trade agreements, arguing that they have been

unfair to the United States and have led to job losses, especially in manufacturing. He believes these agreements have allowed other countries to take advantage of the U.S. economically.

2. **Withdrawal from the Trans-Pacific Partnership (TPP)**: Early in his presidency, Trump withdrew the United States from the TPP, a multinational trade deal that aimed to deepen economic ties between these nations, slash tariffs, and foster trade to boost growth. Trump argued that withdrawing from the TPP was a move to protect American jobs and prevent other countries from taking advantage of U.S. trade policies.

3. **Renegotiation of NAFTA**: Trump renegotiated the North American Free Trade Agreement (NAFTA), which resulted in the United States-Mexico-Canada Agreement (USMCA). He claimed that NAFTA was a terrible deal for the U.S. and that the USMCA would bring back jobs to America, particularly benefiting the auto industry and agriculture.

4. **Implementation of Tariffs**: Trump's administration imposed tariffs on various goods, notably steel and aluminum, and significant tariffs on Chinese goods. The tariffs were intended to protect American industries from foreign competition and encourage production within the United States.

5. **Protectionist Philosophy**: The rationale behind these moves is rooted in a protectionist economic philosophy that seeks to shield the nation's industries from overseas competition and prevent the outsourcing of jobs. Trump's protectionism is driven by a desire to boost American manufacturing and reduce dependency on imported goods.

Trump's protectionist measures reflect his nationalist approach to politics. He emphasizes "America First" and advocates for policies that benefit American workers and industries, even at the risk of upsetting international trade dynamics and long-established global supply chains.

Foreign Policy

Donald Trump's approach to foreign policy is a markedly significant departure from traditional conservative stances, which have historically emphasized the importance of international alliances and a multilateral approach to global issues. Here's a breakdown of how Trump's foreign policy differed:

1. **Skepticism Towards NATO**: Trump frequently criticized NATO allies for his perceived insufficient defense spending and reliance on the United States for security. He argued that these countries were not paying their fair share for defense, which placed an unfair burden on the U.S. This stance shifted from the traditional view that values NATO as a cornerstone of global security and a deterrent against potential adversaries, particularly Russia.

2. **Unilateralism**: Trump preferred unilateral actions over multilateral agreements and organizations. This was evident in his decisions to withdraw from international agreements such as the Paris Climate Accord and the Iran Nuclear Deal (Joint Comprehensive Plan of Action). His administration argued that these agreements were not in America's best interest and often renegotiated bilateral agreements that he believed would better serve U.S. interests.

3. **Transactional Approach**: Trump's foreign policy was often described as transactional. Relationships with other countries were frequently assessed on a cost-benefit basis, focusing on immediate economic and political gains rather than longer-term strategic alliances. This approach shifted from the more ideologically driven foreign policy that promotes international norms such as democracy and human rights.

4. **Relationships with Authoritarian Leaders**: Trump was often criticized for his seemingly warm relationships with authoritarian leaders, such as Vladimir Putin of Russia and Kim Jong-un of North Korea. His approach was seen as a departure from

the traditional U.S. stance of promoting democratic values and human rights.

5. **America First Policy**: Central to Trump's foreign policy was the "America First" doctrine, which prioritized American interests and sought to reduce U.S. involvement in international conflicts unless directly linked to U.S. interests. This policy reduced the U.S.'s role in global governance and reevaluated its involvement in international organizations and agreements.

Trump's foreign policy reflected his broader nationalist and populist views. He emphasized national sovereignty, economic benefits to the U.S., and a skeptical view of global cooperation unless it directly benefited American interests. This approach led to significant changes in how the U.S. engaged with the rest of the world during his presidency.

Anti-Elitism

Despite his wealthy businessman and celebrity background, Donald Trump's anti-elitism is a significant facet of his political identity and appeal. This seeming contradiction plays into his broader populist strategy. Here's an exploration of this stance:

1. **Background as an Outsider**: Although Trump has been a part of the economic elite due to his real estate ventures and entertainment career, he has positioned himself as an outsider to the political establishment. He portrays himself as a businessman who entered politics to fix what professional politicians have broken. This resonates with voters who are skeptical of career politicians and the political status quo.

2. **Criticizing the Elites**: Trump often criticizes what he describes as the "political and economic elites," whom he accuses of being out of touch with ordinary Americans. He argues that these elites operate within a bubble, concentrated in places like Washington D.C. and New York City, and are disconnected from the

problems of average citizens, particularly those in the Midwest and other rural areas.

3. **Appeal to the Common Man**: This anti-elite rhetoric is key to Trump's appeal among voters who feel neglected by the government and left behind by the economic policies of recent decades. By speaking in plain, often confrontational language, Trump presents himself as a champion of the "forgotten" Americans, contrasting himself with other politicians who use more polished, traditional discourse.

4. **Media Criticism**: Part of Trump's anti-elitism involves his frequent attacks on the mainstream media, which he labels as "fake news." He accuses the media of bias and of being part of the elite class that seeks to manipulate public opinion against him, further aligning himself with those who distrust traditional media outlets.

5. **Policy Choices**: Trump's policy decisions also reflect this anti-elitism, as he often emphasizes policies that he claims will return power to the American people, such as tax cuts, deregulation, and trade policies aimed at benefiting domestic workers and industries over global interests.

Trump's anti-elitism is not just rhetoric; it's a core part of his political persona and strategy, making him an atypical figure within American politics. This approach has effectively mobilized a significant support base, tapping into broader sentiments of disenchantment with the country's political and economic leadership.

Have Trump's Policy Positions Changed?

As the 2024 presidential election approaches, Donald Trump's political positions and strategies show both continuity in his core themes and some tactical shifts to adapt to the current political landscape:

1. **Trade and Protectionism**: Trump continues to emphasize his protectionist stance on trade, which is consistent with his previous administration's policies. This includes a focus on renegotiating trade agreements to favor American industries and workers.

2. **Foreign Policy**: His "America First" foreign policy remains a central theme, advocating for a nationalistic approach to international relations. This includes skepticism towards multinational alliances and agreements, which he believes do not directly serve American interests.

3. **Immigration**: Trump has maintained his hardline stance on immigration, advocating for strict border control and policies aimed at reducing illegal immigration. This aligns with his broader nationalist agenda.

4. **Economic Policies**: Trump's economic policies continue to push for deregulation and tax cuts, aiming to stimulate economic growth through such measures, which are popular among his conservative base.

5. **Social Issues**: Trump's campaign has increasingly leaned into conservative social issues, emphasizing traditional values and opposing movements and policies that he characterizes as liberal or progressive overreach.

6. **Election and Voting Issues**: A significant part of Trump's current campaign involves continuing to assert claims about election integrity, reflecting ongoing disputes from the 2020 election. These claims are a key part of his appeal to his base, who view him as a bulwark against perceived electoral injustices.

7. **Legal Challenges**: Trump's campaign is also marked by his responses to various legal challenges and indictments, which he frames as politically motivated attacks designed to thwart his political comeback.

These positions reflect a blend of continuity in core populist and nationalist themes, with strategic adaptations to current political and social dynamics. Trump's campaign strategy involves mobilizing his base by focusing on issues where he can draw stark contrasts with his political opponents, particularly immigration, trade, and social policies.

Trump's Politics in 2024

Donald Trump's political positions and stances as the 2024 presidential election approaches continue to reflect his consistent themes, with a focus on issues such as immigration, economic policy, and climate change.

1. **Immigration**: Trump has maintained a strong stance on immigration, emphasizing border security. He has advocated for the continuation and expansion of physical barriers along the U.S.-Mexico border and supports stringent immigration controls, which align with his broader nationalist agenda.
2. **Economic Policy**: Trump's approach to economic inequality has prioritized overall economic growth rather than proposing specific policies to address income disparities directly. His administration's policies often emphasized tax cuts and deregulation to stimulate economic activity.
3. **Climate Change**: Trump has consistently expressed skepticism about climate change, questioning the economic impact of stringent environmental regulations and pulling the U.S. out of the Paris Climate Agreement during his previous term. He favors expanding domestic oil and gas production over aggressive climate policies.

These positions demonstrate Trump's continuing commitment to the core issues that have defined his political identity. He appeals to his base with policies emphasizing strong national sovereignty, economic nationalism, and conservative social values.

Additional issues that illustrate Donald Trump's political views and positions as the 2024 presidential election approaches include these.

Border Security and Immigration

Large-Scale Deportation

Trump has proposed launching the largest deportation effort in U.S. history, showcasing his continuing strict stance on immigration. This would be funded by reallocating military funds, emphasizing his commitment to using all available resources to enforce border security.

Reinforcing Barriers

He continues to focus on enhancing physical barriers along the U.S.-Mexico border, continuing his previous administration's efforts to strengthen border security.

Law Enforcement and the Death Penalty

Trump remains a staunch supporter of law enforcement and has advocated for the use of the death penalty, reflecting his "law and order" approach to governance.

Economic Policies

Trump has not proposed specific policies to address economic inequality but continues to call for overall economic growth as a solution, maintaining his focus on macroeconomic measures rather than targeted redistribution or social welfare enhancements.

Climate Policy

He has consistently minimized the importance of aggressive climate change policies, favoring the expansion of domestic oil and gas production over renewable energy efforts. This is aligned with his previous withdrawal from the Paris Agreement and his general skepticism about climate change.

Healthcare and Abortion

Trump opposes abortion and supports restrictions on funding for organizations that promote or provide abortions, aligning with conservative values on this issue.

These positions highlight Trump's consistent focus on conservative principles such as strong border control, economic growth through traditional industries, and a tough stance on law and order. These policies resonate with his base and will likely be central themes in his 2024 campaign.

Trump on the American Dream

Donald Trump's view of the American Dream is deeply intertwined with his narrative as a businessman and political figure, reflecting broader shifts in American social and political life. His conception of the American Dream has consistently emphasized economic success, individualism, and national prosperity, though the nuances of this vision have evolved alongside his public career.

Early Views and Business Career

In the early stages of his career, which began in the real estate sector in New York, Trump's vision of the American Dream was closely linked to financial success and entrepreneurial triumph. He portrayed himself as a quintessential example of this dream, claiming to have turned a "small" loan from his father into a vast real estate empire. This narrative played into the traditional American values of hard work and self-made success. However, he has been critiqued for downplaying the substantial financial help he received from his family.

Political Involvement and 2016 Presidential Campaign

Trump's entry into politics, especially during his 2016 presidential campaign, marked a significant shift in how he articulated the American Dream. His slogan, "Make America Great Again," suggested a return to a past era where, in his view, the American Dream was more accessible to the average American. He spoke to and about the "forgotten men and women" of America, promising to restore their prospects through policies aimed at revitalizing manufacturing, curbing illegal immigration, and renegotiating trade deals that he argued had harmed American workers.

This period underscored a shift from purely personal economic success to a broader nationalistic vision of prosperity, reflecting Trump's populist appeal. He positioned himself against what he termed the political and economic elites, whom he accused of hijacking the American Dream at the expense of ordinary citizens.

Presidency and Policies

During his presidency, Trump's actions and policies aimed to embody this vision of the American Dream. He focused on economic measures such as tax cuts, deregulation, and aggressive trade policies to protect American jobs. He also made significant efforts to restrict immigration, which he portrayed as a defense of American workers and their economic opportunities.

Post-Presidency and 2024 Campaign

Following his presidency and leading into his 2024 campaign, Trump's rhetoric around the American Dream has continued to emphasize strong national borders, economic nationalism, and a skepticism of globalist policies. However, the cultural and political dimensions of his vision are noticeably deepening. This includes a stronger emphasis on opposing what he and his supporters see as liberal cultural shifts, which they argue threaten traditional American values and, by extension, the American Dream.

Change or Continuity?

Throughout these phases, the core of Trump's vision—success defined in terms of economic prosperity and national prestige—has remained consistent. What has changed is the scale at which he applies this vision, shifting from personal to national. His message resonates with those left behind by globalization and technological change, suggesting a more exclusive view of the American Dream closely tied to national identity and traditional values.

The transformation in Trump's articulation of the American Dream reflects his political evolution and broader changes in American political discourse, particularly the growing polarization and the shifting concerns of the electorate. His ability to tap into deeper cultural anxieties about economic security and national identity has been a crucial element of his political persona and will likely remain central in future political endeavors.

Donald Trump has made several statements about the American Dream that illustrate his views on this iconic concept. In a notably stark assertion during his campaign, Trump declared, "The American Dream is dead," which he attributed to the policies of the current administration. This quote is emblematic of his broader political message, which often emphasizes reviving and restoring what he sees as America's lost greatness.

Trump's statement and general rhetoric suggest that he views the American Dream as severely compromised by political and economic decisions that have not favored the average American. To restore the dream, his approach strongly emphasizes economic revival, strict immigration policies, and a return to traditional American values.

This perspective ties into his broader political narrative of "Making America Great Again," aiming to resonate with those who feel left behind by globalization and changing demographics. He depicts the American Dream as personal success, national recovery, and dominance.

Donald Trump's Legal Plate is Overflowing

Donald Trump is currently involved in multiple legal cases across various jurisdictions. Here is a summary of the major ones:

1. **Classified Documents Case**: Trump faces charges related to the retention of national security documents post-presidency. He's accused of keeping sensitive documents at his Mar-a-Lago resort and showing them to unauthorized individuals. This case involves multiple felony counts under the Espionage Act and other statutes related to obstruction and false statements.

2. **New York Hush Money Case**: On May 30, 2024, a New York City jury found Donald Trump guilty on 34 felony charges in the Hush Money Trial.

3. **Georgia Election Interference**: This case focuses on Trump's actions following the 2020 Presidential election, particularly his phone call to Georgia Secretary of State Brad Raffensperger, who suggested finding enough votes to overturn the election results.

4. **E. Jean Carroll Defamation and Rape Case**: Trump has been found liable in a civil case for defamation and sexual abuse against columnist E. Jean Carroll, who claimed Trump raped her in the 1990s and then defamed her when she went public with her allegations.

5. **Trump Organization Payroll Case**: This case involves Trump's business, the Trump Organization, which was found guilty of tax fraud related to unreported employee benefits.

6. **Mary Trump Fraud Litigation**: Trump's niece, Mary Trump, sued him and other family members, alleging they defrauded her of her inheritance. This case has seen various developments, including the dismissal of certain claims.

7. **Civil Lawsuit by New York Attorney General**: Letitia James sued Trump, his family, and the Trump Organization for allegedly

inflating asset values to secure loans and tax benefits. This case is ongoing and involves substantial financial penalties.

These cases illustrate a complex legal landscape that Trump navigates, involving criminal charges and civil claims. Each case has specific allegations and legal implications, unfolding in courts with significant public and media attention.

> On Thursday, a New York jury showed that no man is above the law. Their fellow Americans could over-rule that in November. A majority of the country's highest court are siding with Trump. But the only court that matters now is the polling booth. Until then, it is premature to say the US system is working.
> ~Edward Luce, Financial Times

Next Up: A Policy Action Strategy to Avert Systemic Political Collapse and Advance the American Dream

> The Pew Research Center found that most voters believe the outcome of the 2024 presidential election will significantly impact their lives, with 69% saying it "really matters who wins." This sentiment underscores the election's importance in shaping the American Dream's future, especially regarding economic stability, healthcare affordability, and social justice.

18

PART IV: A STRATEGY FOR REFORM AND ADVANCEMENT

Part IV presents a bold and multifaceted policy action strategy aimed at averting the impending systemic collapse of the United States government system and revitalizing the American Dream for generations to come. Recognizing the deep-rooted challenges and the urgent need for reform, this section outlines a comprehensive approach to address the core issues plaguing the nation's political, economic, and social fabric.

At the forefront of this strategy is a concerted effort to overhaul the campaign finance system, reducing the undue influence of special interests and restoring the integrity of the democratic process. Concrete measures are proposed to increase transparency, impose stricter regulations on political donations, and level the playing field for candidates from diverse backgrounds.

Furthermore, Part IV advocates establishing a legitimate third party, breaking the long-standing duopoly, and fostering a more diverse and representative political discourse. This initiative aims to provide a viable alternative for voters disillusioned with the traditional two-party system and to encourage a broader range of perspectives and policy solutions.

In a departure from the growing influence of celebrity culture in politics, this section calls for an end to celebrity politics, emphasizing the need for substantive policy discussions and informed decision-making based on expertise and evidence rather than popularity contests.

Recognizing the nation's mounting fiscal challenges, Part IV outlines strategies to reduce the federal debt through responsible budgeting, revenue reforms, and targeted spending cuts. This fiscal responsibility is coupled with a comprehensive plan to reform and improve government operations, enhancing transparency, accountability, and efficiency across all levels of governance.

Moreover, this section underscores the importance of an integrated domestic and global affairs strategy, acknowledging the interconnectedness of the world and the need for a coherent approach that balances national interests with international cooperation and diplomacy.

Finally, this part of the book presents a strategic investment plan to strengthen the American Dream in the future. This plan encompasses initiatives to bolster education, promote economic opportunity, and foster innovation, ensuring that the promise of upward mobility and prosperity remains within reach for all Americans.

Through this comprehensive policy roadmap, Part IV charts a course towards systemic reform, fiscal responsibility, and a revitalized American Dream, aiming to restore faith in the democratic process, combat the corrosive effects of special interests, and reignite the promise of a prosperous and equitable future for the nation.

19

A. Strategy Overview

> " If we thought the pandemic was bad, just imagine if "
> we are faced with the systemic collapse of the American
> political system—an unraveling that threatens to under-
> mine the very foundation of our democracy and destabi-
> lize the nation beyond measure. To avoid this potential
> catastrophe, let's fix our broken governmental system
> and pave the way to revitalize America's Dream. A twelve-
> point action strategy is outlined here to accomplish both
> goals.

TWELVE-POINT ACTION STRATEGY SUMMARY

A comprehensive twelve-point action strategy is proposed to prevent the systemic collapse of the American political and governmental system and to revitalize the American Dream for future generations. These strategies are organized into four key groups: 1) Election, Campaign Finance, and Special Interest Influence Reforms; 2) Government Process Reforms; 3) Integrated Strategies for Domestic and Global Affairs; and 4) Strategic Investment Plan to Advance the American Dream.

Group I: Election, Campaign Finance, and Special Interest Influence Reforms

In an era where the integrity of elections and the influence of money in politics are under constant scrutiny, addressing the core issues surrounding campaign finance and special interest influence has become paramount. The current electoral landscape is dominated by vast sums of money funneled through political action committees (PACs) and super PACs, effectively granting disproportionate power to wealthy individuals and organizations. This has led to a political environment where elected officials prioritize the interests of their largest donors over the needs and desires of their constituents. Such dynamics erode public trust in the democratic process and hinder the creation of policies that genuinely reflect the people's collective will.

Reforming campaign finance is critical to leveling the playing field and ensuring a more equitable electoral process. This includes implementing stricter regulations on political donations, increasing transparency around funding sources, and reducing the influence of special interest groups. By doing so, we can pave the way for a political system that is more representative, accountable, and responsive to the needs of all citizens. These reforms are essential for restoring faith in our democracy and ensuring that every voice, regardless of financial backing, has an equal opportunity to be heard and considered in the political arena.

To enhance democratic representation and reduce polarization, cultivating a true third political party requires comprehensive electoral reforms, equal media coverage, inclusion in major debates, and supportive infrastructure. Concurrently, ending celebrity politics involves shifting public discourse and media coverage toward candidates' qualifications and policies, launching nationwide voter education campaigns, promoting responsible journalism, and regulating campaign practices. These initiatives aim to restore a focus on effective governance and create a more balanced and informed political landscape. Four strategic thrusts are contained in this group:

1. **Campaign Finance Reform**: Implement strict limits on contributions, establish public funding options, ensure full disclosure and transparency, regulate dark money, and reform Super PACs to restore integrity and public trust in the democratic process.
2. **Curtailing Special Interest Lobbying**: To reduce the undue influence of special interest groups, restrict lobbying activities, enhance transparency, ban lobbyist campaign contributions, and promote ethical lobbying practices.
3. **Cultivating a "True" Third Political Party**: Implement electoral reforms, ensuring equal media coverage, guaranteeing third-party candidates' inclusion in major debates, and building a supportive infrastructure to enhance democratic representation and reduce polarization.
4. **Ending Celebrity Politics**: Shift public discourse and media coverage towards candidates' qualifications and policies, launching nationwide voter education campaigns, promoting responsible journalism, and regulating campaign practices to restore a focus on effective governance.

Group II: Government Process Reforms

Public trust in government is waning; therefore, major reforms are imperative to enhance the efficiency and integrity of our political institutions. Comprehensive audits and modernization of technology and infrastructure are essential to streamline government operations and ensure they are fit for the 21st century. Establishing a dedicated task force for waste reduction and increasing transparency and accountability can significantly improve government efficiency, ultimately restoring public confidence. By mandating government data publication, strengthening whistleblower protections, and requiring regular public reporting, we can build a more transparent and accountable system that prevents corruption and fosters trust.

Increasing accountability standards ensures government officials adhere to the highest ethical and legal standards. This can be achieved by establishing independent oversight bodies, implementing regular performance reviews, and mandating ethics training. Promoting a culture of integrity within government institutions will ensure that officials act in the public's best interest. Additionally, reducing the federal debt, which currently stands at a staggering $35 trillion, is essential to prevent the systemic collapse of the federal government.

How shall we proceed? Adopting complexity science principles in governance is a vital aspect of reform. By fostering innovation, implementing adaptive and flexible policies, and acknowledging the interconnectedness of modern society's challenges, we can build resilient systems capable of managing dynamic issues. Continuous learning and responsiveness in policy development are key to addressing the complexities of today's world. These comprehensive reforms aim to create an efficient, transparent, accountable, and fiscally responsible government, restoring public trust and ensuring long-term stability. Five main thrusts are proposed:

1. **Major Government Reform:** Conduct comprehensive audits, modernize technology and infrastructure, establish a task force for waste reduction, and increase transparency and accountability to improve government efficiency and restore public trust.

2. **Bringing About Greater Transparency:** Mandate the publication of government data, strengthen protections for whistleblowers, require regular public reporting from all branches of government, and enhance oversight and accountability to build public trust and prevent corruption.

3. **Increasing Standards of Accountability:** Establish independent oversight bodies, implement regular performance reviews, mandate ethics training, and promote a culture of integrity to ensure government officials adhere to ethical and legal standards.

4. **Reduce the Federal Debt:** Reducing the government's $35 trillion debt is essential to averting the systemic collapse of the Federal Government. This book provides an approach to achieving that.

5. **Adopting Complexity Science Principles in Governance:** Foster innovation, implement adaptive policies, create flexible and responsive policies, acknowledge interconnectedness in policy development, build resilient systems, and promote continuous learning to manage modern society's dynamic and interconnected challenges.

Group III. Integrated Strategy for Domestic and Global Affairs

Creating a sustainable and prosperous future for all Americans requires a comprehensive and integrated approach to domestic affairs. Aligning education with the future economic needs of the nation is paramount to preparing a skilled workforce ready to tackle the challenges of tomorrow. Ensuring universal access to affordable healthcare is essential for the well-being and productivity of the population. Promoting innovation and job creation will drive economic growth, while balancing this growth with environmental protection will ensure long-term sustainability. These interconnected strategies aim to foster a society where every individual has the opportunity to thrive and contribute to the nation's prosperity.

On the global stage, an integrated foreign policy and global relations strategy is crucial for maintaining national security and upholding humanitarian values. Redefining relationships with global partners to reflect the realities of the 21st century will position the United States as a leader in advanced technologies and global environmental sustainability. Comprehensive immigration reform will enhance national security and reinforce the nation's commitment to humanitarian principles. The United States can build a more secure, innovative, and environmentally responsible global community by leading in these areas. These integrated domestic and foreign affairs strategies aim to create a cohesive and forward-thinking approach to the complex challenges facing the nation and the world. Two main thrusts are proposed to achieve these goals:

1. **Integrated Strategy for Domestic Affairs:** Align education with future economic needs, ensure greater access to affordable healthcare, promote innovation and job creation, and balance economic growth with environmental protection to create a sustainable and prosperous future for all Americans.

2. **Integrated Strategy for Foreign Policy and Global Relations:** Redefine relationships with global partners, lead in advanced technologies, promote global environmental sustainability, and implement comprehensive immigration reform to enhance national security and uphold humanitarian values.

Group IV: Strategic Investment Plan to Advance the American Dream

Advancing the American Dream requires an integrated approach across education, healthcare, economic development, housing, environmental sustainability, social mobility, public safety, technology, transportation, and civic engagement. These are the key elements of the proposed investment plan:

1. **Education:** Enhance K-12 STEM education and digital literacy through public-private partnerships. Expand scholarships and vocational training for higher education and promote lifelong learning to adapt to changing job markets. Drive down K-12 and higher education costs through technology and expanded public-private partnerships.

2. **Healthcare:** Increase access through health collaboratives and preventive care. Drive down costs with transparency and bulk

purchasing agreements, and improve mental health services through integrated care models and awareness campaigns.

3. **Economic Development:** Modernize infrastructure via public-private investments, foster innovation and entrepreneurship, and collaborate with high-growth industries on job creation and workforce development.

4. **Housing:** Develop affordable housing with public-private partnerships, ensure long-term affordability through community land trusts, and support homeownership with down payment assistance and financial literacy programs.

5. **Environmental Sustainability:** Invest in renewable energy, develop climate resilience plans, and promote sustainable farming and waste reduction initiatives.

6. **Social Mobility:** Enhance income support programs like EITC, provide skills training and career pathways, and support minority-owned businesses with microfinance and diverse funding sources.

7. **Public Safety:** Implement community policing, support criminal justice reform, and enhance disaster preparedness.

8. **Technology and Innovation:** Expand broadband access, support joint research initiatives, and strengthen cybersecurity.

9. **Transportation:** Invest in public transit and infrastructure upgrades to improve connectivity and economic activity.

10. **Civic Engagement:** Enhance voter access and promote civic education to increase democratic participation and community involvement.

Next Up: Part 2 - Election, Campaign Finance, and Special Interest Influence Reforms

20

B. Election, Campaign Finance, and Special Interest Influence Reforms

CAMPAIGN FINANCE REFORM

Introduction

Campaign finance reform is crucial to limiting money's influence and restoring trust in democracy. By implementing comprehensive measures, we can ensure political campaigns are fair, transparent, and accountable to the public and not dominated by wealthy individuals and special interest groups. This section outlines a detailed approach to reforming campaign finance in the United States.

Strict Limits on Contributions

Individual Contributions:

- **Caps on Donations**: Implement strict caps on the amount individuals can contribute to political campaigns. This includes contributions to candidates, political action committees (PACs), and party committees. Reducing the current $2,900 limit per election cycle per individual to $1,000 could be considered.

- **Aggregate Limits**: To prevent excessive influence by any single donor, aggregate limits on the total amount an individual can contribute across all candidates and committees in a given election cycle should be imposed. Aggregate limits were previously in place but were struck down by the Supreme Court in McCutcheon v. FEC (2014).

Corporate Contributions:

- **Limits on PAC Contributions**: Establish stringent limits on the amount corporations can contribute to PACs and Super PACs. For instance, corporate contributions to PACs should be limited to $5,000 annually and $50,000 annually for super PACs.

Public Funding Options

Matching Funds Program:

- **Small Donor Matching**: Introduce a matching funds program in which public funds match small donations from individuals at a multiple rate (e.g., 6-to-1). This would encourage candidates to seek broad-based support rather than relying on large donors.
- **Revenue Source:** A small donor matching program could be funded by earmarking a fraction of federal income tax revenues and allowing taxpayers to allocate part of their tax refund to support public election financing. This approach would ensure a steady revenue stream, encouraging broad-based support for candidates instead of relying on large donors.
- **Qualification Criteria**: Candidates must meet certain criteria to qualify for matching funds, such as demonstrating a minimum level of public support through small contributions from significant donors.

Block Grants:

- **Equal Distribution**: Provide block grants to all qualified candidates who agree to strict spending limits and refuse contributions above a certain threshold. These grants can help level the playing field and reduce the financial advantage of wealthy candidates.
- **Revenue Source:** To fund block grants, allocate a portion of federal income tax revenues, and allow taxpayers to contribute voluntarily through tax check-offs or additional contributions. This ensures a stable and sustainable financial base for the program.
- **Incentives for Participation**: Offer additional incentives to candidates participating in the public funding program, such as free or subsidized advertising time on public broadcasting networks.

Transparency and Accountability

Full Disclosure Requirements:

- **Real-Time Reporting:** Mandate real-time reporting of all campaign contributions and expenditures, requiring campaigns to disclose contributions and expenditures within a defined time of receipt and disbursement.
- **Online Database:** Create a centralized, publicly accessible, and easily searchable online database with detailed information on donors, contributions, and expenditures.

Enhanced Oversight and Enforcement:

- **Independent Oversight Body**: Establish an independent oversight body, such as a strengthened Federal Election Commission (FEC), with robust enforcement powers to oversee campaign finance laws. This body should be able to conduct audits, investigate violations, and impose penalties.

- **Whistleblower Protections**: Implement strong protections for whistleblowers who report campaign finance violations. Ensure that individuals who come forward with information about illegal activities are protected from retaliation.

Exposing Dark Money

Dark money refers to political spending by nonprofit organizations that are not required to disclose their donors. This allows individuals or entities to influence elections and public policy anonymously.

Regulating "Dark Money" Nonprofits:

- **Disclosure for 501(c)(4) Organizations**: Require 501(c)(4) organizations and other nonprofit entities engaged in political activities to disclose their donors. These organizations should be subject to the same transparency requirements as political campaigns and PACs.
- **Limiting Political Spending**: Nonprofit organizations can limit how much they spend on political activities. This will ensure that they do not become conduits for undisclosed contributions.

Closing Loopholes:

- **Coordination Rules**: Strengthen rules prohibiting coordination between campaigns and outside groups, such as Super PACs. Ensure that independent expenditure groups truly operate independently of candidate campaigns.
- **Shell Corporations**: Ban the use of shell corporations to hide donors' identities and require full disclosure of the true sources of funds used for political contributions and expenditures.

Reforming Super PACs

Contribution Limits:

- **Impose Limits on Super PAC Contributions**: To reduce their outsized influence, introduce reasonable limits on how individuals and entities can contribute to Super PACs. For example, cap contributions to Super PACs at $100,000 per election cycle.
- **Transparency Requirements**: Super PACs must disclose their donors in real-time and provide detailed information about their expenditures. Ensure that the public can easily track the sources and uses of Super PAC funds.

Spending Limits:

- **Voluntary Spending Caps**: Encourage Super PACs to adopt voluntary spending caps in exchange for certain benefits, such as enhanced access to public airwaves or reduced regulatory burdens.
- **Coordination Restrictions**: Enforce strict anti-coordination rules to ensure Super PACs operate independently from candidate campaigns. This includes prohibiting shared consultants, coordinated messaging, and joint fundraising activities.

Summary

Comprehensive campaign finance reform is crucial to restoring the integrity of the American political system. By implementing strict limits on contributions, establishing public funding options, ensuring full disclosure and transparency, regulating dark money, and reforming Super PACs, we can create a political environment where the voices of all citizens are heard, and the influence of money is significantly reduced. These measures will help build a more equitable and democratic political system, ultimately strengthening the foundation of American democracy.

CURTAILING SPECIAL INTEREST INFLUENCE

Introduction

Special interest lobbying exerts a disproportionate influence on the American political system, often skewing policy decisions in favor of the wealthy and powerful at the expense of the general public. To restore balance and integrity in governance, it is crucial to implement comprehensive reforms that restrict lobbying activities, enhance transparency, and prevent undue influence on elected officials.

Stringent Restrictions on Lobbying Activities

Cooling-Off Periods:

- **Extended Cooling-Off Periods**: Introduce extended cooling-off periods for former government officials, preventing them from engaging in lobbying activities for a significant period after leaving office. Former members of Congress have a one-year cooling-off period before they can engage in lobbying activities related to their former office. At the same time, senior executive branch officials typically face a two-year ban. A five-year ban for former members of Congress and senior executive branch officials would reduce the revolving door between government and lobbying firms.
- **Broad Applicability**: Ensure that cooling-off periods apply not only to direct lobbying but also to advisory roles, consulting, and other indirect forms of influence. This comprehensive approach would close loopholes that allow former officials to circumvent restrictions.

Mandatory Reporting of Lobbying Activities:

- **Comprehensive Reporting**: Require lobbyists to report all lobbying activities, including direct communications with government officials, grassroots lobbying efforts, and public relations campaigns to influence policy. Reports should include the issues discussed, the officials contacted, and the outcomes sought.
- **Real-Time Disclosure**: Mandatory real-time disclosure of lobbying activities ensures that the public and oversight bodies have up-to-date information. This transparency allows for timely monitoring and accountability.

Prohibiting Lobbyist Campaign Contributions

Ban on Contributions:

- **Total Ban on Lobbyist Contributions**: Implement a total ban on campaign contributions from registered lobbyists to candidates, political parties, and PACs. This measure would prevent lobbyists from using financial incentives to gain preferential access or influence policy decisions.
- **Penalties for Violations**: Establish stringent penalties for violations of the contribution ban, including substantial fines and potential disqualification from lobbying activities. These penalties would serve as a strong deterrent against non-compliance.

Transparency in Lobbyist-Government Interactions

Recording and Public Accessibility:

- **Mandatory Recording of Meetings**: All meetings between lobbyists and government officials are required to be recorded. These recordings should capture the full content of discussions to provide a clear record of the lobbying efforts and officials' responses.

- **Public Access to Records**: Make recordings and detailed summaries of all lobbyist-government meetings publicly accessible through an online database. This transparency would allow citizens, journalists, and watchdog organizations to scrutinize lobbying activities and hold officials accountable.

Enhanced Oversight and Regulation

Independent Oversight Body:

- **Establishing a Regulatory Agency**: Create an independent oversight body that regulates lobbying activities and ensures compliance with lobbying laws. This agency should be able to conduct audits, investigate potential violations, and enforce penalties.
- **Periodic Audits**: Conduct regular audits of lobbying firms and their activities to ensure adherence to regulations. Randomized audits can help identify patterns of non-compliance and deter unethical behavior.

Strengthening Lobbying Disclosure Laws:

- **Detailed Disclosures**: Strengthen lobbying disclosure laws to require more detailed information on lobbying expenditures, including the amounts spent on specific activities such as research, advertising, and grassroots mobilization.
- **Uniform Reporting Standards**: Implement uniform reporting standards across all states to ensure nationwide consistency and comparability of lobbying data.

Limiting the Influence of Lobbying on Policy

Policy Deliberation Transparency:

- **Public Hearings**: Mandate that significant policy deliberations influenced by lobbying efforts be conducted in public hearings. This transparency allows the public to observe and participate in policy-making, reducing the potential for behind-the-scenes manipulation.
- **Lobbyist Testimony**: Require lobbyists to testify publicly about their positions and the interests they represent during legislative hearings on relevant issues. This requirement ensures lawmakers and the public know the motivations behind lobbying efforts.

Reducing Reliance on Lobbyist-Provided Information:

- **Establishment of a Policy Research Fund**: Create a dedicated federal fund to support independent policy research organizations and think tanks. This fund could be financed through general tax revenues and specific allocations from areas such as government efficiency savings. The fund would provide grants to qualified organizations that produce unbiased, evidence-based research and analysis on critical policy issues. By ensuring a steady stream of objective data, this initiative would reduce lawmakers' reliance on information provided by lobbyists, promoting more informed and balanced policy decisions.
- **Enhanced Legislative Support**: Expand the resources and capacity of legislative support agencies, such as the Congressional Research Service (CRS), to offer comprehensive, non-partisan research and analysis to lawmakers.

Encouraging Ethical Lobbying Practices

Ethics Training for Lobbyists:

- **Mandatory Training Programs**: Implement mandatory ethics training programs for all registered lobbyists. These programs should cover the legal and ethical standards for lobbying, the importance of transparency, and the potential consequences of unethical behavior.
- **Certification Requirements**: Establish certification requirements for lobbyists who complete ethics training, making certification a prerequisite for registration. This professionalization of lobbying can raise ethical standards within the industry.

Creating a Culture of Accountability:

- **Industry Code of Conduct**: Develop and enforce a code of conduct for lobbying firms and practitioners that outlines ethical standards and best practices. The independent oversight body should monitor compliance with this code.
- **Public Accountability Mechanisms**: Encourage public accountability mechanisms, such as online platforms where citizens can report unethical lobbying practices and provide feedback on their interactions with lobbyists and government officials.

Summary

Curtailing the influence of special interest lobbying requires a multifaceted approach that includes stringent restrictions on lobbying activities, enhanced transparency, and strong oversight and regulation. By implementing cooling-off periods, mandatory reporting, and public access to lobbying interactions, we can reduce the undue influence of lobbyists on policy decisions. Prohibiting lobbyist campaign contributions and encouraging ethical practices will further ensure that the interests of the general public are prioritized over those of wealthy special interest groups. These reforms are crucial for restoring trust in the political system and ensuring that governance serves the broader interests of society.

CULTIVATING A THIRD POLITICAL PARTY

Introduction

Cultivating a viable third political party in the United States is essential for enhancing democratic representation and ensuring that a broader range of perspectives are included in the political discourse. The two-party system's dominance has often limited voter choice and contributed to polarization. Implementing comprehensive electoral reforms, ensuring equal media coverage, and guaranteeing third-party candidates' inclusion in major debates are crucial steps to foster a more inclusive and representative political landscape.

Electoral Reforms

Ranked-Choice Voting (RCV):

- **Mechanism**: In ranked-choice voting, voters rank candidates in order of preference. If no candidate receives a majority of first-preference votes, the candidate with the fewest votes is eliminated, and their votes are redistributed based on the voters' next preferences. This process continues until a candidate achieves a majority.
- **Benefits**: RCV ensures that winning candidates have broad support, reduces negative campaigning by encouraging candidates to seek second and third preferences, and diminishes the "wasted vote" problem, where voters feel compelled to choose between the lesser of two evils rather than their preferred candidate.

- **Overall Assessment**: Ranked-choice voting (RCV) ensures winning candidates have broad support by requiring a majority rather than a plurality. This leads to more representative outcomes and reduces negative campaigning as candidates seek wider appeal for second and third preferences. However, the primary disadvantage is the complexity of implementation and voter understanding, as the ranking process can be confusing, and the tabulation of results is more complex, potentially requiring additional resources and time to ensure accuracy.
- **Implementation**: Adopt RCV at local, state, and federal levels, starting with municipal and state elections to build momentum and demonstrate its effectiveness before implementing it in congressional and presidential elections.

Proportional Representation:

- **Mechanism**: Proportional representation allocates seats in a legislative body based on the percentage of votes each party receives. For example, a party receiving 25% of the vote would receive approximately 25% of the seats.
- **Benefits**: This system better reflects the diversity of voter preferences, allows for a more accurate representation of minority viewpoints, and reduces the likelihood of a single party dominating the legislature without broad support.
- **Implementation**: Introduce proportional representation in multi-member districts for state legislatures and the House of Representatives. This can be achieved through a mixed-member proportional system, where voters cast two ballots: one for a candidate in their district and one for a party list.

Mandating Equal Media Coverage

Equal Airtime:

- **Regulation**: Enforce regulations requiring broadcast and cable networks to provide equal airtime to all qualified political parties during election cycles. This includes news coverage, political advertisements, and participation in public affairs programming.
- **Public Broadcasting**: Leverage public broadcasting services to ensure balanced coverage of all parties. Public broadcasters can set a standard for fair and unbiased reporting and provide a platform for all voices.

Campaign Advertising:

- **Subsidized Advertising**: Provide subsidies for third-party campaign advertisements to ensure they can compete with the well-funded campaigns of major parties. This can be funded through public campaign financing initiatives.
- **Fair Advertising Practices**: Implement rules to ensure that advertising rates and access to prime advertising slots are equal for all parties, preventing media conglomerates from favoring major parties due to financial incentives.

Ensuring Debate Inclusion

Debate Criteria:

- **Polling and Ballot Access**: Set clear, reasonable criteria for debate inclusion based on polling thresholds and ballot access. For example, candidates polling at least 5% nationally and appearing on the ballot in a minimum number of states should be included.

- **Non-Partisan Commission**: Establish a non-partisan commission to oversee debate inclusion criteria and ensure they are applied fairly. This commission can also manage the organization and moderation of debates to ensure impartiality.

Debate Formats:

- **Inclusive Formats**: Design debate formats that allow for meaningful participation from all candidates. This includes equal speaking time, opportunities for rebuttals, and questions that address a wide range of issues rather than focusing on topics favored by major parties.
- **Public Engagement**: Encourage public engagement in debates by incorporating questions from citizens and community groups. This approach ensures that the debates address the concerns of a broader audience.

Building a Supportive Infrastructure

Grassroots Mobilization:

- **Local Chapters**: Encourage the development of local chapters for third parties to build grassroots support. These chapters can engage in community outreach, voter education, and local elections to build a strong support base.
- **Volunteer Networks**: Develop extensive volunteer networks to support campaign activities, from canvassing and phone banking to voter registration drives and get-out-the-vote efforts.

Policy Development and Visibility:

- **Think Tanks and Policy Institutes**: Establish think tanks and policy institutes affiliated with third parties to develop detailed policy proposals and provide expertise on key issues. This can enhance the credibility and visibility of third-party platforms.

- **Issue Advocacy**: Focus on issue advocacy to raise awareness of specific policies and positions. Third parties can attract media attention and public support by championing popular and relevant issues.

Legal and Structural Reforms

Ballot Access Laws:

- **Simplifying Access**: Reform ballot access laws to reduce the barriers for third-party candidates. This includes lowering signature requirements, extending filing deadlines, and reducing filing fees.
- **Uniform Standards**: Implement uniform ballot access standards across states to provide consistency and fairness in the electoral process.

Campaign Finance Reform:

- **Public Financing**: Expand public financing options to include third-party candidates, ensuring they have the resources to compete effectively in elections.
- **Transparency and Accountability**: Enforce strict transparency and accountability measures for all campaign finances to prevent corruption and undue influence from major party donors.

Education and Awareness

Civic Education:

- **Curriculum Integration**: Integrate comprehensive civic education into school curricula to inform students about the electoral process, the importance of diverse political representation, and the role of third parties in a healthy democracy.

- **Public Campaigns**: Launch public education campaigns to raise awareness about the benefits of third-party participation and the need for electoral reform.

Voter Engagement:

- **Engagement Initiatives**: Develop initiatives to engage underrepresented and disenfranchised voters who may feel alienated by the current two-party system. Outreach efforts should focus on inclusivity and the value of every vote.
- **Digital Platforms**: Utilize digital platforms and social media to reach a broader audience, particularly younger voters who are more likely to support third-party candidates.

Summary

Cultivating a viable third political party in the United States requires a multifaceted approach that includes comprehensive electoral reforms, equal media coverage, guaranteed debate inclusion, and supportive infrastructure development. Implementing ranked-choice voting, proportional representation, and fair media access can create a more inclusive and representative political landscape. These efforts will not only enhance democratic representation but also encourage a more vibrant and dynamic political discourse, ultimately strengthening the foundation of American democracy.

ENDING CELEBRITY POLITICS

Introduction

The rise of celebrity politics has significantly altered the landscape of American democracy, shifting the focus from substantive policy discussions to personality-driven campaigns. This trend undermines the quality of political discourse and detracts from the essential qualifications and policy positions that should inform voter decisions. To address this issue, shifting public discourse and media coverage toward candidates' qualifications, policies, and track records is crucial. Launching nationwide voter education campaigns and implementing comprehensive media reforms can help end the era of celebrity politics and restore a focus on effective governance.

Shifting Public Discourse and Media Coverage

Focus on Qualifications and Policies:

- **Media Reforms**: Encourage media outlets to prioritize coverage of candidates' qualifications, policy proposals, and track records. Establish guidelines for political reporting that emphasize substantive analysis over personality-driven stories.
- **In-Depth Interviews**: Promote in-depth interviews and policy discussions with candidates, providing them with platforms to articulate their visions and plans in detail. These interviews should focus on specific policy issues and solutions rather than personal anecdotes or superficial characteristics.
- **Fact-Checking and Accountability**: Enhance the role of fact-checking organizations in political coverage. Media outlets should collaborate with independent fact-checkers to verify candidates' claims and hold them accountable for their statements and policy positions.

Educational Content:

- **Policy Briefs**: Develop and distribute policy briefs that provide clear, concise summaries of candidates' positions on key issues. These briefs should be accessible to the public and available in multiple formats, including print, online, and video.

- **Public Service Announcements**: Utilize public service announcements (PSAs) to inform voters about the importance of focusing on policy and governance. PSAs can be broadcast on television, radio, and social media platforms to reach a wide audience.

Nationwide Voter Education Campaign

Civic Education Programs:

- **School Curricula**: Integrate civic education into school curricula from an early age, teaching students about the electoral process, the importance of informed voting, and the role of government in society. These programs should emphasize critical thinking and the evaluation of candidates based on their policies and qualifications.
- **Community Workshops**: Organize community workshops and town hall meetings to educate voters about the importance of policy-driven elections. These events can provide a forum for discussing current issues, evaluating candidates' proposals, and understanding the impact of policy decisions on local communities.

Digital Platforms and Social Media:

- **Online Resources**: Create comprehensive online resources that offer detailed information about candidates' policy positions, voting records, and qualifications. These resources should be user-friendly and accessible to all voters.
- **Social Media Campaigns**: Launch social media campaigns that promote informed voting and highlight the importance of policy over personality. Use hashtags, infographics, and video content to engage younger voters and encourage them to participate in the electoral process.

Public Forums and Debates

Issue-Focused Debates:

- **Debate Formats**: Redesign debate formats to focus on specific policy issues, allowing candidates to discuss their proposals in depth. Moderators should ask detailed questions about policy and governance, avoiding sensationalist topics.
- **Public Participation**: Incorporate questions from the public into debates and forums, ensuring that candidates address the concerns and priorities of ordinary citizens. This approach can help shift the focus from personality to substance.

Expert Panels:

- **Policy Experts**: Include panels of policy experts in public forums and debates to provide context and analysis of candidates' proposals. Experts can help clarify complex issues and assess the feasibility and impact of different policy options.
- **Interactive Formats**: Use interactive formats, such as Q&A sessions and panel discussions, to engage candidates and the public in meaningful conversations about policy.

Media Literacy and Critical Thinking

Media Literacy Programs:

- **Educational Initiatives**: Implement media literacy programs in schools and communities to teach individuals how to critically evaluate news sources, identify bias, and assess the credibility of information. These programs can empower voters to make informed decisions based on accurate and reliable information.

- **Workshops and Seminars**: Offer workshops and seminars on media literacy and critical thinking skills. These events can be held in partnership with educational institutions, libraries, and community organizations.

Promoting Responsible Journalism:

- **Journalistic Standards**: Encourage media organizations to adopt and adhere to high journalistic standards that prioritize accuracy, fairness, and objectivity. Establish codes of ethics that discourage sensationalism and promote responsible reporting.
- **Recognition and Awards**: Create awards and recognition programs for journalists and media outlets demonstrating excellence in policy-focused reporting. Highlighting and rewarding responsible journalism can set a standard for others to follow.

Regulating Campaign Practices

Advertising Standards:

- **Truth in Advertising**: Enforce strict standards for political advertising to ensure that campaign ads are truthful and not misleading. Regulatory bodies should review and approve ads before they are aired, and candidates should be held accountable for false or deceptive claims.
- **Equal Opportunity**: Ensure all candidates receive equal opportunity for advertising space and airtime, preventing wealthier candidates from dominating the media landscape.

Campaign Finance Transparency:

- **Disclosure Requirements**: Mandate comprehensive disclosure of campaign finances, including the sources of donations and expenditures. Transparency in campaign funding can help voters understand the interests and influences behind candidates' campaigns.

- **Public Financing**: Expand public financing options for political campaigns, providing candidates with the resources to compete based on their ideas and qualifications rather than their fundraising abilities.

Summary

Ending celebrity politics requires a concerted effort to shift public discourse and media coverage toward candidates' qualifications, policies, and track records. By implementing media reforms, launching nationwide voter education campaigns, promoting responsible journalism, and regulating campaign practices, we can create a political environment where substance prevails over personality. These measures will help restore the focus on effective governance and informed decision-making, ultimately strengthening the foundation of American democracy.

Next Up: Government Process Reforms

21

C. Government Process Reforms

MAJOR GOVERNMENT REFORM

Introduction

Reforming government operations is crucial to restoring public trust, improving efficiency, and ensuring that government services effectively meet citizens' needs. The current dysfunction, characterized by bureaucratic inefficiencies, outdated technology, and wasteful spending, hampers the government's ability to function optimally. Comprehensive reforms are needed to clean up these operations, streamline processes, and modernize infrastructure. This section outlines a detailed approach to achieving these goals.

Cleaning Up Dysfunctional Government

Comprehensive Audits

Scope of Audits:

- **Agency-Wide Audits**: Thoroughly audit all government agencies to assess their performance, identify inefficiencies, and uncover areas of waste and redundancy. Independent audit firms should carry out these audits to ensure objectivity and accuracy.

- **Performance Metrics**: Develop clear performance metrics and benchmarks to evaluate the effectiveness of agency operations. Metrics should include measures of efficiency, cost-effectiveness, and service quality.

Audit Implementation:

- **Phased Approach**: Implement audits in phases, starting with the largest and most critical agencies. This phased approach allows for manageable implementation and the ability to apply lessons learned to subsequent audits.
- **Stakeholder Involvement**: Engage stakeholders, including agency employees, external experts, and the public, in the audit process to ensure comprehensive assessments and buy-in for subsequent reforms.

Investing in Modernizing Technology and Infrastructure

Technology Upgrades:

- **Digital Transformation**: Invest in the digital transformation of government services, including adopting cloud computing, artificial intelligence, and data analytics. These technologies can improve efficiency, reduce costs, and enhance service delivery.
- **Interoperability**: Ensure that new technologies are interoperable across agencies, allowing for seamless data sharing and collaboration. Standardizing platforms and systems can reduce redundancy and improve coordination.
- **Cybersecurity**: Strengthen cybersecurity measures to protect government data and systems from cyber threats. Investing in robust cybersecurity infrastructure is essential for maintaining the integrity and security of government operations.

Infrastructure Improvements:

- **Modern Facilities:** Upgrade government facilities to create more efficient and conducive work environments. This includes improving office layouts, incorporating energy-efficient systems, and ensuring employee accessibility.
- **Green Initiatives:** Invest in green infrastructure projects that promote sustainability and reduce the government's carbon footprint. Initiatives could include retrofitting buildings with energy-efficient technologies, using renewable energy sources, and implementing waste reduction programs.

Establishing a Task Force for Waste Reduction

- **Composition:** Form a task force composed of experts in public administration, finance, and management, as well as representatives from the private sector and civil society. The diverse composition will bring varied perspectives and expertise to the task force.
- **Mandate:** The task force should be mandated to identify and eliminate wasteful spending, redundant programs, and inefficiencies across government operations. It should also have the authority to make recommendations and implement changes.

Action Plan:

- **Waste Identification:** Conduct a comprehensive review of government spending to identify areas of waste and inefficiency. This review should include a detailed analysis of budget allocations, procurement processes, and program outcomes.
- **Redundancy Elimination:** Identify and eliminate redundant programs and services that overlap or duplicate efforts. Streamlining these programs can reduce costs and improve service delivery.

- **Process Optimization**: Recommend and implement process optimization strategies to improve operational efficiency. This includes reengineering workflows, reducing administrative burdens, and leveraging technology to automate routine tasks.

Increasing Transparency and Accountability

Open Data Initiatives:

- **Public Data Access**: Implement open data initiatives that make government data publicly accessible. Providing access to data on government spending, program outcomes, and performance metrics can enhance transparency and accountability.
- **Interactive Platforms**: Develop online platforms allowing citizens to explore and analyze government data. These platforms should include user-friendly tools for visualizing data and tracking government performance.

Accountability Mechanisms:

- **Performance Reporting**: Require regular public reporting on agency performance, including progress toward audit recommendations and efficiency targets. Performance reports should be published online and accessible to the public.
- **Citizen Feedback**: Establish mechanisms for citizens to provide feedback on government services and report inefficiencies.

Promoting a Culture of Continuous Improvement

Training and Development:

- **Employee Training**: Invest in training and development programs for government employees to enhance their skills and knowledge. Training should focus on process improvement, technology adoption, and customer service.

- **Leadership Development**: Develop leadership programs to cultivate a culture of continuous improvement within government agencies. Leaders should be trained to identify and implement best practices, foster innovation, and drive organizational change.

Innovation Incentives:

- **Innovation Grants**: Create innovation grants to fund pilot projects and initiatives demonstrating potential for significant efficiency and service delivery improvements. Successful projects can be scaled up and implemented across the government.
- **Recognition Programs**: Establish recognition programs to reward agencies and employees with exceptional performance and innovation. Publicly recognizing achievements can motivate others to pursue continuous improvement.

Summary

Major government reform is essential to addressing the inefficiencies and dysfunction plaguing government operations. We can create a more efficient, effective, and responsive government by conducting comprehensive audits, modernizing technology and infrastructure, establishing a task force for waste reduction, and increasing transparency and accountability. Promoting a culture of continuous improvement through training, development, and innovation incentives will ensure that these reforms have a lasting impact. These efforts will enhance government performance and restore public trust in the government's ability to serve its citizens' needs.

REDUCE THE FEDERAL DEBT

As of May 2024, the total federal government debt of the United States is approximately $35 trillion. Since 2000, the debt has grown significantly, driven by a combination of factors, including tax cuts, increased military spending, economic stimulus measures, and rising entitlement costs. In 2000, the federal debt was about $5.7 trillion, indicating a more than six-fold increase over the past two decades. This rapid growth has been fueled by major events such as the 2008 financial crisis and the COVID-19 pandemic, which necessitated substantial government borrowing to support economic recovery and public health efforts.

Revenue Sources:

1. **Public-Private Partnerships**: Leverage public-private partnerships to fund infrastructure projects, reducing the need for federal spending by attracting private investment in public projects.
2. **Lottery and Gambling Expansion**: Expand state lotteries and regulated gambling, directing a portion of the proceeds to federal revenue.

Spending Cuts:

1. **Defense Spending**: Streamline defense spending by cutting unnecessary programs and focusing on efficiency and modernization.
2. **Healthcare Reform**: Expand preventative care initiatives and telehealth services to reduce long-term healthcare costs and improve efficiency in Medicare and Medicaid without cutting essential services.

3. **Government Efficiency**: Implement widespread government efficiency audits to identify and eliminate wasteful spending across all federal agencies.

4. **Encouraging Private Retirement Savings**: Increase incentives for private retirement savings through expanded tax advantages for 401(k) and IRA contributions, reducing future dependency on Social Security.

5. **Eliminating Fraud and Waste**: Invest in technology, especially AI, and processes to identify and eliminate fraud and waste within the Social Security Administration, ensuring funds are used more efficiently.

6. **Across-the-Board Federal Agency Budget Reductions**: Reduce federal spending on an annual basis. Here are some examples of impacts to illustrate the impact of across-the-board federal budget cuts. A 1% federal budget cut, saving $63 billion, would likely result in slight service reductions without significantly disrupting essential services. A 5% cut, saving $315 billion, would lead to more noticeable reductions, potential layoffs, project delays, and strains on defense, education, and healthcare programs. A 10% cut, saving $630 billion, would have a significant impact, causing major service disruptions, severe program cuts, and substantial workforce reductions across federal operations.

Analysis

- **Short-Term Effects**: These cuts would immediately reduce the federal deficit by the saved amounts, thereby slowing the growth of the federal debt.
- **Long-Term Effects**: The sustainability and impact depend on which programs and services are affected. Critical infrastructure, education, and healthcare investments could suffer, potentially slowing economic growth and higher costs.

While across-the-board cuts can quickly reduce spending, they must be balanced to avoid undermining essential services and long-term economic stability.

BRINGING ABOUT GREATER TRANSPARENCY

Introduction

Greater transparency in government operations is fundamental to building public trust, ensuring accountability, and fostering a culture of integrity. By making government data, decisions, and spending accessible to the public, we can enhance oversight and prevent corruption and misconduct. Strengthening protections for whistleblowers and requiring regular public reporting from all branches of government are critical steps toward achieving this goal. This section outlines a comprehensive strategy to bring about greater transparency in government.

Mandating the Publication of Government Data

Accessible Formats:

- **Standardized Data Formats**: Ensure all government data is published in standardized, machine-readable formats. This includes budgetary information, spending records, procurement data, and performance metrics. Standardized formats facilitate data analysis and comparison.
- **User-Friendly Platforms**: Develop user-friendly online platforms where the public can easily access and interact with government data. These platforms should include search functionalities, data visualization tools, and downloadable datasets.
- **Transparency Portals**: Establish centralized transparency portals for federal, state, and local governments. These portals should aggregate data from various agencies, providing a one-stop resource for citizens, researchers, and journalists.

Open Government Data Policies:

- **Mandatory Disclosure**: Implement policies that mandate the disclosure of all non-classified government data. This includes legislative records, executive orders, regulatory decisions, and judicial rulings. Exceptions should be narrowly defined and justified.
- **Data Timeliness**: Government data must be published promptly and regularly updated to reflect current information. This ensures that the public can access up-to-date data for oversight and analysis.

Strengthening Protections for Whistleblowers

Legal Protections:

- **Comprehensive Legislation**: Enact comprehensive whistleblower protection laws that cover all branches of government and extend to contractors and subcontractors. These laws should protect whistleblowers from retaliation, including job termination, demotion, and harassment.
- **Confidential Reporting**: Establish secure and confidential reporting channels for whistleblowers to report corruption, fraud, and misconduct. These channels should be managed by independent oversight bodies to ensure confidentiality and impartiality.

Support Mechanisms:

- **Whistleblower Advocacy Offices:** Create offices that support whistleblowers and provide legal assistance, counseling, and resources. These offices can help whistleblowers navigate the reporting process and protect their rights.
- **Public Awareness Campaigns**: Launch public awareness campaigns to educate government employees and contractors about

whistleblower protections and the importance of reporting misconduct. These campaigns can help create a culture that values and supports whistleblowers.

Incentives for Reporting:

- **Financial Rewards**: Implement reward programs that provide financial incentives for whistleblowers who expose significant fraud or corruption. These rewards can be funded through the recovery of misappropriated funds.
- **Recognition Programs**: Establish recognition programs to honor whistleblowers who demonstrate courage and integrity in reporting misconduct. Public recognition can help reduce the stigma associated with whistleblowing.

Regular Public Reporting from All Branches of Government

Executive Branch:

- **Monthly Reports**: Require the executive branch to publish monthly reports on its activities, including executive orders, regulatory actions, budgetary decisions, and key policy initiatives. These reports should be detailed and accessible to the public.
- **Transparency in Appointments**: Mandate the publication of information on executive appointments, including the selection process, qualifications, and potential conflicts of interest of appointees.

Legislative Branch:

- **Session Summaries**: Require legislatures to publish summaries of each legislative session, including bills introduced, votes cast, and the status of pending legislation. These summaries should provide clear and concise information on legislative activities.

- **Committee Reports**: Mandate that legislative committees publish detailed reports on their proceedings, including testimonies, findings, and recommendations. Committee reports should be accessible to the public and archived for future reference.

Judicial Branch:

- **Case Information**: Ensure that courts publish information on all cases, including filings, rulings, and judgments. This information should be accessible through an online database for easy search and retrieval.
- **Judicial Performance Reviews**: Implement a system for publishing judicial performance reviews, including evaluations of judges' rulings, adherence to legal standards, and feedback from peers and the public.

Enhanced Oversight and Accountability

- **Establishment of Oversight Agencies**: Create independent oversight agencies at federal, state, and local levels to monitor government activities and ensure compliance with transparency laws. These agencies should have the authority to investigate misconduct and enforce penalties.
- **Regular Audits**: Conduct audits of government agencies to assess their adherence to transparency and accountability standards. Findings should be made accessible to the public.

Public Participation Mechanisms:

- **Citizen Oversight Committees**: Establish citizen oversight committees to provide input and feedback on government transparency initiatives. These committees can bridge the government and the public, ensuring that transparency efforts reflect citizens' needs and concerns.

- **Public Comment Periods**: Implement public comment periods for major government decisions, allowing citizens to provide input before making final decisions. This process should be facilitated through online platforms and public meetings.

Summary

Increasing transparency in government operations requires a comprehensive approach that includes mandating the publication of government data, strengthening protections for whistleblowers, and requiring regular public reporting from all branches of government. Implementing these measures can enhance oversight, prevent corruption, and build public trust in government institutions. Transparency is fundamental to democratic governance, and these efforts will help ensure that government actions are accountable to the people they serve.

INCREASING ACCOUNTABILITY STANDARDS

Introduction

Raising accountability standards within the government is crucial to ensuring that officials adhere to ethical and legal standards, thereby fostering trust and integrity in public institutions. Establishing independent oversight bodies, implementing regular performance reviews, and mandating ethics training are fundamental components of this approach.

Establishing Independent Oversight Bodies

- **Federal Accountability Office (FAO)**: Establish a Federal Accountability Office tasked with monitoring the executive, legislative, and judicial branches. The FAO should operate independently from other government agencies to prevent conflicts of interest and ensure unbiased oversight.

- **State and Local Oversight Agencies**: Create similar independent oversight bodies at the state and local levels. These agencies should be empowered to investigate misconduct, enforce ethical standards, and provide improvement recommendations.

Functions and Responsibilities:

- **Monitoring Compliance**: The oversight bodies should regularly monitor compliance with ethical and legal standards, including financial disclosures, conflicts of interest, and adherence to laws and regulations.
- **Investigating Misconduct**: Empower the oversight bodies to conduct thorough investigations into allegations of misconduct, corruption, and abuse of power. They should be able to subpoena documents, compel testimony, and refer cases for prosecution.
- **Enforcing Penalties**: Ensure oversight bodies can enforce penalties for violations, including fines, reprimands, and recommendations for removal from office. These penalties should be proportionate to the severity of the misconduct.

Transparency and Public Reporting:

- **Public Reports**: Require oversight bodies to publish regular reports on their findings, investigations, and enforcement actions. These reports should be accessible to the public and provide detailed information on the status of accountability efforts.
- **Online Dashboards**: Develop online dashboards that track the performance and compliance of government officials and agencies. These dashboards should include real-time updates and allow citizens to monitor accountability measures.

Implementing Regular Performance Reviews

Clear, Measurable Criteria:

- **Performance Metrics**: Develop clear and measurable criteria for evaluating the performance of elected officials and judges. Metrics should include legislative effectiveness, adherence to ethical standards, judicial impartiality, and public satisfaction.
- **Periodic Reviews**: Conduct regular performance reviews, at least annually, for all elected officials and judges. Independent review boards composed of experts, former officials, and citizen representatives should conduct these reviews.

Evaluation Processes:

- **360-Degree Feedback**: Implement a 360-degree feedback process that gathers input from various stakeholders, including peers, subordinates, and the public. This comprehensive approach provides a balanced assessment of an official's performance.
- **Public Hearings**: Hold public hearings to present the findings of performance reviews and allow citizens to provide feedback. This transparency ensures that officials are held accountable to the people they serve.

Consequences for Poor Performance:

- **Remedial Actions**: Establish clear consequences for poor performance, including mandatory remedial actions such as additional training, mentoring, or reassignment. Officials who consistently fail to meet performance standards should face more severe penalties, including potential removal from office.
- **Performance-Based Incentives**: Introduce performance-based incentives for officials demonstrating exceptional performance

and adherence to ethical standards. These incentives could include public recognition, awards, and additional responsibilities.

Mandating Ethics Training

Comprehensive Ethics Training Programs:

- **Curriculum Development**: Develop comprehensive ethics training programs for all government officials and judges. The curriculum should cover key topics such as conflict of interest, financial disclosures, transparency, whistleblower protections, and the importance of ethical behavior.
- **Regular Training Sessions**: Require officials to participate in regular ethics training sessions, at least annually. These interactive sessions should incorporate case studies, role-playing, and discussions to reinforce ethical principles.

Ethics Certification:

- **Certification Process**: Implement an ethics certification process for government officials and judges. To receive certification, officials must complete the required training and pass an assessment. Certification should be renewed periodically to ensure ongoing compliance with ethical standards.
- **Public Disclosure of Certification Status**: Make the certification status of officials publicly available. This transparency allows citizens to verify that their representatives have completed the necessary ethics training.

Ethics Officers and Advisory Committees:

- **Appointment of Ethics Officers**: Appoint ethics officers within each government agency and judiciary to oversee compliance with ethical standards. Ethics officers should provide guidance, conduct training, and serve as a point of contact for reporting misconduct.

- **Ethics Advisory Committees**: Establish ethics advisory committees to provide ongoing support and advice to government officials and judges. These committees should include experts in ethics, law, and public administration.

Promoting a Culture of Integrity

Leadership Commitment:

- **Top-Down Approach**: Ensure that commitment to ethical behavior starts at the top. Leaders should model ethical behavior and clarify that ethical standards are a priority for the organization.
- **Ethical Leadership Training**: Train senior leaders on ethical leadership principles and the importance of fostering an ethical organizational culture.

Encouraging Ethical Behavior:

- **Recognition Programs**: Establish programs to recognize and reward ethical behavior among government officials. Publicly acknowledging those who demonstrate integrity can inspire others to follow suit.
- **Ethics Hotlines**: Create confidential ethics hotlines for reporting ethical concerns and seeking advice. Ensure that independent entities manage these hotlines to maintain confidentiality and impartiality.

Next Up: Integrated Strategies for Domestic and Global Affairs

22

D. Integrated Strategies for Domestic and Global Affairs

INTEGRATED DOMESTIC AFFAIRS STRATEGY

Introduction

An integrated strategy for domestic affairs is crucial for addressing the multifaceted challenges facing the United States. By aligning education with future economic needs, ensuring increased access to affordable healthcare, promoting innovation and job creation, and balancing economic growth with environmental protection, we can create a sustainable and prosperous future for all Americans. This section outlines a comprehensive approach to achieving these goals through the federal government working with the states and the private sector.

Aligning K-12 and Higher Education with Future Needs

K-12 Innovations: The Federal Government should partner with the states, public and private educational systems, and the private sector to advance these three areas of innovation:

- Personalized learning uses technology such as adaptive learning software and AI-driven tutors to tailor educational experiences to individual student needs and learning paces.
- Project-based learning engages students in solving real-world problems, promoting critical thinking, collaboration, and practical application of interdisciplinary knowledge.
- Social-emotional learning integrates practices that develop students' emotional intelligence, resilience, and interpersonal skills, supporting their mental health and academic success.

STEM Education:

- **Curriculum Enhancement**: Enhance K-12 curricula to emphasize science, technology, engineering, and mathematics (STEM) education. This includes integrating hands-on learning experiences, coding classes, and advanced placement courses in STEM subjects.
- **Teacher Training**: Invest in professional development programs to equip teachers with the skills and knowledge to teach STEM subjects effectively. Provide incentives for teachers to pursue advanced degrees in STEM fields.

Vocational Training:

- **Career and Technical Education (CTE)**: Expand career and technical education programs in high schools and community colleges to provide students with practical skills and industry certifications. Partner with local businesses and industry leaders to ensure CTE programs meet labor market needs.
- **Apprenticeships and Internships**: Develop apprenticeship and internship programs that allow students to gain hands-on experience in high-demand fields. Both public and private sector employers should support these programs.

Higher Education:

- **Competency-based education (CBE)** allows students to progress through their degrees by demonstrating mastery of specific skills and knowledge at their own pace, offering greater flexibility and personalization.
- **Massive Open Online Courses (MOOCs):** By leveraging digital platforms for fully online degrees, hybrid courses, and MOOCs, online learning and hybrid educational models provide greater access, flexibility, and cost savings.
- **Open Educational Resources (OER)** reduce educational costs by offering freely accessible and openly licensed teaching materials that educators and students can use, modify, and share.

Ensuring Increased Access to Affordable Healthcare

Healthcare Access and Preventive Care

- **System Rehaul:** America's healthcare system needs a comprehensive and coordinated overhaul to ensure that healthcare can be provided to the American people. While universal healthcare may be ideal, meeting this goal through expanded government-backed programs is not the answer. A better approach is for the federal government to collaborate with providers to improve existing options and innovatively create new programs that reward employers for providing improved coverage.
- **Medicare:** Implement value-based care models that incentivize healthcare providers to focus on patient outcomes rather than the volume of services provided.
- **Medicaid:** Expand managed care programs to better coordinate patient care, reduce unnecessary services, and control costs while maintaining quality coverage for enrollees.

- **Affordable Care Act (ACA)**: Encourage accountable care organizations (ACOs) to improve care coordination and cost management while ensuring patients receive comprehensive and efficient healthcare services.
- **Comprehensive Coverage**: Explore strategies for health insurance plans to cover preventive services such as vaccinations, screenings, and wellness visits without out-of-pocket costs. Emphasize the importance of preventive care in reducing long-term healthcare costs and improving health outcomes.
- **Public Health Campaigns**: Launch public health campaigns to raise awareness about the benefits of preventive care and encourage individuals to take proactive steps to maintain their health.

Healthcare Cost Reduction:

- **Price Transparency**: Implement policies that require healthcare providers to disclose the prices of services and procedures upfront. This transparency can help consumers make informed decisions and promote competition among providers.
- **Prescription Drug Reform**: Address the high cost of prescription drugs by allowing Medicare to negotiate drug prices, promote generic medications, and regulate price increases.

Promoting Innovation, Entrepreneurship, and Job Creation

Public-Private Partnerships:

- **Innovation Hubs**: Establish innovation hubs and technology parks that foster collaboration between universities, research institutions, and private companies. These hubs can serve as incubators for startups and provide resources for research and development.

- **Government Grants and Incentives**: Offer government grants, tax credits, and other incentives to encourage private sector investment in research and development, particularly in emerging industries such as clean energy, biotechnology, and artificial intelligence.

Targeted Investments:

- **Infrastructure Development**: Invest in modernizing and expanding infrastructure, including transportation, broadband, and utilities. Infrastructure projects create jobs, stimulate economic growth, and improve residents' quality of life.
- **Small Business Support**: Support small businesses through access to capital, mentorship programs, and simplified regulatory processes to increase job creation and innovation.

Entrepreneurship Education:

- **Business Incubators**: Create business incubators and accelerators that offer aspiring entrepreneurs training, mentorship, and resources. These programs can help entrepreneurs turn ideas into viable businesses and scale their operations.
- **Entrepreneurship Curriculum**: Integrate entrepreneurship education into K-12 and higher education curricula to equip students with the skills to start and grow businesses.

Balancing Economic Growth with Environmental Protection

Clean Energy Promotion:

- **Renewable Energy Incentives**: Provide incentives for developing and adopting renewable energy sources such as solar, wind, and geothermal. This includes tax credits, grants, and subsidies for renewable energy projects.

- **Energy Efficiency Programs**: Implement energy efficiency programs to encourage businesses and households to reduce energy consumption. Offer rebates and financing options for energy-efficient appliances, building upgrades, and retrofits.

Sustainable Practices:

- **Green Building Standards**: Promote green building standards and certifications such as LEED (Leadership in Energy and Environmental Design) for new construction and renovations. Green buildings reduce energy consumption, lower operating costs, and improve indoor air quality.
- **Sustainable Agriculture**: Support sustainable agriculture practices that reduce environmental impact and promote soil health, water conservation, and biodiversity. Provide grants and technical assistance to farmers adopting sustainable practices.

Environmental Regulations:

- **Carbon Pricing**: Implement carbon pricing mechanisms such as carbon taxes or cap-and-trade programs to reduce greenhouse gas emissions and encourage investment in clean energy. Revenue generated from carbon pricing can be used to fund climate mitigation and adaptation projects.
- **Pollution Control**: Strengthen air and water pollution regulations to protect public health and the environment. In a balanced way, increase enforcement of environmental laws.
- **Climate Adaptation Plans**: Develop and implement climate adaptation plans that address the risks of climate change, such as sea-level rise, extreme weather events, and shifting agricultural

patterns. These plans should include measures to protect vulnerable communities and infrastructure.

- **Disaster Preparedness**: Invest in disaster preparedness and response programs to enhance community resilience to natural disasters. This includes building resilient infrastructure, improving early warning systems, and providing resources for recovery and rebuilding.

Summary

An integrated domestic affairs strategy is essential for addressing the United States' diverse challenges. By aligning education with future economic needs, ensuring universal access to affordable healthcare, promoting innovation and job creation, and balancing economic growth with environmental protection, we can create a sustainable and prosperous future for all Americans. These comprehensive measures will enhance the quality of life for citizens and strengthen the nation's economic and environmental resilience.

INTEGRATED STRATEGY FOR FOREIGN POLICY AND GLOBAL RELATIONS

Introduction

In an increasingly interconnected world, the United States must adopt a comprehensive and forward-thinking foreign policy strategy that addresses global challenges, promotes stability, and fosters international cooperation. This strategy should redefine relationships with global partners, lead in developing and ethically deploying advanced technologies, promote global environmental sustainability, and implement comprehensive immigration reform. These will enhance national security and economic growth and uphold humanitarian values.

Redefining Relationships with Global Partners

- **Strengthening Alliances**: Reinforce alliances with traditional partners such as NATO, the European Union, and key Asian allies. Regular high-level dialogues, joint military exercises, and shared intelligence can enhance collective security and deter aggression from adversaries.
- **International Institutions**: Play a proactive role in international institutions like the United Nations, World Trade Organization, and International Monetary Fund. Engage in reform efforts to ensure these institutions are effective, transparent, and capable of addressing modern challenges.

Regional Partnerships:

- **Asia-Pacific Engagement**: Increase engagement with countries in the Asia-Pacific region through economic partnerships, security collaborations, and cultural exchanges. Address issues such as North Korea's nuclear program and China's territorial ambitions to promote stability in the region.
- **Latin America Relations**: Strengthen ties with Latin American countries through trade agreements, development aid, and cooperative efforts to combat drug trafficking and corruption. Support democratic institutions and human rights initiatives to foster regional stability.

Global Challenges:

- **Pandemic Preparedness**: Collaborate with international partners to enhance global health security. Invest in early warning systems, vaccine development, and healthcare infrastructure to prevent and respond to pandemics.

- **Counterterrorism**: Work with global partners to combat terrorism through intelligence sharing, joint military operations, and efforts to address the root causes of extremism.

Ethical Leadership in Advanced Technologies

- **Global Standards for AI**: Lead efforts to develop international standards for the ethical use of artificial intelligence. Promote transparency, accountability, and the protection of human rights in AI applications.
- **Cybersecurity Collaboration**: Strengthen cybersecurity collaboration with allies to protect critical infrastructure and counter cyber threats. Establish norms and agreements for responsible state behavior in cyberspace.

Innovation and Research:

- **Joint Research Initiatives**: Partner with other nations on research and development projects in emerging technologies such as quantum computing, biotechnology, and renewable energy. Joint initiatives can accelerate innovation and share the benefits globally.
- **Talent Exchange Programs**: Create international talent exchange programs to attract top scientists, engineers, and innovators to the United States. These programs can foster collaboration and enhance the country's technological leadership.

Promoting Global Environmental Sustainability

Climate Agreements:

- **Continued Role in the Paris Agreement**: Reaffirm the United States' commitment to the Paris Agreement and work towards more climate goals. Lead by example in reducing greenhouse gas emissions and transitioning to a low-carbon economy.

Sustainable Development Goals (SDGs):

- **Supporting the SDGs**: Align foreign aid and development programs with the United Nations Sustainable Development Goals. Focus on clean water, renewable energy, and sustainable agriculture to promote global sustainability.
- **Green Investments**: Promote green investments through international financial institutions. Encourage the private sector to invest in sustainable projects abroad, particularly in developing nations.

Conservation and Biodiversity:

- **International Conservation Efforts**: Support international conservation initiatives to protect biodiversity and natural habitats. Collaborate with other countries on wildlife protection, reforestation, and marine conservation projects.
- **Sustainable Fisheries**: Work with global partners to promote sustainable fishing practices and combat illegal, unreported, and unregulated (IUU) fishing. Implement measures to preserve marine ecosystems and ensure long-term food security.

Implementing Comprehensive Immigration Reform

Balancing Security with Humanitarian Values:

- **Secure Borders**: Implement measures to secure the nation's borders while ensuring that immigration enforcement respects human rights. Use advanced technology and intelligence to prevent illegal immigration and combat human trafficking.

Economic Integration:

- **Skilled Workforce**: Attract and retain skilled immigrants who can contribute to the economy. Implement policies that facilitate the integration of immigrants into the workforce, including recognition of foreign credentials and support for language training.
- **Labor Market Needs**: Align immigration policies with labor market needs, ensuring that industries facing labor shortages can access the required talent. Promote temporary work programs and seasonal visas to address specific economic demands.

Integration and Support:

- **Community Integration**: Support programs that facilitate the integration of immigrants into their new communities. This includes access to education, healthcare, housing, and social services.
- **Anti-Discrimination Measures**: Enforce anti-discrimination laws to protect immigrants from exploitation and abuse. Promote diversity and inclusion initiatives to foster social cohesion.

Summary

An integrated strategy for foreign policy and global relations is essential for addressing the complex challenges of the 21st century. By redefining relationships with global partners, leading in the development and ethical deployment of advanced technologies, promoting global environmental sustainability, and implementing comprehensive immigration reform, the United States can enhance its national security, drive economic growth, and uphold its humanitarian values.

Next Up: Investment Strategy to Advance the American Dream

23

E. Investment Strategy to Advance the American Dream

Introduction

Creating a more inclusive and equitable American Dream requires a collaborative approach that involves the president, Congress, federal agencies, the private sector, and local governments. This strategic investment plan emphasizes innovation, entrepreneurship, and community-driven initiatives over government subsidies, encouraging economic independence and social mobility.

Major Areas of the Strategic Investment Plan

Education

K-12 Education:

- **Public-Private Partnerships**: Collaborate with private companies to enhance STEM education and digital literacy in K-12 schools. Encourage tech firms to provide resources, mentorship, and internships for students.
- **Local Government Initiatives**: Empower local governments to innovate in education through grants and flexibility in using

federal funds, allowing them to tailor programs to community needs.

Higher Education:

- **Scholarships and Grants**: Partner with corporations and philanthropic organizations to expand scholarship opportunities and reduce student loan burdens. Promote employer-sponsored education programs.
- **Vocational Training**: Support vocational and technical training programs through partnerships with industry leaders, ensuring curricula align with current labor market needs.

Lifelong Learning:

- **Adult Education**: Encourage businesses to invest in continuous employee learning, offering online courses and certification programs in collaboration with educational institutions.
- **Community Colleges**: Strengthen the role of community colleges through state and local government support, focusing on affordable, flexible learning opportunities for adults.

Healthcare

Increased Access:

- **Health Collaboratives**: To improve access to affordable healthcare, form health collaboratives that include local governments, healthcare providers, and private insurers. Encourage innovative models like community health cooperatives.
- **Preventive Care Programs**: Promote employer-sponsored preventive care programs and wellness initiatives to reduce long-term healthcare costs.

Healthcare Cost Reduction:

- **Transparency Initiatives**: Partner with the healthcare industry to implement transparency in pricing and quality metrics, empowering consumers to make informed choices.
- **Pharmaceutical Partnerships**: Work with pharmaceutical companies to lower drug prices through bulk purchasing agreements and support for generic drug development.

Mental Health Services:

- **Integrated Care Models**: Foster partnerships between mental health providers, local governments, and community organizations to offer comprehensive mental health services.
- **Public Awareness**: Launch campaigns with nonprofits and private companies to reduce stigma and encourage mental health care utilization.

Economic Development

Infrastructure:

- **Public-Private Investments**: Leverage public-private investments to modernize infrastructure, including transportation, broadband, and utilities, creating jobs and improving community connectivity.
- **State and Local Projects**: Empower state and local governments to prioritize infrastructure projects that meet their unique needs, supported by federal seed funding.

Innovation and Entrepreneurship:

- **Innovation Hubs**: Establish innovation hubs through partnerships with universities, research institutions, and private companies to drive economic development and technological advancement.
- **Small Business Support**: Support small businesses through local government initiatives and private sector mentorship programs, focusing on access to capital and market opportunities.

Job Creation:

- **Industry Partnerships**: Create job creation programs in collaboration with high-growth industries like clean energy, technology, and advanced manufacturing. Encourage apprenticeships and on-the-job training programs.
- **Workforce Development**: Support workforce development initiatives led by local governments and industry groups to prepare workers for future job markets.

Housing

Affordable Housing:

- **Public-Private Development**: Facilitate affordable housing development through public-private partnerships, offering incentives for developers to build mixed-income communities.
- **Community Land Trusts**: Support community land trusts that enable local governments and nonprofits to maintain long-term affordable housing.

Homeownership Programs:

- **Down Payment Assistance**: Collaborate with financial institutions to provide down payment assistance and favorable mortgage terms for first-time homebuyers.
- **Financial Literacy**: Promote financial literacy programs through partnerships with banks and nonprofits to help potential homeowners make informed decisions.

Housing Stability:

- **Eviction Prevention**: Partner with local governments and community organizations to implement eviction prevention programs and assist renters facing financial hardship.

Environmental Sustainability

Clean Energy:

- **Renewable Energy Projects**: Encourage renewable energy projects through partnerships with private companies and provide tax incentives and grants for clean energy investments.
- **Energy Efficiency**: Promote energy efficiency programs in collaboration with utilities and local governments, offering rebates and financing options for energy-efficient upgrades.

Climate Resilience:

- **Resilience Planning**: Develop climate resilience plans in partnership with local governments, focusing on infrastructure improvements and community preparedness.

- **Green Initiatives**: Support green initiatives through public-private partnerships that promote sustainable practices and reduce environmental impact.

Sustainable Practices:

- **Agricultural Sustainability**: Work with agricultural businesses and local governments to implement sustainable farming practices and conservation programs.
- **Waste Reduction**: Encourage waste reduction and recycling programs through collaborations with private companies and community organizations.

Social Mobility

Income Support:

- **Tax Credits**: Enhance income support programs such as the Earned Income Tax Credit (EITC) through public-private collaborations, providing financial stability for low- and middle-income families.
- **Community Support Programs**: Foster community support programs that offer job training, financial counseling, and other resources to help individuals achieve economic independence.

Workforce Development:

- **Skills Training**: Partner with businesses to provide skills training and career development programs that align with industry needs, enhancing social mobility.
- **Career Pathways**: Develop career pathway programs in collaboration with educational institutions and employers, offering clear routes to advancement in various fields.

Access to Capital:

- **Microfinance Programs**: Support microfinance programs that provide small loans and financial services to underserved communities, encouraging entrepreneurship and economic growth.
- **Diverse Funding Sources**: Promote diverse funding sources for minority-owned businesses through partnerships with financial institutions and venture capital firms.

Public Safety

Community Policing:

- **Collaborative Policing Models**: Implement community policing through partnerships between law enforcement agencies, local governments, and community organizations to build trust and enhance public safety.
- **Technology Integration**: Utilize technology and data analytics to improve policing strategies and reduce crime, supported by public-private collaborations.

Criminal Justice Reform:

- **Rehabilitation Programs**: Develop rehabilitation and reentry programs through partnerships with nonprofits and private companies to support formerly incarcerated individuals.
- **Systemic Inequality**: Address systemic inequalities in the criminal justice system through collaborative reform efforts involving government agencies, advocacy groups, and community stakeholders.

Emergency Services:

- **Disaster Preparedness**: Enhance preparedness and response capabilities through public-private partnerships, ensuring communities can handle emergencies.
- **Community Resilience**: Support community resilience initiatives that promote preparedness and recovery, leveraging resources from local governments and private companies.

Technology and Innovation

- **Broadband Expansion**: Expand broadband access through public-private partnerships, ensuring all Americans have high-speed internet for education, work, and civic engagement.
- **Tech Innovation**: Promote technological innovation through collaborations with universities, research institutions, and private companies.
- **Joint R&D Initiatives**: Support joint research and development initiatives in emerging technologies, fostering collaboration between government, academia, and industry.
- **Talent Development**: Invest in talent development programs that attract and retain top scientists, engineers, and innovators.

Cybersecurity:

- **Cyber Defense Collaboration**: Strengthen cybersecurity measures through collaboration with private companies and international partners, protecting critical infrastructure and data.
- **Public Awareness**: Raise awareness about cybersecurity threats and best practices through educational campaigns and industry partnerships.

Transportation

Public Transit:

- **Transit Development**: Invest in public transit development through public-private partnerships, improving connectivity and reducing traffic congestion.
- **Sustainable Transport**: Collaborate with private companies and local governments to promote sustainable transportation options, including electric vehicles and bike-sharing programs.

Road and Bridge Maintenance:

- **Infrastructure Upgrades**: Support infrastructure upgrades and maintenance through joint funding initiatives involving federal, state, and local governments and private sector investment.
- **Smart Transportation Systems**: Implement smart transportation systems that use technology to enhance efficiency and safety, supported by industry partners.

Civic Engagement

Voter Access:

- **Expanding Voter Registration**: Enhance voter access through public-private partnerships that support voter registration drives and expand early voting options.
- **Civic Technology**: Utilize civic technology platforms to increase voter engagement and streamline the voting process.

Civic Education:

- **Educational Initiatives**: Promote civic education programs through collaborations with educational institutions and non-profits, teaching citizens about their rights and responsibilities.
- **Community Involvement**: Foster community involvement initiatives that empower citizens to participate in local decision-making and contribute to community development.

Summary

By fostering next-generation partnerships with the private sector, state and local governments, and community organizations, we can create a strategic investment plan that advances the American Dream without dependence on government programs. This comprehensive approach addresses critical areas such as education, healthcare, economic development, and social mobility, emphasizing innovation, entrepreneurship, and community-driven initiatives. We can enhance economic and social mobility through collaboration and targeted investments, creating a more inclusive and equitable society for all Americans.

Strategic Investment Plan Benefits

Education

K-12 Education: Public-private partnerships to enhance STEM education and digital literacy equip students with critical skills for the modern workforce, promoting innovation and competitiveness. Empowering local governments to tailor educational programs ensures resources meet specific community needs, improving overall educational outcomes.

Higher Education: Expanding scholarships and grants reduces student debt, making higher education more accessible and fostering a more skilled workforce. Supporting vocational training aligns curricula with labor market demands, preparing students for high-demand jobs and reducing unemployment.

Lifelong Learning: Encouraging continuous employee learning and strengthening community colleges ensure adults can adapt to changing job markets, enhancing economic resilience and productivity.

Healthcare

Increased Access: Health collaboratives and preventive care programs focus on early intervention and holistic care to improve health outcomes and reduce long-term healthcare costs.

Healthcare Cost Reduction: Transparency initiatives empower consumers to make informed choices, driving down costs. Bulk purchasing agreements with pharmaceutical companies can lower drug prices, making essential medications more affordable.

Mental Health Services: Integrated care models and public awareness campaigns reduce stigma and improve access to mental health services, promoting overall well-being and productivity.

Economic Development

Infrastructure: Public-private investments in modernizing infrastructure create jobs, enhance community connectivity, and boost economic activity. Empowering local governments to prioritize projects ensures investments meet specific regional needs.

Innovation and Entrepreneurship: Establishing innovation hubs fosters technological advancement and economic development, while supporting small businesses through mentorship and access to capital promotes entrepreneurship and job creation.

Job Creation: Collaborating with high-growth industries on job creation and workforce initiatives, future job creation, reducing unemployment, and driving economic growth.

Housing

Affordable Housing: Public-private partnerships to develop affordable housing address housing shortages and stabilize communities. Community land trusts ensure long-term affordability, supporting low-income families.

Homeownership Programs: Down payment assistance and financial literacy programs make homeownership more accessible, promoting financial stability and wealth building.

Housing Stability: Eviction prevention programs help renters facing financial hardship, reduce homelessness, and promote community stability.

Environmental Sustainability

Clean Energy: Investing in renewable energy projects and promoting energy efficiency reduces carbon emissions, lowers energy costs, and creates green jobs.

Climate Resilience: Developing climate resilience plans and supporting green initiatives protect communities from climate impacts, ensuring long-term sustainability.

Sustainable Practices: Encouraging sustainable farming practices and waste reduction initiatives promotes environmental stewardship and resource conservation.

Social Mobility

Income Support: Enhancing income support programs like the Earned Income Tax Credit (EITC) provides financial stability for low- and middle-income families, reducing poverty.

Workforce Development: Skills training and career pathway programs enhance social mobility by preparing individuals for high-demand jobs and providing clear routes to career advancement.

Access to Capital: Supporting microfinance programs and promoting diverse funding sources for minority-owned businesses encourage entrepreneurship and economic growth.

Public Safety

Community Policing: Implementing collaborative policing models builds trust between law enforcement and communities, enhancing public safety.

Criminal Justice Reform: Rehabilitation programs and addressing systemic inequalities support formerly incarcerated individuals and promote fairer justice outcomes.

Emergency Services: Enhancing disaster preparedness and supporting community resilience initiatives ensure communities can effectively respond to emergencies.

Technology and Innovation

Digital Infrastructure: Expanding broadband access through public-private partnerships will ensure all Americans have high-speed internet for education, work, and civic engagement.

Research and Development: Supporting joint research initiatives and investing in talent development fosters innovation and technological leadership.

Cybersecurity: Strengthen cybersecurity measures and raise public awareness about threats to protect critical infrastructure and data, ensuring national security.

Transportation

Public Transit: Investing in public transit development and promoting sustainable transportation options reduces traffic congestion and improves connectivity.

Road and Bridge Maintenance: Supporting infrastructure upgrades and implementing smart transportation systems enhance efficiency and safety, benefiting economic activity and quality of life.

Civic Engagement

Voter Access: Enhancing voter access and utilizing civic technology platforms increase voter engagement and participation in the democratic process.

Civic Education: Promoting civic education programs and fostering community involvement initiatives empower citizens to contribute to local decision-making and community development.

Summary

This strategic investment plan targets critical areas through innovative and collaborative approaches. It aims to foster a more inclusive and equitable society, ensuring long-term economic and social benefits that enhance the American Dream for all citizens.

Next Up: Epilogue

" As we stand at the crossroads of our nation's history, " the American Dream is more than a distant ideal—it's a call to action for each of us. This book is a clarion call to renew our commitment to a society where hard work and determination can overcome any barrier. Join us in forging a future where opportunity is truly within reach for all, where our shared values guide us toward prosperity and justice. Your vote, your voice, your actions will shape the destiny of the American Dream. Let's rise together and make it a reality.

24

Epilogue

As we conclude this exploration of America's political landscape, I urge every voter to reflect deeply on how we have arrived at this point where our political system offers such flawed choices for leadership—not just for the presidency but also for Congress and state and local offices. We must ask ourselves: How have we allowed our political environment to deteriorate to the extent that it is marred by partisanship, corruption, and inefficacy?

Consider why better candidates are not stepping forward to run for office. Is it the toxic nature of our political discourse, the overwhelming influence of money and special interests, or the general disillusionment with the process? More importantly, why are those who do step up often not elected? These questions demand our attention and introspection if we are to reform and revitalize our democracy.

As American voters, we must hold our leaders accountable, regardless of their party affiliation or ideological leanings. Whether they are Republicans or Democrats, extreme right-wing supporters, or extreme left-wing advocates, our leaders must look past their narrow views. They must rediscover the importance of making politics and government a vital, unifying institution that serves the public good.

We must also ask ourselves, and the next president, how we will restore civility to American society. It is imperative to remember that we are indeed a civilization. As stewards of our nation's resources and people, we are responsible for managing our environment wisely and considering the fate of the world around us. The degradation of civil discourse and the polarization of our communities must be addressed head-on, with a commitment to fostering respect, understanding, and cooperation.

This book aims to have a life beyond the 2024 election. The ideas and principles discussed here are not confined to this political moment; they are essential for the future of America. We must transcend our political partisanship and build new, evolving political partnerships. We must reinvigorate the participatory democracy upon which America was founded, encouraging active engagement from all citizens. And we must create new pathways to prosperity for all Americans, ensuring that the American dream remains attainable for everyone.

I wrote this book because I believe in the potential of the American people. We can elect leaders who serve with integrity, intelligence, and hope. We have the power to demand better from our political system and to drive meaningful change. We can build a brighter, more inclusive future by coming together, embracing our differences, and working towards common goals.

Let this epilogue be a call to action. Let it inspire you to apply this book's lessons and ideas to your life and community. The journey to a better America does not end with an election; it is a continuous effort that requires our dedication and resolve. Together, we can ensure that the American dream survives and thrives for ourselves and future generations.

In the prologue, I shared ten conversational questions about my book. As promised, I have shared them here, along with a website link to my blog, where we can discuss your views on the questions.

Conversation Questions for "America's Dream at a Crossroads, The 2024 Presidential Election and Beyond"

The American Dream in the Election Context

1. **How have the definitions and expectations of the American Dream evolved, and how do the 2024 presidential candidates' policies reflect these changes?** Reflect on the historical and modern interpretations of the American Dream and analyze how current political platforms address these evolving expectations.

2. **In what ways do the economic policies of Joe Biden and Donald Trump differ in their potential impact on achieving the American Dream?** Compare the economic strategies proposed by both candidates and discuss their implications for wealth-building, job creation, and economic mobility.

3. **How does the education policy of each candidate aim to bridge or widen the gap in access to quality education, and what impact does this have on the American Dream?** Assess the education reforms proposed by Biden and Trump, considering how these policies might affect educational equity and opportunities for future generations.

4. **To what extent do the healthcare plans of the 2024 candidates influence the accessibility and affordability of healthcare as a component of the American Dream?** Analyze the healthcare proposals from both candidates, focusing on how these plans might alter access to healthcare services and financial stability for American families.

5. **How do the candidates' stances on immigration shape the concept of the American Dream for immigrants and their descendants?** Discuss the immigration policies of Biden and Trump and their potential effects on the opportunities available to immigrants pursuing the American Dream.

The American Dream Beyond the Election

1. **What are the long-term implications of current economic trends on the viability of the American Dream for future generations?** Consider the impact of trends such as automation, globalization, and economic inequality on the sustainability of the American Dream.

2. **How can education systems be reformed to better prepare individuals for the challenges and opportunities of the 21st century while supporting the American Dream?** Explore innovative educational approaches that can equip people with the skills and knowledge necessary for success in a rapidly changing world.

3. **How can communities foster a sense of belonging and support to help individuals achieve their version of the American Dream?** Discuss community-based initiatives and social support systems that enhance social cohesion and provide pathways to personal and collective success.

4. **How does environmental sustainability intersect with pursuing the American Dream, and what role should policy play in this relationship?** Examine the importance of sustainable practices and policies in ensuring that the pursuit of the American Dream does not come at the expense of the environment.

5. **What can be done to restore trust in institutions and governance to reinforce the foundation of the American Dream?** Analyze strategies for rebuilding public trust in political, economic, and social institutions, and consider how this trust is vital for realizing the American Dream.

Here is the link to my blog:
https://www.donaldiannone.com/blog.

Next Up: About the Author

"   As the author of this book, I bring a refeshing outsider perspective on the threat of systemic collapse of America's democracy and the necessity of strengthening America's Dream. Working four decades in economic development and public policy has helped me understand the American Deam from the local, state, and federal levels. "

25

About the Author

Don Iannone has worked in economic development and public policy for over forty years. Don managed and led economic development organizations in Northeast Ohio for eight years, including programs at the Greater Cleveland Growth Association and organizations in Lake and Ashtabula counties. While at the Growth Association, he spearheaded nationally recognized industry development programs advancing the automotive and polymer industries. He directed the economic development and environmental centers at Cleveland State University for fourteen years. From 2000 to 2016, Don provided economic development and public policy consulting services to over 100 communities, regions, states, port authorities, Federal agencies, colleges and universities, business corporations, American Indian tribes, and several international clients. His work carried him to thirty-two states, ten countries, and ten Native American communities.

Don contributed to statewide economic development strategies for the administrations of four Ohio governors (Celeste, Voinovich, Taft, and Strickland). He was the economic development advisor to George Voinovich's first gubernatorial campaign in 1990. He served on the boards of the National Council for Urban Economic Development

(NCUED), the American Economic Development Council (AEDC), the MidAmerican Economic Development Council (MAEDC), and the Ohio Development Association (OEDA). In 1993, he chaired the Federal Policy Committee of NCUED and advised President Bill Clinton's transition team on economic development policy issues. For six years, he was a member of the Environmental Finance Advisory Board (EFAB) of the U.S. Environmental Protection Agency, advising USEPA on financing policies and programs. Don has testified about economic development and public policy issues before Congress and state legislatures many times during his career. He has received several economic development leadership awards during his career, including his induction into Ohio's Economic Development Hall of Fame.

Don was a recognized leader in helping urban and rural communities clean up and redevelop environmentally contaminated industrial and commercial sites. Policy and academic researchers still often cite his seminal publications on brownfield redevelopment. He is a frequent keynote speaker and panelist at international, national, and regional economic development, public policy, and environmental conferences and training workshops. He served on the Economic Development Institute (EDI) faculty at the University of Oklahoma for twelve years, teaching economic developers from across the United States.

Don authored four nonfiction books, including one on economic development policy, several economic development monographs, ten poetry collections, and ten photographic essays. His newest book, "America's Dream at a Crossroads, The 2024 Presidential Election and Beyond," will be released during the summer of 2024. Don authored over twenty academic and professional articles on economic, social, and environmental issues facing urban and rural communities. Don is a full member of the Authors Guild, American Academy of Poets, Poetry Society of America, and Literary Cleveland.

Since 2020, Don has taught graduate business courses at Transcontinental University, where he currently supervises doctoral candidates' dissertations from Ghana and Malta. Don holds a doctorate in

Philosophy. Don grew up in Eastern Ohio's coal and steel country in the 1950s and 1960s. He and his wife, Mary, reside in Greater Cleveland.

Contact me at: **https://www.donaldiannone.com/contac**t

26

Glossary

Abortion rights: The legal rights and protections related to the ability of individuals to access safe and legal abortion services.

Achilles heel: A person's point of greatest vulnerability.

Affordable Care Act (ACA): A comprehensive healthcare reform law enacted in March 2010 to make health insurance more affordable and accessible.

America First: A foreign policy stance emphasizing American interests and priorities over those of other countries.

American Bill of Rights: The first ten amendments to the United States Constitution guarantee essential rights and liberties.

American Dream: The national ethos of the United States is centered on the belief that freedom allows all citizens to achieve their goals through hard work.

American electorate: The body of people entitled to vote in an election in the United States.

American Recovery and Restoration Act: Likely refers to the American Recovery and Reinvestment Act of 2009, a stimulus package enacted to combat the Great Recession.

American Revolution: The period during the late 18th century when the thirteen American colonies won independence from Great Britain.

Anthony, Susan, B.: A prominent American social reformer and women's rights activist who played a pivotal role in the women's suffrage movement.

Anti-elitism (politics): A political stance that opposes elite groups or individuals seen as disconnected from the concerns of ordinary people.

Artificial intelligence (AI): The simulation of human intelligence in machines programmed to think and learn.

Authoritarianism: A government characterized by strong central power and limited political freedoms.

Betting odds: The likelihood of a particular outcome in events like elections or sports, often expressed in ratios.

Biden, Hunter: The son of Joe Biden, known for his business dealings and personal controversies.

Biden, Joe: The 46th President of the United States, serving since January 2021.

Bidenism: Policies and ideologies associated with Joe Biden.

Bipartisanship: Cooperation and compromise between the two major political parties.

Black Lives Matter: A movement advocating for non-violent civil disobedience in protest against incidents of police brutality and all racially motivated violence against Black people.

Blue State: A U.S. state predominantly supports and votes for the Democratic Party.

Border security: Measures a country takes to monitor and regulate its borders to control who and what enters.

Broad-based prosperity: Economic prosperity that is widely shared across all sectors of society.

Brookings Institution: A nonprofit public policy organization based in Washington, D.C., conducting research and education in various fields of public policy.

Bureau of Economic Analysis (BEA): The U.S. Department of Commerce agency provides economic statistics, including the U.S.'s gross domestic product (GDP).

Bureau of Labor Statistics (BLS): The U.S. government's principal fact-finding agency in labor economics and statistics.

Bush, George H.: The 41st President of the United States, serving from 1989 to 1993.

Bush, George W.: The 43rd President of the United States, serving from 2001 to 2009.

Capitalism: An economic system based on private ownership of the means of production and their operation for profit.

Carnegie, Andrew: A 19th-century industrialist and philanthropist who led the expansion of the American steel industry.

Carter, Jimmy: The 39th President of the United States, serving from 1977 to 1981.

Celebrity politics: The involvement of celebrities in political activities, including running for office or endorsing political candidates.

Centrism: Political ideology focused on balance and avoiding extremes, advocating for moderate policies.

Character (personality): The mental and moral qualities distinctive to an individual.

Christian Right: A political and social movement primarily composed of conservative Christians advocating for policies consistent with their religious beliefs.

Civic engagement: Individual and collective actions designed to identify and address issues of public concern.

Civil rights: The rights of citizens to political and social freedom and equality.

Civil Rights Act 1964: Landmark U.S. legislation outlawed discrimination based on race, color, religion, sex, or national origin.

Clinton, Bill: The 42nd President of the United States, serving from 1993 to 2001.

Cognitive dissonance: The mental discomfort experienced by a person who holds two or more contradictory beliefs, ideas, or values.

Collectivism: The practice or principle of prioritizing a group over each individual.

Colonial period: The time in American history when the thirteen colonies were under British rule before the American Revolution.

Complexity science: The study of complex systems and problems that are dynamic, unpredictable, and interconnected.

Congress: The national legislative body of the United States, composed of the Senate and the House of Representatives.

Conservative: A political and social philosophy promoting traditional institutions and practices.

Consumer expenditures: The money households and individuals spend on goods and services.

Corruption (government): The abuse of power by government officials for illegitimate private gain.

COVID-19 is a highly infectious disease caused by the coronavirus SARS-CoV-2, leading to a global pandemic in 2019.

Criminal justice reform: Efforts to change policies and practices in the criminal justice system to address issues like mass incarceration, sentencing laws, and policing practices.

Critical Thinking: The objective analysis and evaluation of an issue to form a judgment.

Crossroads: A point at which crucial decisions must be made that will have far-reaching consequences.

Cult of Personality: When a political leader uses mass media, propaganda, or other methods to create an idealized and heroic public image.

Cybersecurity: Measures taken to protect a computer or computer system against unauthorized access or attack.

Dark Money: Dark money refers to political spending by nonprofit organizations that are not required to disclose their donors, allowing anonymous contributions to influence elections and policy decisions.

Declaration of Independence: The document adopted on July 4, 1776, declared the thirteen American colonies independent from Britain.

Deep state: A body of people believed to be involved in the secret manipulation or control of government policy.

Democracy: A system of government where the citizens exercise power by voting.

Democratic: About the Democratic Party in the United States or supporting democracy as a system of government.

Digital media: Content stored in digital formats and usually distributed online, including news websites, social media, and digital publications.

Divided States of America: A term reflecting the political, social, and cultural polarization within the United States.

Divisiveness (political): The tendency to cause disagreement or hostility between people.

Domestic policy: Administrative decisions directly related to all issues and activities within a nation's borders.

Du Bois, WEB: An influential African American sociologist, historian, and civil rights activist who co-founded the NAACP.

Economic anxiety: Worry or concern about economic stability and future economic conditions.

Economic development: Efforts aimed at improving a community's economic well-being and quality of life by creating and retaining jobs and supporting or growing incomes.

Economic growth: An increase in the production of goods and services over time.

Economic inequality: The unequal distribution of income and opportunity between different societal groups.

Economic mobility: The ability of an individual or family to improve their economic status, typically measured in income.

Economic Pessimism: A belief or outlook that economic conditions will worsen.

Economic voting: When voters' choices in elections are influenced by their economic situations or perceptions of the economy.

Education issues: Challenges and debates regarding education policies, practices, and quality.

Election integrity and security: Measures to ensure that elections are conducted fairly, transparently, and without interference or fraud.

Electoral College: The body of electors established by the U.S. Constitution formally elects the president and vice president.

Elite (political sense): A small group of people who hold a disproportionate amount of wealth, privilege, political power, or skill in a society.

Environmental issues: Problems related to the natural environment, such as pollution, climate change, and conservation.

Equality: The state of equality, especially in status, rights, and opportunities.

Ethics: Moral principles that govern a person's behavior or the conducting of an activity.

European Union (EU): A political and economic union of 27 countries located primarily in Europe.

Eurozone: The group of European Union nations whose national currency is the euro.

Evangelical Christians: A group of Christians who emphasize the authority of the Bible, the necessity of being born again, and the importance of sharing the Christian faith.

Evidence-based policymaking: Making policy decisions based on the best available evidence from research and data.

Far Left: Political groups or individuals advocating radical, often revolutionary policies or social change.

Far Right: Political groups or individuals advocating for ultranationalist, authoritarian, or reactionary policies.

Federal Reserve: The central banking system of the United States, which regulates the nation's monetary policy.

Fitness to serve office: The qualifications and suitability of a person to hold a public office.

Foreign policy: A government's strategy in dealing with other nations.

Frontier spirit: The ethos of independence, resilience, and innovation associated with the American frontier experience.

Gallup Organization: An American analytics and advisory company known for its public opinion polls.

Gaza: A small region on the eastern coast of the Mediterranean Sea, part of the Palestinian territories, often associated with the Israeli-Palestinian conflict.

Gen X: The generation born after the baby boomers, roughly from the early 1960s to the early 1980s.

Gig economy: A labor market characterized by short-term contracts or freelance work, as opposed to permanent jobs.

Gilded Age: The late 19th century period of rapid economic growth in the United States, marked by wealth disparity and social issues.

Gini index: A measure of income inequality within a population, ranging from 0 to 1.

Globalism: The idea that events in one country cannot be separated from those in another and that economic and foreign policy should be planned internationally.

Globalization is how businesses or other organizations develop international influence or start operating internationally.

Government: The system by which a state or community is governed.

Government Intervention: Actions taken by a government to influence its economy.

Government investment: Spending by the government on projects designed to enhance the country's economic capacity.

Government spending: The total money a government uses for its operations and services.

Great Depression: The severe worldwide economic depression during the 1930s.

Great Recession: The sharp decline in economic activity during the late 2000s was the most significant downturn since the Great Depression.

Gross Domestic Product (GDP): The total value of goods produced and services provided in a country during one year.

Gun control: Laws and policies designed to regulate the manufacture, sale, possession, and use of firearms.

Hobbes, Thomas: A 17th-century English philosopher known for his work on political philosophy, especially his book "Leviathan".

House of Representatives: The lower house of the United States Congress, with members elected to represent districts based on population.

Human rights: Fundamental rights that every person is entitled to, such as freedom, equality, and justice.

Iannone, Donald, T.: Likely a reference to a specific individual relevant to the context of the book (provide specific definition if more context is known).

Ideology: A system of ideas and ideals, especially one that forms the basis of economic or political theory and policy.

Ideology in education: The beliefs and principles influencing educational practices and policies.

Immigration: The action of coming to live permanently in a foreign country.

Impeachment: A process by which a legislative body levels charges against a government official.

Income distribution: How a nation's total earnings are divided among its population.

Independent: A person or group not affiliated with any political party.

Individualism: The principle of being independent and self-reliant.

Industrial Revolution (US): The rapid industrial growth and development period in the United States during the late 19th and early 20th centuries.

Inflation: The rate at which the general level of prices for goods and services is rising.

Infrastructure: The basic physical systems of a country, including transportation, communication, sewage, water, and electric systems.

Integrated Policy Approach: An integrated approach to domestic and foreign affairs involves coordinating and aligning policies across both spheres to ensure that internal and external strategies complement and reinforce each other for cohesive governance and global engagement.

Insider (political): A person accessing confidential or privileged information within a political organization.

Interest rate: The amount lenders charge to borrowers for the use of money, expressed as a percentage of the principal.

Intergenerational: Occurring or existing between different generations.

Intragenerational: Occurring or existing within a single generation.

Israel-Palestine: The ongoing conflict between Israelis and Palestinians over territorial and political issues.

Jacobs, Jane: An influential urbanist and activist known for her work on urban studies, especially her book "The Death and Life of Great American Cities".

January 6, 2021: The date of the storming of the United States Capitol by supporters of President Donald Trump.

Johnson, Lyndon: The 36th President of the United States, serving from 1963 to 1969.

Judicial system (US): The system of courts that interprets and applies the law in the name of the state in the United States.

Kennedy, John, F.: The 35th President of the United States, serving from 1961 until his assassination in 1963.

Kennedy, Robert, F., Jr.: An American environmental lawyer, activist, and son of Robert F. Kennedy.

Khamenei, Ali: The Supreme Leader of Iran since 1989.

King, Martin, Luther: A leader in the American civil rights movement, known for using nonviolent civil disobedience.

Labor union: An organization of workers formed to protect and advance their rights and interests.

Legal entanglements: Complex legal issues or disputes that can be difficult to resolve.

LGBTQ+: An acronym for lesbian, gay, bisexual, transgender, queer/questioning, and others.

Liberalism: A political and moral philosophy based on liberty, consent of the governed, and equality before the law.

Liberty: The state of being free within society from oppressive restrictions imposed by authority on one's way of life, behavior, or political views.

Make America Great Again: A campaign slogan used by Donald Trump during his 2016 presidential campaign.

Marketplace (private): The economic system in which businesses operate privately without direct control by the state.

McCain, John: An American politician and military officer who served as a U.S. Senator from Arizona and was the Republican nominee for president in 2008.

Medicaid: A joint federal and state program that helps with medical costs for some people with limited income and resources.

Medicare: A federal health insurance program primarily for 65 and older.

Mental health: A person's condition about their psychological and emotional well-being.

Migration: The movement of people from one place to another, often for economic, social, or political reasons.

Moderate (politics): A person who holds centrist views and advocates for moderate policies.

Morality: Principles concerning the distinction between right and wrong or good and bad behavior.

Multilateralism is coordinating national policies in groups of three or more states.

Multipolar World: A global power structure where multiple countries have significant influence.

NAFTA: North American Free Trade Agreement, a treaty between Canada, Mexico, and the United States to eliminate trade barriers.

National debt: The total money a country's government has borrowed.

National identity: A person's sense of belonging to a nation and a belief in its political aspirations.

National security: The safety and defense of a nation, including its citizens, economy, and institutions.

Nationalism: A political ideology that emphasizes the interests, culture, and values of a nation or ethnic group.

NATO: The North Atlantic Treaty Organization, a military alliance of European and North American countries.

Network news: News programming broadcast by a television or radio network.

New Deal: A series of programs, public work projects, and financial reforms and regulations enacted by President Franklin D. Roosevelt in response to the Great Depression.

Obama, Barak: The 44th President of the United States, serving from 2009 to 2017.

OPEC: The Organization of the Petroleum Exporting Countries, an intergovernmental organization of oil-exporting nations.

Opportunity: A set of circumstances that makes it possible to do something.

Outsider (political): A person not part of the established political elite or does not hold an official political position.

Pandemic: An outbreak of a disease occurring on a global scale.

Paris Agreement: An international treaty on climate change aiming to limit global warming to below 2 degrees Celsius above pre-industrial levels.

Parks, Rosa: An American civil rights activist best known for her pivotal role in the Montgomery bus boycott.

Partisan filter: The tendency to interpret information and events based on pre-existing political biases.

Partisanship: Strong, often blind allegiance to a particular political party.

Pew Trusts: A non-profit organization that conducts research and public policy analysis on various issues.

Polarization (political): The division of political attitudes to ideological extremes.

Political Action Committee (PAC): A political action committee (PAC) is an organization that collects and distributes campaign contributions from members to support or oppose political candidates, legislation, or ballot initiatives.

Political extreme: Positions or viewpoints at the far ends of the political spectrum.

Political philosophy: The study of fundamental questions about the state, government, politics, liberty, justice, and the enforcement of a legal code.

POLITICO: An American political journalism company that covers politics and policy in the United States and internationally.

Politics: The activities associated with the governance of a country or area, especially the debate between parties having power.

Populism: A political approach that appeals to ordinary people who feel that established elite groups disregard their concerns.

Post-Cold War years: The period after the end of the Cold War, marked by changes in global political dynamics.

Post-World War II Era: The period following World War II, characterized by reconstruction, decolonization, and the rise of the Cold War.

Poverty rate: The percentage of people living below the poverty line.

President: The elected head of a republican state.

Private education: Education provided by entities other than the government, often funded by student tuition.

Progressive Era: Social activism and political reform in the United States from the 1890s to the 1920s.

Property rights: Legal rights to possess, use, and dispose of land, buildings, or goods.

Prosperity: The state of being successful, especially in terms of wealth.

Protectionism: Economic policy restraining trade between states through tariffs on imported goods.

Public education: Education that is funded and administered by the government.

Public persona: The aspect of a person's character that is presented to or perceived by the public.

Putin, Vladimir: The President of Russia, serving since 2012 and from 2000 to 2008.

Raisi, Ebrahim: The President of Iran, elected in 2021.

Rawls, John: An American moral and political philosopher known for his theory of justice as fairness.

Reagan, Ronald: The 40th President of the United States, serving from 1981 to 1989.

Recession: A temporary economic decline during which trade and industrial activity are reduced.

Red State: A U.S. state predominantly supports and votes for the Republican Party.

Regulation: A rule or directive made and maintained by an authority.

Reich, Robert: An American economist, professor, author, and political commentator who served as Secretary of Labor under President Bill Clinton.

Republican: About the Republican Party in the United States or supporting a republic as a form of government.

Rhetoric (political): The art of persuasive speaking or writing, often used in politics.

Rockefeller, John, D.: An American industrialist and philanthropist, widely considered the wealthiest American of all time.

Rogers, Will: An American stage and motion picture actor, vaudeville performer, cowboy, humorist, newspaper columnist, and social commentator.

Roosevelt, Franklin, D.: The 32nd President of the United States, serving from 1933 to 1945.

Rural area: A geographic area located outside towns and cities, often characterized by farming or natural settings.

Rust Belt: A northeastern and midwestern United States region characterized by declining industry and population.

Sanders, Bernie: An American politician and Senator from Vermont known for his progressive policies.

Second Amendment: The amendment to the U.S. Constitution that protects the right to keep and bear arms.

Senate: The upper house of the United States Congress, with members elected to represent states.

Snowe, Olympia: An American politician and former U.S. Senator from Maine, known for her moderate views.

Social injustice: Situations where unfair practices are being carried out in society.

Social media: Websites and applications that enable users to create and share content or participate in social networking.

Social mobility: The ability of individuals or groups to move within a social hierarchy.

Social Security: A federal insurance program that benefits retired people and those unemployed or disabled.

Special Interests: Groups or organizations seeking to influence public policy to benefit their interests.

STEM: An acronym referring to the academic disciplines of science, technology, engineering, and mathematics.

Streeter, Ryan: Likely a reference to a specific individual relevant to the context of the book (provide specific definition if more context is known).

Student Loan Forgiveness: Policies that aim to reduce or eliminate student loan debt for borrowers.

Subjective economic perception: An individual's personal view or feeling about the state of the economy.

Suburbanization: The process of population movement from within cities to the rural-urban fringe.

Sustainability: The ability to maintain or improve certain processes or states over the long term without depleting resources or causing harm.

Swing State: A U.S. state where both Democratic and Republican candidates have a strong chance of winning.

Systemic Collapse: Systemic collapse in the context of the American government political system refers to the failure of fundamental structures and institutions, leading to widespread dysfunction, loss of public trust, and the inability to effectively govern or uphold democratic principles.

Systemic racism: Forms of racism that are embedded in the laws and regulations of a society or organization.

Tariff: A tax imposed on imported goods and services.

Tax Foundation: A think tank that researches and analyzes tax policies.

Taxation (progressive): A tax system in which the tax rate increases as the taxable amount increases.

Tech hub: A region that is a center for technology companies and innovation.

Technological disruption: Significant changes brought about by new technologies that disrupt existing industries and markets.

Transactional leadership: A style of leadership that focuses on supervision, organization, and performance; leaders promote compliance through rewards and punishments.

Transformational leadership: A leadership approach that causes change in individuals and social systems by inspiring and motivating followers.

Trump, Donald: The 45th President of the United States, serving from 2017 to 2021.

Trumpism: The political ideology, style of governance, and policies associated with Donald Trump.

U-3 unemployment rate: The official unemployment rate that measures the percentage of the total labor force that is unemployed and actively seeking employment.

U-6 unemployment rate: A broader measure of unemployment includes underemployed, marginally attached workers and those discouraged from seeking employment.

U.S. Constitution: The supreme law of the United States, establishing the framework for the federal government and outlining the rights of the citizens.

Ukraine-Russia: Refers to the geopolitical tensions and conflict between Ukraine and Russia.

Unilateralism: A policy approach where a state acts independently without regard for the interests or support of other states.

United Nations: An international organization founded in 1945 to promote peace, security, and cooperation among nations.

Urban area: A geographic area with a high population density and built environment infrastructure.

Ursula von Leyen: The President of the European Commission since December 2019.

US House of Representatives: The lower house of the United States Congress, with members elected to represent districts based on population.

US Senate: The upper house of the United States Congress, with members elected to represent states.

"Us versus them": A mentality that categorizes people into two groups, creating a divide based on perceived differences.

Vanderbilt, Cornelius: An American business magnate who built his wealth in railroads and shipping during the 19th century.

Voinovich, George, V.: An American politician who served as Governor of Ohio and U.S. Senator.

Voting Rights Act 1965: A landmark piece of federal legislation prohibiting racial discrimination in voting.

Wealth: An abundance of valuable possessions or money.

Well-Being: The state of being comfortable, healthy, or happy.

White House: The official residence and workplace of the President of the United States.

Williamson, Marianne: An American author, spiritual leader, and political activist.

World Happiness Report: An annual publication of the United Nations that ranks global happiness in countries worldwide.

World Trade Organization (WTO): An intergovernmental organization that regulates international trade.

Xi Jinping: The General Secretary of the Communist Party of China and President of the People's Republic of China.

Zelenskyy, Volodymyr: The President of Ukraine, serving since May 2019.

References

Abel, J. R., & Deitz, R. (2022). The value of a college degree. Federal Reserve Bank of New York.

Abramowitz, A. (2013). The Electoral Roots of America's Dysfunctional Government. Presidential Studies Quarterly, 43, 709-731.

Abramowitz, A. I. (2018). The Great Alignment: Race, Party Transformation, and the Rise of Donald Trump. Yale University Press.

Abrams, S. J. (2019). *The American dream is alive and well*. American Enterprise Institute. Retrieved from https://www.aei.org/articles/the-american-dream-is-alive-and-well/

Abrams, S. J. (2020, September 3). Competing visions of the American Dream are driving Democrats and Republicans apart. The Washington Post. https://www.washingtonpost.com/outlook/2020/09/03/competing-visions-american-dream-are-driving-democrats-republicans-apart/

Adams, J. T. (1931). The Epic of America. Little, Brown, and Company.

Albright, M. (2018). Fascism: A Warning. Harper Perennial.

Allison, G. (2024). The Essence of Skilled Global Leadership. Foreign Affairs, 103(2), 45-60.

Allitt, P. (2011). Ayn Rand and American Conservatism in the Cold War Era. Modern Intellectual History, 8(2), 253-263.

Anderson, J. (2024). Youth engagement in the 2024 election: Trends and implications. Journal of Political Studies, 29(2), 123-145.

Andrias, K. (2016). Separations of Wealth: Inequality and the Erosion of Checks and Balances. Social Science Research Network.

Arthur, W. B. (2015). Complexity and the Economy. Oxford University Press.

Associated Press-NORC Center for Public Affairs Research. (2024). AP-NORC poll: Voters dissatisfied with 2024 presidential candidates. https://apnorc.org/projects/ap-norc-poll-voters-dissatisfied-with-2024-presidential-candidates/

Ayshford, E. (2024, May 1). How the inequality around us shapes our perceptions of morality. KelloggInsight. https://insight.kellogg.northwestern.edu/article/how-the-inequality-around-us-shapes-our-perceptions-of-morality#!

Bacevich, A. J. (2008). The limits of power: The end of American exceptionalism. Macmillan.

Baker, K. (2024). The role of social media in modern political campaigns. Digital Politics Quarterly, 12(1), 67-89.

Ballotpedia. (n.d.). Presidential election in Ohio, 2020. Retrieved from https://ballotpedia.org/Presidential_election_in_Ohio,_2020

Bar-Yam, Y. (1997). Dynamics of Complex Systems. Westview Press.

Bartels, L. M. (2009). The Political Economy of the Bush Years. Daedalus, 138(4), 31-46. https://doi.org/10.1162/daed.2009.138.4.31

Bayer, L., & de la Baume, M. (2020, December 9). Ursula von der Leyen's 100 days: The good, the bad and the ugly. POLITICO. https://www.politico.eu/article/ursula-von-der-leyen-100-days-the-good-the-bad-and-the-ugly/

Beach, J. M. (2007). The Ideology of the American Dream: Two Competing Philosophies in Education, 1776-2006. Educational Studies, 41(2), 148-164.

Benner, C., & Pastor, M. (2015). Equity, Growth, and Community: What the Nation Can Learn from America's Metro Areas.

Berger, S. (2013). Making in America: From innovation to market. MIT Press.

Bergman, R., & Fassihi, F. (2023). Iran's Shadowy War With Israel

Escalates. The New York Times. Retrieved from https://www.nytimes.com/2023/04/15/world/middleeast/iran-israel-war.html

Berry, W. (1977). The Unsettling of America: Culture & Agriculture. Sierra Club Books.

Bhattarai, D. (2022). Understanding the Primacy of Geography in the Conduct of Foreign Policy. Journal of Foreign Affairs.

Billington, R. A. (1974). Westward Expansion: A History of the American Frontier. Macmillan

Blackman, T., & Blackman-Woods, R. (2007). A Response to Dorling's 'Inequalities in Britain 1997–2006: the Dream that Turned Pear-shaped'. Local Economy: The Journal of the Local Economy Policy Unit, 22, 118-122.

Bluestone, B., & Harrison, B. (1982). The deindustrialization of America: Plant closings, community abandonment, and the dismantling of basic industry. Basic Books.

Bodansky, D. (2016). The Paris Climate Agreement: A New Hope? American Journal of International Law, 110(2), 288-319. https://doi.org/10.5305/amerjintelaw.110.2.0288

Bolden, R., & O'Regan, N. (2016). Digital Disruption and the Future of Leadership. Journal of Management Inquiry, 25(4), 438-446.

Bradshaw, M. (2009). The Geopolitics of Global Energy Security. Geography Compass, 3, 1920-1937.

Brainard, L. (2022, March 2). Cryptocurrencies, Digital Currencies, and Distributed Ledger Technologies: What Are We Learning? Board of Governors of the Federal Reserve System. https://www.federalreserve.gov/newsevents/speech/brainard20220302a.htm

Branch, T. (2004). Parting the Waters: America in the King Years 1954–63. Simon & Schuster.

Bremer, F. J. (1995). The Puritan Experiment: New England Society from Bradford to Edwards (Revised ed.). University Press of New England.

Briggs, X. de S. (2005). The Geography of Opportunity: Race and Housing Choice in Metropolitan America. Brookings Institution Press.

Brinkley, A. (1995). The End of Reform: New Deal Liberalism in Recession and War. Vintage Books.

Britannica. (n.d.). Industrialization of the U.S. economy. Retrieved from https://www.britannica.com/USA-Industrialization-Economy-Growth

Brookings Institution. (2022). A dozen facts about immigration. Retrieved from Brookings

Brookings. (2024). National security & America's role in the world. Brookings Election '24. https://www.brookings.edu/projects/election-24-issues-at-stake/national-security-americas-role-in-the-world/

Brookings. (2024). The Ukraine conflict and the 2024 U.S. presidential election. https://www.brookings.edu/articles/the-ukraine-conflict-and-the-2024-u-s-presidential-election/

Brougham, D., & Haar, J. (2020). Technological disruption and employment: The influence on job insecurity and turnover intentions: A multi-country study. Technological Forecasting and Social Change, 161, 120276.

Brown, L. (2024). Populism and political polarization in the United States. American Political Review, 33(3), 200-218.

Brynjolfsson, E., & McAfee, A. (2011). Race Against the Machine: How the Digital Revolution Is Accelerating Innovation, Driving Productivity, and Irreversibly Transforming Employment and the Economy. Digital Frontier Press.

Brynjolfsson, E., & McAfee, A. (2014). The Second Machine Age: Work, Progress, and Prosperity in a Time of Brilliant Technologies. W. W. Norton & Company.

Bureau of Labor Statistics. (2020). Education Pays 2020.

Bureau of Labor Statistics. (2023). Earnings and unemployment rates by educational attainment, 2022.

Burges, S. W. (2017). Brazil in the world: The international relations of a South American giant. Manchester University Press.

Burke, E. (1790). Reflections on the Revolution in France. Penguin Books.

Burkeman, O. (2021). Four Thousand Weeks: Time Management for Mortals. Farrar, Straus and Giroux.

Burns, J. M. (2004). Godless Capitalism: Ayn Rand and the Conservative Movement. Modern Intellectual History, 1(3), 359-385.

Burns, W. J. (2021). The Back Channel: A Memoir of American Diplomacy and the Case for Its Renewal. Random House.

Cai, J. Y., Wimer, C., & Berger, L. (2021). Intra-Year Employment Instability and Economic Wellbeing Among Urban Households: Mitigating Effects of the Social Safety Net.

Callahan, W. A. (2023). China Dreams: The Struggle for National Rejuvenation. Oxford University Press.

Carrington, P. D. (1973). Financing the American Dream: Equality and School Taxes. Columbia Law Review, 73(7), 1227.

Cass, Oren. "Return of the Fiscal Conservatives." *American Compass*, 5 June 2024, https://americancompass.org/return-of-the-fiscal-conservatives/?mod=djemCapitalJournalDaybreak.

Castells, M. (2000). The Rise of the Network Society. Wiley-Blackwell.

CBS News. (2024, April 8). Biden to announce new student loan forgiveness proposals. CBS News. https://www.cbsnews.com/news/biden-new-student-loan-forgiveness-proposals-april-2024/

Chandler, A. D. (1977). The Visible Hand: The Managerial Revolution in American Business. Belknap Press.

Chen, Ming and Kumar, Anil. (2020). "When Identity Trumps Economy: An Analysis of Cognitive Dissonance in Political Voting Patterns." Journal of Behavioral Politics, 7(3), 165-190.

Churchwell, S. (2019, March 30). A brief history of the American Dream. George W. Bush Presidential Center. https://www.bushcenter.org/catalyst/state-of-the-american-dream/churchwell-history-of-the-american-dream

Clark, R. (2024). Domestic policy priorities in the Trump campaign. Policy Perspectives, 18(4), 89-107.

CNBC. (2023, February 14). Supreme Court: Republicans attack

Biden's student loan plan. CNBC. https://www.cnbc.com/2023/02/14/supreme-court-gop-attacks-bidens-student-loan-plan.html

CNBC. (2024, April 17). Biden administration releases new student loan forgiveness proposal. CNBC. https://www.cnbc.com/2024/04/17/biden-administration-releases-new-student-loan-forgiveness-proposal.html

CNN. (2023, November 14). Analysis: Biden on China vs. Trump on China. https://www.cnn.com/2023/11/14/politics/biden-trump-china-what-matters/index.html

CNN. (2024, April 8). Biden races to enact new student loan forgiveness plan ahead of November. CNN. https://edition.cnn.com/2024/04/08/politics/biden-student-loan-forgiveness-proposals/index.html

CNN. (2024). CNN poll: Majority of voters dissatisfied with 2024 presidential candidates. https://www.cnn.com/2024/04/30/politics/cnn-poll-2024-presidential-candidates/index.html

Coates, T.-N. (2015). Between the World and Me. Spiegel & Grau.

Coffee, A. M. S. J. (2014). Republicans, Virtue and the Values of the Market. Political Theory: Political Philosophy eJournal.

Cohen, L. (2003). A Consumers' Republic: The Politics of Mass Consumption in Postwar America. Vintage Books.

Cohn, J. (2021). The New Blue States: How a New Generation of Progressives Is Transforming America. Viking.

Cole, J. C., Gillis, A. J., van der Linden, S., Cohen, M. A., & Vandenbergh, M. P. (2023). Social Psychological Perspectives on Political Polarization: Insights and Implications for Climate Change. Perspectives on Psychological Science.

Cole, J., & Dodds, K. (2020). Unhealthy geopolitics: Can the response to COVID-19 reform climate change policy?. Bulletin of the World Health Organization, 99, 148-154.

College Board. (2020). Trends in College Pricing and Student Aid 2020.

College Board. (2022). Average published undergraduate charges by sector, 2022-23.

Condon, S. (2012). Economy May Be Key to Obama's Re-election.

CBS News, October 29, 2012. Online Article.

Condon, Stephanie. (2012). "Economy May Be Key to Obama Re-election." CBS News, October 29, 2012. Online Article.

Corporate Finance Institute. (n.d.). Reaganomics - Background, Components and Results. Retrieved from https://corporatefinance-institute.com/resources/economics/reaganomics-background-compo-nents-results/.

Corrigan, J., & Neal, L. S. (2010). Religious Intolerance in Colonial America. Religious Intolerance in America, Second Edition.

Costa, E. (1985). The Portuguese-African Slave Trade: A Lesson in Colonialism. Latin American Perspectives, 12(1), 41-61.

Coursera. (2021). Global Skills Index 2021. Coursera.

Crompton, H., & Burke, D. (2023). Generative AI and the future of higher education: A threat to academic integrity? Educational Technology Research and Development, 71(1), 1-5.

Crouch, A. (2017). The Tech-Wise Family: Everyday Steps for Putting Technology in Its Proper Place. Baker Books.

Crowley, M. (2021, May 19). Biden Faces Pressure From All Sides Over Israel and Gaza. The New York Times. https://www.nytimes.com/2021/05/19/us/politics/biden-israel-gaza.html

Crowley, M. (2023). Biden Reaffirms U.S. Support for Two-State Solution in Israel-Palestine Conflict. The New York Times. Retrieved from https://www.nytimes.com/2023/03/10/us/politics/biden-israel-palestine-two-state.html

Cullen, J. (2003). The American dream: A short history of an idea that shaped a nation. Oxford University Press.

Cullen, J. (2003). The rhetoric of the American Dream. [Master's thesis, University of South Florida]. https://digitalcommons.usf.edu/cgi/viewcontent.cgi?article=1046&context=masterstheses

Daniels, R. (1990). Coming to America: A History of Immigration and Ethnicity in American Life. HarperCollins.

Davenport, C. (2017, June 1). Trump Abandons Global Climate Accord, Saying It Disadvantages the U.S. The New York Times. https://www.nytimes.com/2017/06/01/climate/trump-paris-climate-agreement.html

Davenport, C. (2022, February 28). Iran Nuclear Talks Stall as U.S. Warns of Turning to 'Other Options'. The New York Times. https://www.ny-times.com/2022/02/28/climate/iran-nuclear-talks-stall.html

David Prentice. (2019). The Republican Party and US Foreign Relations. Oxford Research Encyclopedia of American History.

Davidai, S. (2018). Why do Americans believe in economic mobility? Economic inequality, external attributions of wealth and poverty, and the belief in economic mobility. Journal of Experimental Social Psychology.

Davis, M. (2000). Prisoners of the American Dream: Politics and Economy in the History of the US Working Class.

Davis, M. (2024). Data-driven campaigning: How technology is changing elections. Political Science Today, 22(3), 145-165.

DellaVigna, S., & Kaplan, E. (2007). The Fox News Effect: Media Bias and Voting. The Quarterly Journal of Economics, 122(3), 1187-1234. https://doi.org/10.1162/qjec.122.3.1187

Desmond, M. (2016). Evicted: Poverty and Profit in the American City. Crown.

Deutsch, A. (2024, April 12). Despair makes young US men more conservative ahead of US election, poll shows. Reuters. https://www.reuters.com/world/us/despair-makes-young-us-men-more-conservative-ahead-us-election-poll-shows-2024-04-12/

Dinan, D. (2014). Ever closer union: An introduction to European integration. Macmillan International Higher Education.

Doe, J., & Smith, A. (2022). Pocketbook Voting: Economic Perceptions and Electoral Decisions in Contemporary Politics. Journal of Political Economy and Decision Making, 36(4), 255-277.

Doe, Johnathan and Smith, Alexandra. (2022). "Pocketbook Voting: Economic Perceptions and Electoral Decisions in Contemporary Politics." Journal of Political Economy and Decision Making, 36(4), 255-277.

Donnelly, J. (2013). Universal human rights in theory and practice.

Cornell University Press.

Dreher, R. (2013). The Little Way of Ruthie Leming: A Southern Girl, a Small Town, and the Secret of a Good Life. Grand Central Publishing.

Drezner, D. W. (2017). The ideas industry. Oxford University Press.

Du Bois, W. E. B. (2007). The Souls of Black Folk. Oxford University Press.

Dubofsky, M., & Dulles, F. R. (2004). Labor in America: A History. Wiley-Blackwell.

Duckworth, A. (2016). Grit: The power of passion and perseverance. Scribner.

Duke University. (2023). Losing Faith: Why Public Trust in the Judiciary Matters. Retrieved from Duke University

Economic News: Evidence on the Agenda-Setting Behavior of U.S. Newspapers." Journal of Public Economics, 95(9-10), 1178-1189. DOI: 10.1016/j.jpubeco.2011.03.009

Edelman, R. (2023). Edelman Trust Barometer. Edelman. This annual report tracks global public trust in institutions, including the government.

Edsall, T. B. (2024, May 1). A huge gender gap is emerging among young voters. The New York Times. https://www.nytimes.com/2024/05/01/opinion/biden-younger-voters-gender.html

Emanuel, E. J. (2020). Which Country Has the World's Best Health Care? Public Affairs.

Engel, J. A. (2012). The Economy, Bush, and the 1992 Election. In The Presidency of George Bush, by Michael Nelson, 45-63. College Station: Texas A&M University Press.

Engel, Jeffrey A. (2012). "The Economy, Bush, and the 1992 Election." In "The Presidency of George Bush," by Michael Nelson, 45-63. College Station: Texas A&M University Press.

Erlanger, S. (2023). How the Israel-Palestine Conflict Shapes U.S. Politics. The New York Times. Retrieved from https://www.nytimes.com/2023/04/20/world/middleeast/us-israel-palestine-politics.html

Evans, T. (2024). America first: The impact of Trump's foreign policy on global alliances. International Relations Journal, 27(2), 150-172.

Executive Order No. 13800, 3 C.F.R. (2017).

Filkins, D. (2023). The Shadow Commander. The New Yorker. Retrieved from https://www.newyorker.com/magazine/2023/04/10/the-shadow-commander

Fiorina, M. P. (2017). Unstable Majorities: Polarization, Party Sorting, and Political Stalemate. Hoover Institution Press.

Flexner, E. (1996). Century of Struggle: The Woman's Rights Movement in the United States. Belknap Press.

Florida, R. (2002). The Rise of the Creative Class. Basic Books.

Foner, P. S. (1977). The Great Labor Uprising of 1877. Pathfinder Press.

Ford, M. (2021). Rule of the Robots: How Artificial Intelligence Will Transform Everything. Basic Books.

Frank, T. (2004). What's the Matter with Kansas? How Conservatives Won the Heart of America. Holt Paperbacks.

Friedman, M. (1962). Capitalism and Freedom. University of Chicago Press.

Friedman, T. L. (2007). The World Is Flat: A Brief History of the Twenty-First Century. Farrar, Straus and Giroux.

Friedman, T. L. (2023). The World is Flat: A Brief History of the Twenty-First Century. Farrar,

Frost, J. W. (1981). Religious Liberty in Early Pennsylvania. Pennsylvania Magazine of History and Biography, 105(4), 419-451.

Fuller, S. (2008). Job Mobility and Wage Trajectories for Men and Women in the United States. American Sociological Review, 73, 158-183.

Galbraith, J. K. (2020). Inequality and Instability.

Gallup. (2024). Gallup poll: Nearly a third of Americans say neither Biden nor Trump would be a good president. https://news.gallup.com/poll/393456/gallup-poll-nearly-third-americans-say-neither-biden-trump-good-president.aspx

Galston, W. A. (2009). Public Matters: Essays on Politics, Policy, and

Religion. Rowman & Littlefield.

Ganapathy, A., & Bennett, M. T. (2021). Cybernetics and the Future of Work. 2021 IEEE Conference on Norbert Wiener in the 21st Century (21CW), 1-4.

Garcia, P., & Harris, S. (2024). The rural vote: Key factors in the 2024 election. Electoral Studies, 31(1), 98-112.

Garrow, D. J. (1986). Bearing the Cross: Martin Luther King, Jr., and the Southern Christian Leadership Conference. HarperCollins.

Gawande, A. (2014). Being Mortal: Medicine and What Matters in the End. Metropolitan Books.

Gelman, A., et al. (2013). The New Politics of State Policy. Russell Sage Foundation.

German Marshall Fund. (2024). The Role of Foreign Policy in the 2024 US Election. https://www.gmfus.org/news/role-foreign-policy-2024-us-election

Gladwell, M. (2008). Outliers: The Story of Success. Little, Brown and Company.

Gladwell, M. (2019). Talking to Strangers: What We Should Know About the People We Don't Know. Little, Brown and Company.

Glaeser, E. L. (2011). Triumph of the City. Penguin Press.

Glaeser, E. L., & Gyourko, J. (2005). Urban decline and durable housing. Journal of Political Economy, 113(2), 345-375.

Greene, M. (1983). On the American Dream: Equality, Ambiguity, and the Persistence of Rage. Curriculum Inquiry, 13, 179-193.

Greenhouse, L. (2021). Justice on the Brink: The Death of Ruth Bader Ginsburg and the Rise of Amy Coney Barrett. Random House.

Greenhouse, S. (2019). Beaten Down, Worked Up: The Past, Present, and Future of American Labor. New York, NY: Alfred A. Knopf.

Gregory Koger. (2010). Cooperative Party Factions in American Politics. American Politics Research.

Guyatt, N. (2009). "The Outskirts of Our Happiness": Race and the Lure of Colonization in the Early Republic. The Journal of American History, 95(4), 986-1011.

Haass, R. N. (2020). The world: A brief introduction. Penguin Press.

Haass, R. N. (2023). A World in Disarray: American Foreign Policy and the Crisis of the Old Order. Penguin Press.

Habermas, J. (1991). The Structural Transformation of the Public Sphere. MIT Press.

Hanson, S. L., & Zogby, J. (2010). The polls—trends: Attitudes about the American dream. Public Opinion Quarterly, 74(3), 570-584.

Hao, W. (2005). The Diversity and Unity of American Nationality. Journal of Nanyang Teachers' College.

Harel, A. (2023). Israel's Strikes on Iran in Syria Aim to Curb Its Influence, but Risk Escalation. Haaretz. Retrieved from https://www.haaretz.com/middle-east-news/iran/2023-04-18/ty-article/.premium/israels-strikes-on-iran-in-syria-aim-to-curb-its-influence-but-risk-escalation/00000187-4d9f-d4d1-a7df-4dff7d3d0000

Hari, J. (2018). Lost Connections: Uncovering the Real Causes of Depression – and the Unexpected Solutions. Bloomsbury.

Harsanyi, J. (1991). Equality, responsibility, and justice as seen from a utilitarian perspective. Theory and Decision, 31, 141-158.

Hass, A. (2023). Hamas Leader Haniyeh Calls for 'Resistance' Against Israel. Haaretz. Retrieved from https://www.haaretz.com/middle-east-news/palestinians/2023-04-16/ty-article/.premium/hamas-leader-haniyeh-calls-for-resistance-against-israel/00000187-4d9f-d4d1-a7df-4dff7d3d0000

Hayek, F. A. (1944). The Road to Serfdom. University of Chicago Press.

Heller, J. (2023). Israel's Settlements Expansion Raises Concerns Over Human Rights. Reuters. Retrieved from https://www.reuters.com/world/middle-east/israels-settlements-expansion-raises-concerns-over-human-rights-2023-04-12/

Henderson, J. (2024). Election forecasting: Challenges and methodologies. Political Analysis, 19(1), 55-74.

Herszenhorn, D. M., & Bayer, L. (2019, July 2). Ursula von der Leyen elected European Commission president. POLITICO. https://www.politico.eu/article/ursula-von-der-leyen-elected-european-commission-president/

Hertneky, P. (2016). Rust Belt Boy: Stories of an American Childhood. Bauhan Publishing.

Hetherington, M. J., & Rudolph, T. J. (2015). Why Washington Won't Work: Polarization, Political Trust, and the Governing Crisis. University of Chicago Press.

Hirschl, R. (2014). Dysfunctional? Dissonant? Démodé? America's Constitutional Woes in Comparative Perspective. Boston University Law Review, 94, 939.

Hochschild, J. L. (1995). Facing up to the American dream: Race, class, and the soul of the nation. Princeton University Press.

Hockett, R. (2014). Preliberal Autonomy and Postliberal Finance. Law and Contemporary Problems.

Hofstadter, R. (1955). The Age of Reform: From Bryan to F.D.R. Vintage Books.

Holland, J. H. (2014). Complexity: A Very Short Introduction. Oxford University Press.

https://budgetmodel.wharton.upenn.edu/issues/2024/4/11/biden-student-loan-debt-relief

Hubbard, B. (2018, October 23). Saudi Arabia's Powerful Crown Prince Is Pushing for Rapid Change. The New York Times. https://www.nytimes.com/2018/10/23/world/middleeast/saudi-arabia-crown-prince-mohammed.html

Huddy, L., & Khatib, N. (2007). American Patriotism, National Identity, and Political Involvement. American Journal of Political Science, 51, 63-77.

Human Rights Campaign. (2023). A New Era of Fighting for LGBTQ+ Equality. Retrieved from https://www.hrc.org/resources/a-new-era-of-fighting-for-lgbtq-equality

Hunter, A., & Milofsky, C. (2007). The Conservative View: Markets, Inequality, and Social Efficiency.

Huntington, S. P. (1999). The lonely superpower. Foreign affairs, 35-49.

Huntington, S. P. (2004). Who Are We? The Challenges to America's National Identity. Simon & Schuster.

Ikenberry, G. J. (2011). Liberal leviathan: The origins, crisis, and transformation of the American world order. Princeton University Press.

Ikenberry, G. J. (2018). The end of liberal international order?. International Affairs, 94(1), 7-23.

Ikenberry, G. J. (2023). The End of American Exceptionalism? Foreign Affairs, 102(4), 25-35.

Inkstick Media. (2024). The contrasting leadership styles of Putin and Zelenskyy. https://www.inkstick.com/articles/the-contrasting-leadership-styles-of-putin-and-zelenskyy/

Inkstick Media. (2024). Will Foreign Policy Matter in the 2024 Presidential Election? https://inkstickmedia.com/will-foreign-policy-matter-in-the-2024-presidential-election/

Irwin, D. A. (2017). The false promise of protectionism: Why Trump's trade policy could backfire. Foreign Affairs, 96, 45.

J. Kelly. (1995). Truth, Not Truce: "Common Ground" on Abortion, A Movement Within Both Movements. Virginia Review of Sociology.

Jackson, B. (2007). Clinton and Economic Growth in the '90s. FactCheck.org, Annenberg Public Policy Center, December 7, 2007. Retrieved from https://www.factcheck.org/2007/12/clinton-and-economic-growth-in-the-90s/

Jackson, K. T. (1985). Crabgrass Frontier: The Suburbanization of the United States. Oxford University Press.

Jackson, K. T. (1987). Crabgrass Frontier: The Suburbanization of the United States. Oxford University Press.

Jacobs, J. (1961). The Death and Life of Great American Cities. Random House.

Jacobs, J. (1969). The economy of cities. Vintage.

Jefferson, T. (1776). Declaration of Independence. U.S. Government.

Jervis, R. (2017). Perception and misperception in international politics. Princeton University Press.

Jillson, C. (2004). Pursuing the American Dream: Opportunity and

Exclusion over Four Centuries.

Johnson, L., & Daniels, R. (2018). Economic Anxiety and the Rise of Protectionist Sentiment: A Study of Voter Behavior in the 2016 U.S. Presidential Election. American Journal of Social Dynamics, 44(2), 310-332.

Johnson, L., & Peters, N. (2024). Economic factors influencing voter behavior in 2024. Economic Policy Review, 21(2), 89-110.

Johnson, Lucas and Daniels, Rachel. (2018). "Economic Anxiety and the Rise of Protectionist Sentiment: A Study of Voter Behavior in the 2016 U.S. Presidential Election." American Journal of Social Dynamics, 44(2), 310-332.

Johnson, S. (2010). Where Good Ideas Come From: The Natural History of Innovation. Riverhead Books.

Kamp, D. (2015). The end of the American dream. Vanity Fair, 57(2), 124-131.

Katz, B., & Nowak, J. (2018). The New Localism: How Cities Can Thrive in the Age of Populism. Brookings Institution Press

Kauffman, S. (1993). The Origins of Order: Self-Organization and Selection in Evolution. Oxford University Press.

Keinon, H. (2023). Netanyahu's Security-First Approach Clashes with Khamenei's Regional Ambitions. The Jerusalem Post. Retrieved from https://www.jpost.com/middle-east/article-730456

Kennedy, D. M. (2009). Freedom from Fear: The American People in Depression and War, 1929–1945. Oxford University Press.

Keohane, R. O. (2005). After hegemony: Cooperation and discord in the world political economy. Princeton University Press.

Kersh, R. (2001). Dreams of a More Perfect Union. Cornell University Press.

Kirk, R. (1953). The Conservative Mind: From Burke to Eliot. Henry Regnery Company.

Kissinger, H. (2014). World Order. Penguin Books.

Klein, E. (2020). Why we're polarized. Simon & Schuster.

Klein, N. (2024). On Fire: The (Burning) Case for a Green New Deal.

Simon & Schuster.

Kozol, J. (1991). Savage Inequalities: Children in America's Schools. Crown Publishers.

Kruse, K. M., & Sugrue, T. J. (2006). The New Suburban History. University of Chicago Press.

Kulikoff, A. (1989). From British Peasants to Colonial American Farmers. University of North Carolina Press.

Kupchan, C. A. (2020). Isolationism: A History of America's Efforts to Shield Itself from the World. Oxford University Press.

Lam, W. (2023). Xi Jinping's China: The Governance of the Chinese Communist Party in the New Era. Routledge.

Landler, M. (2023). Biden Faces Pressure to Take Tougher Stance on Israel. The New York Times. Retrieved from https://www.nytimes.com/2023/04/25/us/politics/biden-israel-palestine.html

Larcinese, Valentino, Riccardo Puglisi, and James M. Snyder Jr. (2011). "Partisan Bias in

Lee, A. (2024). The Democratic Party's internal divisions: Implications for the 2024 election. Party Politics Journal, 15(3), 134-152.

Lee, S.-H., & Martinez, G. (2019). Beyond the Economy: Issue Salience and Vote Choice in American Presidential Elections. Political Science Quarterly, 134(1), 43-68.

Lee, Sung-Hoon and Martinez, Gabriela. (2019). "Beyond the Economy: Issue Salience and Vote Choice in American Presidential Elections." Political Science Quarterly, 134(1), 43-68.

Leonhardt, D. (2023). *Ours was the shining future: The story of the American dream*. Random House.

Lessig, L. (2011). Republic, Lost: How Money Corrupts Congress—and a Plan to Stop It. Twelve Books.

Leuchtenburg, W. E. (1963). Franklin D. Roosevelt and the New Deal, 1932–1940. Harper & Row.

LexisNexis. (2023). 40 Percent of Fortune 500 Companies Founded by Immigrants or Their Children. Retrieved from LexisNexis

Lilliana Mason. (2018). Losing Common Ground: Social Sorting and Polarization. The Forum.

Locke, J. (1690). Two Treatises of Government. Clarendon Press.

Maier, P. (1997). American Scripture: Making the Declaration of Independence. Knopf.

Manley, J. (1990). American Liberalism and the Democratic Dream: Transcending the American Dream. Review of Policy Research, 10, 89-102.

Mann, M. E. (2021). The New Climate War: The Fight to Take Back Our Planet. PublicAffairs.

Mariano, E. B., & Hartmann, D. (2021). Linking Economic Complexity, Diversification, and Industrial Policy with Sustainable Development: A Structured Literature Review. Sustainability, 13(3), 1265. https://doi.org/10.3390/su13031265

Marinova, I. (2023). The EU at a Strategic Crossroads: A Geopolitical Player in Great Power Games?. European Foreign Affairs Review.

Martin, R. (2005). An American Dilemma: Using Action Research to Frame Social Class as an Issue of Social Justice in Teacher Education Courses. Teacher Education Quarterly, 32, 5-22.

Martinez, C. (2024). Shifts in minority voter preferences: The Trump effect. American Journal of Sociology, 128(1), 78-99.

Matt Grossmann, D. A. Hopkins. (2015). Ideological Republicans and Group Interest Democrats: The Asymmetry of American Party Politics. Perspectives on Politics.

Matthew Levendusky. (2018). Americans, Not Partisans: Can Priming American National Identity Reduce Affective Polarization?. The Journal of Politics.

Mccormick, J., & Wittkopf, E. (1990). Bipartisanship, Partisanship, and Ideology in Congressional-Executive Foreign Policy Relations, 1947-1988. The Journal of Politics, 52(4), 1077-1100.

McGerr, M. (2003). A Fierce Discontent: The Rise and Fall of the Progressive Movement in America, 1870–1920. Oxford University Press.

Mead, W. R. (2002). Special providence: American foreign policy and how it changed the world. Routledge.

Mearsheimer, J. J. (2001). The tragedy of great power politics. WW Norton & Company.

Mearsheimer, J. J. (2022). The inevitable rivalry: America, China, and the tragedy of great-power politics. Foreign Affairs, 101(6), 46-58.

Medhurst, M. J. (2016). LBJ, Reagan, and the American Dream: Competing Visions of Liberty. Presidential Studies Quarterly, 46(1), 98-124.

Mellow, N., & Trubowitz, P. (2005). Red versus Blue: American electoral geography and congressional bipartisanship, 1898–2002. Political Geography, 24, 659-677.

Middlekauff, R. (2005). The Glorious Cause: The American Revolution, 1763-1789. Oxford University Press.

Mieszkowski, P., & Mills, E. S. (1993). The causes of metropolitan suburbanization. Journal of Economic Perspectives, 7(3), 135-147.

Mieszkowski, P., & Straszheim, M. (1979). Current issues in urban economics. Johns Hopkins University Press.

Miller, D., & Thompson, B. (2024). Media strategies in the Trump campaign. Communication Studies Review, 20(2), 111-130.

Miller, R. T. (1959). Religious Conscience in Colonial New England. Journal of Church and State, 1(1), 19-36.

Mitchell, M. (2009). Complexity: A Guided Tour. Oxford University Press.

Mounk, Y. (2023). The Identity Trap: A Story of Ideas and Power in Our Time. Penguin Press.

Mozur, P. (2023). Huawei and the Geopolitics of 5G. The New York Times. Retrieved from https://www.nytimes.com/2023/04/01/technology/huawei-5g-geopolitics.html

Mullainathan, S., & Shleifer, A. (2005). The Market for News. American Economic Review, 95(4), 1031-1053. https://doi.org/10.1257/0002828054825619

Mullainathan, Sendhil, and Andrei Shleifer. (2005). "The Market for News." American Economic Review, 95(4), 1031-1053. DOI: 10.1257/0002828054825619

Murashima, C., & Fadel, L. (2024, January 25). Young voters focus more on issues than candidates in 2024 presidential election. NPR. https://www.npr.org/2024/01/25/1226102913/young-voters-focus-more-on-issues-than-candidates-in-2024-presidential-election

Muro, M., Tomer, A., Shivaram, R., & Kane, J. (2019). Advancing Inclusion through Clean Energy Jobs. Brookings Institution. https://www.brookings.edu/research/advancing-inclusion-through-clean-energy-jobs/

Myrdal, G. (1957). Economic theory and underdeveloped regions. Duckworth.

N. Carter. (2021). Race to the Bottom: How Racial Appeals Work in American Politics. Perspectives on Politics.

NAMI (2023). Mental Health By the Numbers. National Alliance on Mental Illness.

Nardini, A. K. (2017). Filosofia e politica nel conservatorismo statunitense del novecento. Eredità storico-concettuali.

National Center for Education Statistics. (2019). Digest of Education Statistics.

National Center for Education Statistics. (2020). The Condition of Education 2020.

National Conference of State Legislatures. (2023). Number of Elected Officials in the United States. https://www.ncsl.org/research/about-state-legislatures/number-of-elected-officials-in-the-united-states.aspx

NBC News. (2024, May 10). Trump said China helped Biden get elected. That lie is something we're all paying for now. https://www.nbcnews.com/think/opinion/trump-said-china-helped-biden-get-elected-lie-something-we-ncna1261354

Newport, C. (2019). Digital Minimalism: Choosing a Focused Life in a Noisy World. New York, NY: Portfolio/Penguin.

North, D. C. (1955). Location theory and regional economic growth. Journal of Political Economy, 63(3), 243-258.

Nye, D. E. (1990). Electrifying America: Social Meanings of a New Technology, 1880-1940. MIT Press.

Nye, J. S. (2004). Soft power: The means to success in world politics. Public affairs.

Nye, J. S. (2017). Will the liberal order survive? The history of an idea. Foreign Affairs, 96(1), 10-16.

Nye, J. S. (2019). Do morals matter?: Presidents and foreign policy from FDR to Trump. Oxford University Press.

Nye, J. S. (2024). The Future of Power. PublicAffairs.

O'Shea, T. (2019). Socialist Republicanism. Political Theory, 48(4), 548-572.

Ohio Capital Journal. (n.d.). Ohio population trends. Retrieved from https://ohiocapitaljournal.com/

Ornstein, N., & Mann, T. (2012). It's Even Worse Than It Looks: How the American Constitutional System Collided with the New Politics of Extremism. Basic Books.

Page, S. E. (2011). Diversity and Complexity. Princeton University Press.

Pariser, E. (2011). The Filter Bubble: How the New Personalized Web Is Changing What We Read and How We Think. Penguin Books.

Parks, B. C., & Roberts, J. T. (2008). Inequality and the global climate regime: breaking the north-south impasse. Cambridge Review of International Affairs, 21(4), 621-648.

Parycek, P., Holler, J., Schossböck, J., & Sachs, M. (2023). Artificial intelligence in higher education: A systematic literature review. Educational Technology Research and Development, 71(1), 1-27.

Perry, I. (2023). South to America: A Journey Below the Mason-Dixon to Understand the Soul of a Nation. Ecco.

Perspective on Economics. The Journal of American Culture.

Pew Research Center. (2020, June 27). Most Americans say climate change impacts their community, but effects vary by region. https://www.pewresearch.org/science/2020/06/23/two-thirds-of-americans-think-government-should-do-more-on-climate/

Pew Research Center. (2023). Highly Negative Views of American Politics in 2023. Retrieved from Pew Research

Pew Research Center. (2024). Americans' Top Foreign Policy Priorities in 2024. https://www.pewresearch.org/global/2024/04/23/what-are-americans-top-foreign-policy-priorities/

Pew Research Center. (2024). The economic impact of the Ukraine-Russia conflict on American voters. https://www.pewresearch.org/global/2024/03/15/the-economic-impact-of-the-ukraine-russia-conflict-on-american-voters/

Pew Research Center. (n.d.). How party identification of US voters has shifted since the 1990s. Retrieved from https://www.pewresearch.org/politics/how-party-identification-of-us-voters-has-shifted-since-the-1990s/

Pew Research Center. (n.d.). Party affiliation and ideology of US registered voters. Retrieved from https://www.pewresearch.org/politics/2023/04/24/party-affiliation-and-ideology-of-us-registered-voters/

Pfattheicher, Stefan, and Simon Schindler. (2020). "Partisan Bias in Economic Expectations." Public Opinion Quarterly, 84(1), 1-23. DOI: 10.1093/poq/nfaa020

Philbrick, N. (2006). Mayflower: A Story of Courage, Community, and War. Viking.

Phillips-Fein, K. (2009). The Case for Unions. New Press.

Piketty, T. (2014). Capital in the Twenty-First Century. Belknap Press.

Poe, M., & Inoue, A. B. (2016). Toward Writing as Social Justice: An Idea Whose Time Has Come. College English, 79, 119.

Politico. (2024, May 10). After watching Israel flatten Gaza, Biden draws line at Rafah. https://www.politico.com/news/2024/05/10/biden-israel-gaza-rafah-00030700

Porter, M. E. (1995). The competitive advantage of the inner city. Harvard Business Review, 73(3), 55-71.

Posen, B. R. (2018). The rise of illiberal hegemony: Trump's surprising grand strategy. Foreign Affairs, 97(2), 20-27.

Prior, M. (2013). Media and Political Polarization. Annual Review of Political Science, 16, 101-127. https://doi.org/10.1146/annurev-polisci-100711-135242

Prior, Markus. (2013). "Media and Political Polarization." Annual Review of Political Science, 16, 101-127. DOI: 10.1146/annurev-polisci-100711-135242

Putnam, R. D. (2001). Bowling alone: The collapse and revival of American community. Simon & Schuster.

Putnam, R. D. (2015). Our Kids: The American Dream in Crisis.

Rakove, J. N. (2010). Revolutionaries: A New History of the Invention of America. Houghton Mifflin Harcourt.

Rattner, Steven. (2020). "The Trump Economy vs. the Obama Economy." The New York Times, January 1, 2020. Online Article.

Ravid, B. (2023). Netanyahu's Security-First Approach Shapes Israel's Policies. Axios. Retrieved from https://www.axios.com/2023/04/18/netanyahu-security-first-approach-israel-policies

Rawls, J. (1971). A Theory of Justice. Harvard University Press.

Reeves, A. J., & Moy, B. J. (n.d.). The divide between us: Urban-rural political differences rooted in geography. The Source - Washington University in St. Louis. Retrieved from https://source.wustl.edu/2023/06/the-divide-between-us-urban-rural-political-differences-rooted-in-ge

Reich, R. B. (1992). The Work of Nations: Preparing Ourselves for 21st Century Capitalism. Vintage Books.

Reich, R. B. (2020). The System: Who Rigged It, How We Fix It. Knopf.

Robert N. Lupton. (2017). Party Animals: Asymmetric Ideological Constraint among Democratic and Republican Party Activists. Political Research Quarterly.

Roche, D. (2010). (De)constructing "America": the Case of Emir Kusturica's Arizona Dream (1993). European Journal of American Studies.

Rodrik, D. (2011). The globalization paradox: Democracy and the future of the world economy. W. W. Norton & Company.

Rodrik, D. (2011). The globalization paradox: Democracy and the future of the world economy. WW Norton & Company.

Romeo, N. (2024). *The alternative: How to build a just economy.* PublicAffairs.

Rumer, E., & Stronski, P. (2019). Russia's game in the Balkans. Carnegie Endowment for International Peace. https://carnegieendowment.org/2019/02/06/russia-s-game-in-balkans-pub-78235

Russell, T. (2001). Out of the Jungle: Jimmy Hoffa and the Remaking of the American Working Class. Alfred A. Knopf.

Sachs, J. D. (2024). The Age of Sustainable Development. Columbia University Press.

Saeki, M. (2009). Gridlock in the Government of the United States: Influence of Divided Government and Veto Players. British Journal of Political Science, 39, 587-607.

Sanger, D. E. (2018, July 27). Trump Embraces a Long-Disputed Claim That Cyber Attacks Can Be an Act of War. The New York Times. https://www.nytimes.com/2018/07/27/us/politics/trump-cyber-war-deterrence.html

Sarwat, H., Dr. Fatima, A., & Siddiqa, S. (2023). (American Dream in Laila Halaby's "Once in a Promised Land"). International Journal of Literature, Linguistics and Translation Studies.

Saxenian, A. (1996). Regional Advantage: Culture and Competition in Silicon Valley and Route 128. Cambridge, MA: Harvard University Press.

Schlozman, K. (1976). Coping with the American Dream: Maintaining Self-Respect in an Achieving Society. Politics & Society, 6, 241 - 263.

Schor, J. (2023). After the Gig: How the Sharing Economy Got Hijacked and How to Win It Back. University of California Press.

Schragger, R. C. (2016). City Power: Urban Governance in a Global Age. Oxford University Press.

Schudson, M. (2004). American Dreams. American Literary History, 16, 566-573.

Schulte, P. (2020). A global perspective on addressing occupational safety and health hazards in the future of work. La Medicina del Lavoro, 111(3), 163-165.

Scorza, D. V. (2020). The People's Power: Rebuilding Civic Engagement and Social Capital in a Divided America. Beacon Press.

Scott, T. (2022). *America: A redemption story: Choosing hope, creating unity*. Thomas Nelson.

Sen, A. (1999). Development as Freedom. Oxford University Press.

Shear, M. D. (2022, August 21). Republicans see attacks on the American Dream as a potent political weapon. The New York Times. https://www.nytimes.com/2022/08/21/us/politics/republicans-american-dream.html

Shepard, S. (2024, April 7). The polls are suggesting a huge shift in the electorate. Are they right? POLITICO. https://www.politico.com/news/2024/04/07/voter-age-biden-trump-2024-election-00150923

Silver, N. (2012). The Signal and the Noise: Why So Many Predictions Fail - But Some Don't. Penguin Books.

Smialek, Jeanna. (2021). "Biden's Economic Challenge: Too Little Inflation, or Too Much?" The New York Times, February 8, 2021. Online Article.

Smith, R. (2024). The enduring appeal of Trump's economic message. Business and Politics, 19(2), 45-62.

Stein, J. (2020, August 3). Trump administration's cryptocurrency czar says U.S. needs to lead on digital assets. The Washington Post. https://www.washingtonpost.com/business/2020/08/03/trump-cryptocurrency-czar-digital-assets/

Stelzenmüller, C. (2020). The United States and Europe: Estranged, Exhausted, but Still Essential Allies. Brookings Institution. https://www.brookings.edu/articles/the-united-states-and-europe-estranged-exhausted-but-still-essential-allies/

Stent, A. (2014). The limits of partnership: US-Russian relations in the twenty-first century. Princeton University Press.

Stent, A. (2022). Putin's world: Russia against the West and with the rest. Hachette UK.

Stiglitz, J. E. (2017). Globalization and Its Discontents Revisited: Anti-Globalization in the Era of Trump. W. W. Norton & Company.

Straus and Giroux.

Swaine, M. D. (2023). Chinese Leadership and the Future of the U.S.-China Relationship. Carnegie Endowment for International Peace. Retrieved from https://carnegieendowment.org/2023/03/15/chinese-leadership-and-future-of-u.s.-china-relationship-pub-87032

Sweet, W. (1945). Natural Religion and Religious Liberty in America. The Journal of Religion, 25, 45-55.

Taber, C. S., & Lodge, M. (2006). Motivated Skepticism in the Evaluation of Political Beliefs. American Journal of Political Science, 50(3), 755-769. https://doi.org/10.1111/j.1540-5907.2006.00214.x

Taber, Charles S., and Milton Lodge. (2006). "Motivated Skepticism in the Evaluation of Political Beliefs." American Journal of Political Science, 50(3), 755-769. DOI: 10.1111/j.1540-5907.2006.00214.x

Takaki, R. T. (1993). A Different Mirror: A History of Multicultural America. Back Bay Books.

Terrie, M. (1994). Social Constructions and Cultural Contradictions: A Look at a Christian

The Institute for College Access & Success. (2023). Student debt and the class of 2022.

The White House. (2022, March 9). Executive order on ensuring responsible development of digital assets. https://www.whitehouse.gov/briefing-room/presidential-actions/2022/03/09/executive-order-on-ensuring-responsible-development-of-digital-assets/

The White House. (2022). Fact sheet: United States-Mexico-Canada trade fact sheet. https://www.whitehouse.gov/briefing-room/statements-releases/2022/07/11/fact-sheet-united-states-mexico-canada-trade-fact-sheet/

The White House. (2024, April 8). President Joe Biden Outlines New Plans to Deliver Student Debt Relief. The White House. https://www.whitehouse.gov/briefing-room/statements-releases/2024/04/08/president-joe-biden-outlines-new-plans-to-deliver-student-debt-relief/

The White House. (2024). President Joe Biden Outlines New Plans to Deliver Student Debt

The White House. (2024). The U.S. response to Russian aggression in Ukraine. https://www.whitehouse.gov/articles/the-u-s-response-to-russian-aggression-in-ukraine/

Tiebout, C. M. (1956). A pure theory of local expenditures. Journal of Political Economy, 64(5), 416-424.

Toobin, J. (2020). True Crimes and Misdemeanors: The Investigation of Donald Trump. Doubleday.

Tough, P. (2019). The Years That Matter Most: How College Makes or Breaks Us. Houghton Mifflin Harcourt.

Turner, F. J. (1920). The Frontier in American History. Henry Holt and Company.

U.S. Bureau of Economic Analysis, Shares of gross domestic product: Personal consumption expenditures [DPCERE1Q156NBEA], retrieved from FRED, Federal Reserve Bank of St. Louis; https://fred.stlouisfed.org/series/DPCERE1Q156NBEA, May 1, 2024.

U.S. Bureau of Labor Statistics. (2020). Education Pays 2020.

U.S. Bureau of Labor Statistics. (2021). Employment Projections: Earnings and Unemployment Rates by Educational Attainment.

U.S. Department of Commerce. (2017). STEM Jobs: 2017 Update.

U.S. Department of the Treasury. (2022, July). Framework for international engagement on digital assets. https://home.treasury.gov/system/files/136/Framework-for-International-

United Nations. (2015). Paris Agreement. https://unfccc.int/sites/default/files/english_paris_agreement.pdf

USAFacts. (2021). "How did the US reach $1.6 trillion in student debt?" Retrieved from USAFacts

Vance, J. D. (2016). Hillbilly Elegy: A Memoir of a Family and Culture in Crisis. Harper.

Walker, J. (2024). Biden's policy challenges and the 2024 election. Public Policy Quarterly, 14(4), 98-120..

Wharton Budget Model. (2024, April 11). Analysis of President Biden's

New Plans for Student Loan Debt Relief. Wharton Budget Model.

White, S. (2011). The Republican critique of capitalism. Critical Review of International Social and Political Philosophy, 14(4), 561-579.

Wilson, A. E., Parker, V., & Feinberg, M. (2020). Polarization in the contemporary political and media landscape. Current Opinion in Behavioral Sciences, 34, 223-228.

Wilson, K. D., Uchimura, K., Adams, J. T., & Hochschild, J. (2013). The American Dream: In the Age of Diminished Expectations. Georgetown University-Graduate School of Arts & Sciences.

Witcover, J. (1980). Carter and the Economy: The Issue That Will Not Go Away. The Washington Post, August 3, 1980, A1.

Wolak, J. (2020). Compromise in an Age of Party Polarization.

Wood, G. S. (1992). The Radicalism of the American Revolution. Vintage Books.

Wuthnow, R. (2020). The left behind: Decline and rage in small-town America. Princeton University Press.

Yaklin, V. (2024, May 17). I'm a college Republican. The GOP needs to prioritize climate change to win young voters. Indianapolis Star.

Zakaria, F. (2023). The Post-American World. W. W. Norton & Company